The Roots of Appeasement

Originally published in 1991, *The Roots of Appeasement* outlines the attitudes of the British weekly press and its editors to Nazism and to German and British foreign policies during the 1930s. It analyses and interprets the reasons which underlay those attitudes. Aided by the evidence of the weeklies, it sheds additional light on the roots and development of appeasement. After introducing the weeklies and their editors, the study conveys and examines their attitudes to the European crises of 1935-9 and one chapter focusses on the popular fear of air attack as reflected in the journals. The major conclusion of the book is that a consensus supporting appeasement emerged in the weeklies in the course of 1935 and that it remained virtually intact until September 1938.

The Roots of Appeasement

The British Weekly Press and Nazi Germany
During the 1930s

Benny Morris

Routledge
Taylor & Francis Group

First published in the UK in 1991
by Frank Cass & Co. Ltd

This edition first published in 2022 by Routledge
4 Park Square, Milton Park, Abingdon, Oxon, OX14 4RN
and by Routledge
605 Third Avenue, New York, NY 10158

Routledge is an imprint of the Taylor & Francis Group, an informa business

© 1991 Benny Morris

The right of Benny Morris to be identified as the author of this work has been asserted
by him in accordance with sections 77 and 78 of the Copyright, Designs and Patents
Act 1988.

Publisher's Note
The publisher has gone to great lengths to ensure the quality of this reprint but points
out that some imperfections in the original copies may be apparent.

ISBN 13: 978-1-032-33409-7 (hbk)
ISBN 13: 978-1-003-31959-7 (ebk)
ISBN 13: 978-1-032-33419-6 (pbk)
Book DOI 10.4324/9781032334097

THE ROOTS
OF APPEASEMENT

THE BRITISH WEEKLY PRESS
AND NAZI GERMANY
DURING THE 1930s

BENNY MORRIS

FRANK CASS

First published in 1991 in Great Britain by
FRANK CASS & CO. LTD.
Gainsborough House, Gainsborough Road,
London E11 1RS, England

and in the United States of America by
FRANK CASS
c/o International Specialized Book Services, Inc.
5602 N.E. Hassalo Street, Portland, Oregon 97213

Copyright © 1991 Benny Morris

British Library Cataloguing in Publication Data
Morris, Benny
The roots of appeasement: the British weekly press and
Nazi Germany during the 1930s.
1. Great Britain. Foreign relations with Germany, history.
Influence of press
I. Title
327.41048

ISBN 0-7146-3417-4

Library of Congress Cataloging-in-Publication Data
Morris, Benny, 1948-
The roots of appeasement : the British weekly press and Nazi
Germany during the 1930s / Benny Morris.
Includes bibliographical references and index.
ISBN 0-7146-3417-4 (hardback)
1. Great Britain--Foreign relations--1910-1936. 2. Great Britain-
-Foreign relations--1936-1945. 3. Journalists--Great Britain-
-Attitudes--History--20th century. Government and the press-
-Great Britain--History--20th century. 5. Germany--Politics and
government--1933-1945. 6. Germany--Politics and
government--1918-1933. 7. World War, 1939-1945--Causes. I. Title.
DA578.M617 1991
327.41043--dc20   91-11207
         CIP

Printed in Great Britain by BPCC Wheatons Ltd, Exeter

For Erel, Yagi and Orian

CONTENTS

I

INTRODUCTION

This study aims to outline the attitudes of the British weekly press and of its editors to Nazism and to German and British foreign policies during the 1930s. It attempts to analyse and interpret the reasons which underlay those attitudes. And it hopes, aided by the evidence of the weeklies, to shed additional light on the roots and development of appeasement. Throughout, it is assumed that the weekly press was influential in moulding public opinion and that public opinion affected, and was reflected in, the foreign policy of the National Government. In this respect, the quality weekly press was of especial importance inasmuch as it influenced and reflected the thinking of the nation's intellectual and political elite.

The structure of the study is largely determined by its subject matter and by the argument proposed. After introducing the weeklies and their editors, the study will convey and examine their attitudes to the European crises of 1935–39. A special chapter will focus on the popular fear of air attack as reflected in the journals. The subject has received unjustifiably scant attention in the bulk of works dealing with the period.[1] To judge from the weeklies, the importance of the 'air fear' in the adoption of appeasement cannot be exaggerated.

It will be shown – and this constitutes the major conclusion of this study – that a consensus supporting appeasement emerged in the weeklies in the course of 1935 and that it remained virtually intact until September 1938. The consensus encompassed the supporters of the National Government as well as the bulk of the Liberal and left-wing weeklies ostensibly committed to 'collective Security' and 'resistance to Fascism'. In the course of 1938 this consensus was irreparably undermined; the shock and humiliation of Munich left a permanent mark. The occupation of Prague in March 1939 rendered the continuance of appeasement objectionable to most Britons. It compelled the Government to adopt a posture of resistance to aggression. However, it will be seen that in the weeklies March 1939 did not witness an abrupt and revolutionary change of heart; rather, it marked a stage in the gradual shift, ending in September 1939, from appeasement to resistance.

1

It will be shown that support of appeasement by the Liberal and left-wing weeklies was not only indirect; it was not confined to opposition to rearmament and economic mobilisation. Appeasement by the ostensible advocates of collective security (as by the Government until 1937) was usually pursued by way of omission rather than commission. Thus the Opposition journals refused to condone a blockade of the Suez Canal to Italian shipping during the Abyssinian crisis, supported the denial of arms to the Republic during the Spanish Civil War and, in the main, desisted from backing a British commitment to Czechoslovakia during 1938. 'Positive' appeasement (as practised by Chamberlain from 1937) also was occasionally propounded by these journals. The *New Statesman*'s support of a Sudeten cession in March and August 1938 and its suggestion of a compromise over Danzig and the Corridor in the summer of 1939 are cases in point.

Traditional explanations have seen the Conservatives' pursuit of appeasement as primarily resting on the following assumptions: that Hitler was a rational and tractable statesman; that he desired the revision of the peace treaties rather than the domination of Europe or the world; that he coveted British friendship and was bent upon the avoidance of conflict in the West; that German ambitions in eastern Europe were compatible with Britain's security and vital interests; and that Hitler, like most veterans, abhorred the thought of a new world war. To judge from their representative journals, with none of these assumptions did Liberals and left-wingers normally concur. Yet, by and large, they condoned appeasement and refrained from advocating its alternative before September 1938. This study will attempt to focus on the common ground between Conservatives, Liberals and Socialists which prompted support of appeasement.

The vast majority of Conservatives, Liberals and Socialists in Britain in the 1920s and 1930s were heirs to and, in politics, practitioners of the liberal tradition. Liberalism informed all British political thought and practice; no country boasted so non-violent a General Strike as that of 1926; no country, in the thirties, so completely abjured the political extremes of Fascism and Communism. As Gannon has rightly pointed out, almost all the editors and journalists in the British Press between the wars were 'liberals in the broadest sense of the term'.[2] With the exception of Lady Houston of the *Saturday Review*, Douglas Woodruff of the *Tablet* and, perhaps, Henry Newnham of *Truth*, this was certainly true of the publicists of the weekly press.

Liberalism postulated the rational and 'progressive' evolutionary nature of the historical process. Besides success it upheld pragmatism, tolerance and compromise as the principal political virtues. At the core of the liberal outlook stood the 'idea of limits'. It abhorred excess and extremism; it believed that 'absolutist' thought of any sort assured at least failure if not perdition. All problems and conflicts were seen as soluble with the application of reason; and reason, Liberals believed, ultimately did prevail. Reason, in fact, suffused all and was identified with reality.[3]

To Liberals in the twenties and thirties, the Great War was both a standing reproach and an enigma. Reason had apparently failed. That experience seemingly denied the foundations of liberalism – the belief that men were basically good and that men and nations were essentially rational. Perhaps it was in part to escape from the philosophical dilemma that British Liberals in the inter-war years preferred to explain that holocaust as a consequence of a chain of accidents rather than as a product of the malignity of nations and of their perceived interests and collective will.

The British desire to appease Germany before 1933 is intelligible in the light of the reign of liberalism; appeasement, as an enlightened policy of justice for all, including Germany, was a child of that outlook. For over a decade it was promoted (ineffectually, because of French recalcitrance) by men as diverse as J.M. Keynes and Ramsay MacDonald, Gilbert Murray and Stanley Baldwin. But appeasement did not end with the ascent of Hitler to the chancellorship. In this respect, 1933–35 marked a watershed; appeasement, gradually but perceptibly, changed from a policy based on 'morality' and on a quest for 'justice' to one compelled by fear and expediency. Thus appeasement changed its meaning.[4] In this study, which deals with the later period, the word will normally be used in the latter sense.

Appeasement, in both senses, was fuelled by liberalism. The rule of liberalism in Britain was a pre-condition and a backdrop to the adoption and promotion of appeasement, both before and after 1933. However, it will be seen that whereas before that date the liberal outlook was mainly responsible for the promotion of that policy, after it, and especially from 1935, other factors, whose weight was far greater, obtruded.

Liberalism sired appeasement in three important ways. First, it saw the First World War as mankind's greatest folly and regarded all war as the ultimate evil. Hence, it prescribed the future avoidance of conflict as the highest morality. 'Never again' was the post-1918 liberals' battle-cry. Second, it recognised the peace treaties of 1919 as the spawn of the Great War and as born in its image. It demanded their revision in the name of justice and of expediency. Third, it precluded a full, early and unanimous appreciation of the nature and significance of Nazism. Nazism's postulates, like ideological politics in general, were too alien to the liberal outlook to be comprehensible to the exponents of liberalism.

In England in the twenties and thirties the Great War was seen as the ultimate proof that war was the supreme evil. It was perceived that Britain had fought for four long years without compelling cause and that, in the process, she had lost the flower of a generation and vast wealth. The Empire itself had been shaken to its foundations, as the rumbles from India increasingly indicated. Through the twenties and early thirties a flood of books poured forth vilifying and debunking war; an apogee of publication and consumption was reached between 1929 and 1932.[5] Memoirs recalled the horrors of the front; histories proclaimed the follies of the generals and the politicians; pamphlets and tracts assailed the profits of armaments manufacturers and the expensive credulity of the masses. The survivors of that holocaust, and those grown to maturity in its wake, united under the banner of 'Never again'. Of the editors of the weeklies, only two, Kingsley Martin (the *New Statesman*) and Gerald Barry (the *Week-End Review*), had actually served in the war. But all had lost friends and relatives. J.L. Garvin (the *Observer*), for example, had lost a son on the Somme. The major lesson of the Great War was understood to be that the experience must never, under any pretext, be repeated. There were also some ancillary legacies. Many commentators believed that the Great War had resulted largely from the pursuit by the Powers of an open-ended arms race and from their subscription to military alliances. In the twenties and thirties liberals were nowhere more adamant than in their dual rejection of substantial British rearmament and of British participation in military alliances, secret or otherwise.

The Treaties of Versailles and Saint-Germain were seen by liberals, from Keynes's *Economic Consequences of the Peace* onwards, as the malign progeny of the Great War. The bellicose passions of the war had been translated into the vengeful and unjust strictures of the Peace. A 'guilty conscience' over the treatment of Germany was born. By the end of the twenties most educated Britons had been persuaded of the co-responsibility of all the great Powers in unleashing the catastrophe. Hence, the attribution of sole guilt to Germany was deemed unjust and inexpedient; the treaties' anti-German provisions appeared indefensible and in need of revision. Reparations, territorial penalties, even the discriminatory disarmament – all had to go. From the liberal perspective, the uncompromising, unpragmatic strictures of the Peace seemed to perpetuate the grip of irrationality in world affairs; they promised a new epic of blood-letting. The consensus which arose in Britain in the wake of the Great War opposing the Versailles settlement – and it encompassed

4

Liberals, Socialists and many Conservatives – affords an overwhelming proof of liberalism's sway over British political thinking.

Lastly, liberalism, because of its nature, was unable and unwilling to swiftly and accurately appraise Nazi ideology and its political implications. It attempted to accommodate its perceptions of reality to its pre-conceptions; to view reality as consistent with its premises. What palpably did not 'fit', liberalism misunderstood, ignored or attempted to deny. Of nothing was this more true than of Nazism.

Britain in the 1930s (as before) was an insular society; liberalism was both a product and a cause of that insularity. As attempts to transplant Anglo-Saxon liberalism had failed, so it had immunised Britain against illiberal Continental thought and ideology. In the thirties, a major symptom of this cultural insularity was a general lack of knowledge of German and of German affairs among the educated classes. (France, and the French language, on the other hand, were somewhat better known, in part perhaps because of a measure of shared liberalism in outlook.) An exception was the younger 'Auden generation' which, enthralled with Weimar culture, both knew German and flirted with illiberal Continental ideology. No representative of this generation edited a journal though a number, such as Goronwy Rees (the *Spectator*) and R.H.S. Crossman (the *New Statesman*), filled secondary roles on editorial staffs. The editors of the weeklies were invariably middle-aged or older. Of them, Garvin was exceptional in possessing fluent German and in taking an avid interest in German affairs; he read several German newspapers daily. Kingsley Martin, W.W. Hadley (the *Sunday Times*), Sir Walter Layton (*The Economist*), Henry Wilson Harris (the *Spectator*), Henry Newnham (*Truth*), Lady Rhondda (*Time & Tide*), Lady Houston and John Hutton (the *British Weekly*) – all knew no German. Most did not even visit Germany once during the Hitler years. None, except Garvin, had read *Mein Kampf* before its appearance in English (1939).

To most Liberals, the concept of political ideology was both alien and abhorrent. Liberalism rejected the rule of dogma and absolutes in politics; it refused to believe that unswerving doctrine should or could be translated into policy. It therefore attempted, in the thirties, to dismiss the notion that Germany under Hitler was in fact governed by the ideology and precepts embodied in *Mein Kampf*. Even years of Hitlerite persecution at home and Nazi aggression abroad failed to convince many that here indeed was an ideology on the path of fulfilment. No doubt, the refusal of many Britons to admit this stemmed in some measure from a realisation of the consequences if it were indeed true: if Nazi ideology was as malign as its detractors contended, and was being enacted, then the prospects for Europe were indeed bleak.

Literally thousands of articles on Germany appeared in the weeklies in the course of the thirties. No more than 25 (!) specifically set out to define, explain or analyse Nazi ideology. Most of the editors apparently regarded that ideology as ridiculous, irrelevant or simply intellectually uninteresting. Even those, like Garvin, who displayed an awareness of the connection in German politics between the idea and the action failed to print analyses of Nazi ideology. Most, simply, viewed politics and policies as the product of material forces, interests and ambitions struggling within a context of a changing set of physical circumstances.

In fact, many of the editors displayed a conscious effort to 'disconnect' Nazi ideology from Nazi practice. For that ideology, however obscurely understood, was recognised to be both evil and dangerous. For example, in 1935 Wilson Harris declared:

> It is true, and it is a pity, that that notorious volume [i.e., *Mein Kampf*] is still circulated in unrevised form and regarded as the gospel of the Nazi movement. But even so, if there is some incompatibility between the policies embodied in a volume written in prison by a defeated rebel in 1924 and those proclaimed to the world by the titular head of the German Reich in 1935, it is reasonable to regard the latter as the more authoritative, pending proof to the contrary.[6]

Apparently, the proofs to the contrary already afforded by Hitler – anti-Semitic outrages, the murder of Dollfuss, etc. – had been insufficient. In 1936, following a speech of Hitler's demanding the return of the colonies, Wilson Harris attacked the problem from another angle. He wrote: 'Hitherto, of course, *Mein Kampf* has been the Nazi bible ... Is that so still?' For, he argued, the demand for colonies was contrary to the book's teachings. Wilson Harris therefore concluded that 'in face of the clear evidence that one doctrine in *Mein Kampf* can be superseded at will, the question arises which others can, and how far the volume is to be taken as still embodying the Nazi gospel. This is not unimportant.'[7]

Few editors appeared even troubled, as Wilson Harris obviously was, by the possible nexus between Nazi ideology and practice. Most simply ignored the possibility of a connection between the two and viewed Nazi policies, like those of most states, as unconnected with any body of absolutes.

If most editors preferred to disregard the possible connection between Nazi ideology and policies – refused, in effect, to allow that ideological politics prevailed in Europe – most also simply misunderstood what that ideology was all about. Its essence – race theory – was so remote from the liberal *Weltanschauung* that few were willing or able to come to grips with it.

This failing was noted, and lamented, by a number of perceptive commentators at the time. In mid-1933 *Time & Tide* declared:

> It had been apparent almost from the outset of the Nazi Revolution that the onlooker in the remaining great democracies would fail to grasp what was happening in Germany unless he exercised a conscious imaginative effort. For it all seemed incredible and fantastic.[8]

In August of that year, Garvin wrote to Waldorf Astor (the *Observer*'s proprietor): 'I am staggered here in this country by the utter want of comprehension ... Blind!'[9] Nor, according to Odette Keun, a well-versed observer, had matters improved much by 1935. She wrote: 'The essential nature of Nazism, the thing that constitutes an unprecedented peril for all of us, seems to have completely eluded the comprehension of the English.' In England, she stated, there was 'no consciousness of Nazism as a reality in the public mind. The English man in the street is ignorant; the English intellectuals are apathetic; the English popular press is dumb.'[10]

The blindness of the weeklies towards Nazism was the blindness of liberalism. At the core of Nazi ideology stood the concept of race; it interpreted history as a necessary and perpetual conflict of races; and it conceived of morality as a function of racial well-being. Such doctrine was directly antithetical to the precepts of liberalism. Liberals flatly denied its truth and refused to believe that a 'civilised' nation of 70 millions could subscribe to it, let alone base domestic and foreign policies upon it. When faced with the evidence of Hitler's rule, many looked on with despairing and total incomprehension. Of Nazi displays of anti-Semitism, Sir J. Evelyn Wrench, for example, wrote: 'Personally ... I never shall be able to understand why the [Hitler] Government embarked on an anti-Jew policy.'[11] And Wrench, a Germanophile steeped in German culture, prided himself upon knowing Germany. Yet race theory, the essence of Nazism, was beyond him. In depicting the Third Reich, W. Horsefall Carter was able to write, in 1934, that race doctrine 'is really an aspect that only interests the pundits ... [and] represents a comparatively unimportant element in the complex of forces released by the German Revolution'.[12] Indeed, in the same year, H. Powys Greenwood, writing in the *Spectator*, was 'surprised to find how many Nazis were unorthodox even on the matter of the Aryan race'.[13] The *Week-End Review*, during its brief existence, looked often and thoughtfully at German and European affairs. Yet, in interpreting Nazism it almost never mentioned 'race'.

7

Its description in July 1933 of Nazi ideology was typical. Nazism, it stated, was

> a revolt . . . against years of unemployment . . . and inequality in international status . . . [and] against democratic political machinery which is unsuited to the German people . . . The Nazi Revolution stands for national cleansing, the eradication of corruption and privilege [and] the rule of discipline.[14]

While undoubtedly containing elements of truth, such descriptions missed the racial core of Nazism; Nazi race doctrine went far beyond mere 'national cleansing' (if that was the sense in which the phrase was used). In this respect, liberalism's preconceptions were all-important. Race theory was absurd; hence it was impossible that it suffused Nazism.

What then was Nazism? British Liberals during the 1930s produced a number of interpretations, in part overlapping, in part mutually exclusive and in part true. One major stream of interpretation regarded Nazism as a run-of-the-mill example of nationalism, in no manner qualitatively different from other Continental specimens of the 'disease'. There was, in fact, a tendency in the early thirties in some journals to stress the 'intensive' character of that nationalism. In this view Nazism was primarily an ideology intent upon Germany's internal 'regeneration', economic, political and moral. In 1933 the *New Statesman*, for example, declared that 'the Nazi movement is not primarily directed against the victors of Versailles . . . This sadist nationalism is fully satisfied at home'.[15] *The Economist*, a year later, portrayed Nazism as 'introvert', that is, as concerned with internal German affairs rather than with expansion abroad.[16] Interestingly, it was precisely such Liberal and left-wing journals that denied the Nazi experience the status of a 'Revolution'. While cognisant of the substantial changes Hitler's regime had instituted in all walks of German life, these journals could not perceive them as 'revolutionary': 'Revolution' was the preserve of the Left – a world turned upside down by the Right was always termed 'reaction'.

However, by its actions, Hitler's Germany prevented most liberals from resting on such an 'intensive' interpretation. The Nazis soon exhibited external interests as well; Hitler's nationalism did indeed have a foreign policy and foreign ambitions. What then was the nature of these ambitions? Many Liberals, in 1933 and later, thought these could be defined in terms of 'Versailles' rather than 'race'. If Nazism exhibited an unusual degree of truculence, even by Continental-nationalist standards, then this was due to Germany's memory of defeat and suffering since 1918. According to many Liberals, such as Vernon Bartlett and G.E.G. Catlin[17] of the *Week-End Review*, Nazism was primarily a movement of

8

national liberation aiming to divest Germany of the unjust constraints of Versailles; viewing the phenomenon through their own liberal spectacles, they saw revisionism as the essence of Nazi ideology. Nazi antagonism to Soviet Russia could also be interpreted in the light of legitimate nationalism; nationalism, it was reasoned, always abhorred 'internationalism'. Furthermore, it suited their own anti-Communism. In some measure this also explained Nazi anti-Semitism; nationalism resented 'aliens' and 'cosmopolitans'. The identification of Nazism as essentially nationalism bent on treaty revision was persisted in by many British commentators, such as Herbert Sidebotham ('Scrutator' of the *Sunday Times*), up to the occupation of Prague.

Equating Nazism with 'normal' nationalism rendered it rational and precedented. A derivative of this approach, though less sanguine, was the identification of Nazism with Prussianism. Again, the purpose of the equation was to translate something inexplicable into something known. Seeing Hitler as a new-born Bismarck perhaps somewhat dampened apprehensions. Contrariwise, Germanophobes of Great War vintage, such as Lady Houston and Wickham Steed, favoured this interpretation if only to awaken Britain to the renascent German peril. Certainly it explained the Third Reich's ambitions of German unification and the militarisation of German life. However, the explanation failed to comprehend the full flavour of Nazism – its mystical essence, its universal philosophical pretensions and its social message and make-up.

A second major stream of interpretation of Nazism was 'economic'. All the Liberal and left-wing journals at some point subscribed to one of its variants; some, such as the *New Statesman* and *Tribune*, clung to such interpretation throughout the thirties. In this view, Nazism was seen as the German version of Fascism, a socio-economic ideology of bankrupt capitalism. It served, and was subscribed to by, a coalition of economic 'losers' – industrial and financial barons intent upon preserving their profits and economic empires, the unemployed and *Lumpenproletariat* seeking security and work, and the lower middle classes desirous of retaining their assets now imperilled by big business and political instability. Thus perceived, Nazism was an ideology of class war. German aims and aggressiveness abroad were explicable as well. Seen from this perspective, these were the inevitable results of an economy irreversibly based on rearmament, of an unquenchable need for raw materials, foodstuffs and markets to keep the armaments and civilian economy and its workers on their feet and of the regime's need to externalise pressures and resentment in order to keep afloat. In this interpretation as well, race doctrine was ignored or regarded as mere camouflage designed to conceal the 'real' (economic) motivations of the regime and its backers. Nazi antagonism towards Russia and Bolshevism was explicable as stemming from the class nature of the ideology and from its economic need for eastern European and Ukrainian raw materials, land and markets. Nazi anti-Semitism was attributed to the regime's infinite need of scapegoats and to the cupidity of a middle class covetous of Jewish wealth and jobs.

The attempt, then, was to explain Nazism in the light of something, for liberals, readily identifiable, rational and precedented, be it in economic or political terms. That such explanations contained and imparted a measure of truth is undeniable. But the peculiar admixture of known and unprecedented elements which constituted Nazism produced something novel and alien which was not explicable in the light of each of its parts. Nor was the thrust of Nazi internal and foreign policies intelligible without attending to the ideology's racial core. The failure to understand the ideology resulted in the emergence of secondary misconceptions concerning the workings and policies of the Third Reich. For many years, Nazi excesses were attributed to the first flush of revolutionary zeal or to 'evil counsellors', such as Streicher and Goebbels, with whom the Führer surrounded himself. That the evils and excesses were inherent in the ideology and in the system of government in which it was embodied was thus lost upon many observers.

Thus liberalism's values and preconceptions served as a necessary backdrop to the emergence and adoption of a policy of appeasement towards Nazi Germany. Attitudes to war, attitudes to Versailles and perceptions of Nazism constituted the fabric of the backdrop. But while a necessary pre-condition, they were not the sole or indeed main 'cause' of appeasement. Liberalism was responsible for a mood, anti-war and anti-Versailles, and afforded, when necessary, pretexts for that policy. But it was not the magnanimity or generosity of liberal thought which compelled the successive 'sell-outs' of 1935–39. It is hoped that this will be amply demonstrated in the following study.

II

THE WEEKLIES IN THE 1930s

The Spectator

The *Spectator*, founded in 1828, was the oldest of the serious weeklies in the 1930s. In its politics and personnel, it embodied the liberal Nonconformist conscience of Britain. Sir John Evelyn Wrench, its editor from 1925 until 1932 and a major proprietor through the thirties, possessed, according to Sir J. Angus Watson, 'a deeply religious outlook on life and a "leftish" Liberal outlook in politics'.[1] (Others, perhaps more accurately, thought Wrench a moderate Conservative politically.) Watson, himself the other major proprietor (together they owned 61 per cent of the Spectator Ltd), was a Baptist by upbringing, and a prominent lay preacher and composer of Congregationalist tracts. The non-proprietary editor from 1932 until 1953 was Henry Wilson Harris, a life-long Quaker and Liberal. A former colleague later recalled: 'On great occasions his Quaker principles did not fail him, and they imparted a moral authority to the *Spectator*.'[2]

The *Spectator*'s policies during the 1930s were generally determined by Wilson Harris. His editorship, however, was not free of proprietorial supervision and interference. Wrench especially exercised influence on the journal's outlook in foreign affairs. In 1935, for example, following Hitler's declarations of rearmament, J.M. Keynes approached the editors of the *New Statesman, Time & Tide* and the *Spectator* to issue a conjoint appeal for British firmness; Wilson Harris unenthusiastically consented but Wrench subsequently vetoed the scheme.[3] Wilson Harris later implied the existence of some degree of interference during the 1930s when he recalled that in the early 1940s both Wrench and Watson were away from Britain, and that he was then left 'completely to [himself] so far as the conduct of the *Spectator* on the editorial side was concerned'.[4] Such interference, however, was rarely necessary; in appointing Wilson Harris in 1932, Wrench (and Watson) had been thoroughly cognisant of shared political and philosophical assumptions. As Wilson Harris later put it: 'There were not many questions of policy which caused serious perplexity and none, I think, which involved differences of opinion between Proprietors and Editor.'[5]

Wilson Harris's career is instructive. Born in 1883 to Plymouth Quakers, he read Classics at St John's, Cambridge, and joined the staff of the (Liberal) *Daily News* (later, the *News Chronicle*) in 1903. Successively he served as sub-editor, leader-writer, news editor and diplomatic correspondent. A pacifist, Wilson Harris avoided military service during the Great War. Between 1919 and 1923 he covered the Paris Conference and subsequent European peace gatherings. He developed a passionate devotion to the principles, purposes and works of the League of Nations. In 1923 he left the *Daily News* and joined the League of Nations Union as a fully-paid executive. Until 1932 he edited that body's monthly, *Headway*, and produced annual summaries of the proceedings at Geneva. In 1925 he published *What the League of Nations Is*, a general guide to the origins, structure, aims and accomplishments of that organisation. In the 1920s Wilson Harris often travelled to France and Switzerland but failed to venture any farther eastwards; he learned no German and acquired no appreciable knowledge of German affairs. In the course of the 1930s he visited Germany only once, for ten days (in 1936). (He later recorded that he had then formed 'a sinister impression' of Hitlerism.[6])

Watson and Wrench were also early and firm supporters of the League of Nations. As Sir Angus Watson phrased it in 1935:

> As one of the fruits of the Great War, the League of Nations was founded for the judicial settlement of international aims and ambitions, and that . . . machinery is the only logical way by which the evil of War can be brought to an end. To that system organised Christianity must subscribe without reservation.[7]

This focus on the League as the sole hope and guarantor of world peace was to characterise the *Spectator*'s policy until the Abyssinian debacle of 1935–36. It is well, however, to understand Wilson Harris's early perception of the League's role. In 1919 he wrote: 'it would be a complete mistake to assume that [sanctions mean] of necessity armed force. Unless the League is to fall fatally short of the hopes of its first architects, its sanctions will be less and less military and more and more economic.'[8] This pristine reluctance to contemplate a possible recourse to military sanctions, as time would show, begged the question: What if 'moral' and economic sanctions failed? The jungle politics of the thirties were to demonstrate that an *a priori* rejection of the recourse to war and faithful implementation of the Covenant were irreconcilable postures.

Wrench believed strongly in the crucial importance to Britain of the American and Commonwealth connections. He often pressed these themes upon Wilson Harris.[9] In any case, Wilson Harris's interest in the United States was already well-established by the 1930s. In 1917 he had published an admiring biography of President Woodrow Wilson. Through the twenties and thirties, Wrench, Watson and Wilson Harris believed – in view of America's immense industrial and military prowess – that Britain's security depended upon alignment with America. They greeted America's post-1919 isolationism with despondency; as to a panacea, they clung to a vision of an America once again flexing its political muscles in the international arena. In the thirties, as this prospect recurrently expired, their fear for Britain increased; Britain, they believed, could not go it alone.

Neither was the contribution of the Dominions to the war effort of 1914–18 ever forgotten. The *Spectator* in the thirties always stressed the need to keep the Commonwealth alive. It saw Britain as at once the ultimate protector of far-flung Anglo-Saxon shores and as a potential recipient of Dominions aid should threat materialise to the metropolitan heart. In this respect, British intervention on the Continent, if contrary to the wishes of the Dominions, posed a standing threat and a barely thinkable possibility. Wrench was a founder of the Overseas League and of the English-Speaking Union; indeed it was largely to devote himself to promoting the aims of these associations that he had retired, in 1932, from the time-consuming editorship of the *Spectator*. In his case, concentration on Imperial, Commonwealth and American themes and ties served to hamper his vision regarding the minatory happenings on the Continent. In 1954 he wrote: 'India largely dominated the political horizon for the years up to 1935.'[10]

The events of the thirties starkly illuminated the inconsistency between the *Spectator*'s reliance upon Anglo-Saxon friends and its adherence to the League Covenant. When compelled to choose, the *Spectator* (until 1939) invariably abandoned the Covenant. In 1954 Wilson Harris recalled that in view of America's unwillingness to involve itself, a 'League war' against Japan over 'Manchuria' was 'unthinkable'.[11]

Wilson Harris, Watson and Wrench were all Treaty revisionists. Wilson Harris was the least outspoken of the three, though a member of Lord Allen of Hurtwood's Anglo-German Group, whose primary aim was the overthrow of the Versailles settlement.[12] Perhaps this stemmed from his presence in Paris in 1919, at which time he acquired a perceptive familiarity with the multiple interests, pressures and considerations which had gone into the smithy as the Treaty's clauses were forged. With Wrench, he hoped that the League, over the years, would prove a worthy and efficient instrument for effecting the necessary emendations. In Paris and, later, elsewhere, Wilson Harris formed a strong attachment to Masaryk and Beneš and to their fledgling Republic.

13

Watson and Wrench were more outspoken about the iniquities of Versailles. In 1935 Watson wrote: 'we are bound to recognise that the Treaty of Versailles . . . was not only harsh but unjust in its terms.'[13] In 1940 a badly disabused Wrench wrote in his apologia, *I Loved Germany*: 'I agreed heart and soul with Mr Garvin that the root vice of the whole Treaty was that it left the German race no hope but revenge.'[14]

Wrench was a life-long and prominent Germanophile; he first visited Germany at the age of 12; of that visit he later wrote that it 'made so deep an impression on my consciousness that I am unable to remember my outlook upon life uncoloured by my German experience'.[15] German was both read and spoken at home. Four decades later Wrench wrote that in 1898 he first 'realised the wide implications of the struggle of Teuton versus Slav'.[16] He admired German efficiency, strength, cleanliness, health, outdoor activities, romanticism and idealism; with all these, in the thirties, he was to identify Hitlerism. Though Wilson Harris did not share Wrench's overt Germanophilia, it was to suffuse the *Spectator* for much of the decade.

An abhorrence of war informed all the *Spectator*'s views on Germany and on British foreign policy until 1939. In part, it was based on Wilson Harris's never discarded pacifism; in great measure it was the fruit of memories of the Great War's horrors and of an anticipation of the yet greater horrors a renewed world holocaust would unleash. Wrench and Watson were not pacifists. Watson, in fact, in 1935 – referring to League action against Italy over Abyssinia – specifically denounced pacifism as impractical. But he believed that another world war would lead to the extinction of Western civilisation and, perhaps, of mankind itself.[17] Not surprisingly the philosophical disagreement over pacifism failed to generate any basic divergence over British policy towards Germany among the *Spectator*'s troika.

The journal throughout the thirties expressed a loathing for Communism and all its works. While frequently admitting that the Soviet Union was not bent on aggression or expansion, the editor often even-handedly lamented that Britain and France were fated to entanglement in a 'war of ideologies' (between Russia and Germany) in which none of their vital interests were at stake. A comment of Watson's from 1937 is revealing in its balance. He wrote: 'The *Spectator* is at once opposed to the Fascist form of politics as operating in Germany and Italy to-day and to the Communist ideal dominating Russia, seeing in both policies the same goal of a totalitarian State.'[18]

Such were the assumptions governing the *Spectator*'s policies during the thirties. Their issue, as regards Germany, was overt and conscious appeasement. With Chamberlain, the journal abandoned appeasement only in March 1939. The bulk of the *Spectator*'s articles on the Reich between 1933 and 1937 were distinctly pro-German; Sir Arnold Wilson, Wrench himself, H. Powys Greenwood and others of similar persuasion continuously lauded the internal achievements of the Hitler regime and avowed the Nazis' peaceful intentions abroad. At very worst, they declared, the foreign policy ambitions of the new Germany were limited to the rectification of the grosser injustices of Versailles; thoughts of war and of the use of force were as remote from Hitler's mind as from that of any normal British veteran of the trenches. Only the Nazi persecution of the Jews, pacifists and the Churches was exempted from any trace of adulation or whitewash.

Wilson Harris, in his leaders and editorial notes, was somewhat more balanced. He genuinely deplored Nazism and voiced at least a suspicion that Hitler's actions if not intentions spelt European war. Occasionally, he denounced the Nazi regime roundly and forcefully, taking exception to both its internal and foreign policies. However, usually he took issue with the method rather than the substance of Nazi activities. And the greater loomed the danger of British involvement in war with Germany, the more strident became his advocacy of appeasement.

From 1936, articles critical of the internal workings of the Nazi regime began to appear in the *Spectator*. Such contributions – from R.H.S. Crossman, R.C.K. Ensor and others – by 1938 came to outweigh those from apologists of Germany.

On the political side, Wilson Harris was assisted in the 1930s by R.A. Scott-James and Goronwy Rees. Scott-James served as Assistant Editor and leader-writer from 1933 to the end of 1935; Rees fulfilled these functions from February 1936 until August 1939.

Scott-James was essentially a literary man, and provided little comment on foreign affairs in the pages of the *Spectator* or elsewhere. Rees was a political animal. He was a firm critic of Nazism, his familiarity with the movement and ideology dating from long and frequent stays in late Weimar and early Hitler Germany. He had read *Mein Kampf* in 1932. In common with many of his peers, Rees had found Weimar culture magnetic and the Treaty of Versailles condemnable. With the coming of Hitler, however, he put aside both his Germanophilia and his Versailles-induced 'guilty conscience'.[19]

Comment on international affairs in the *Spectator* was proffered in leaders, in news-review paragraphs ('Notes of the Week'), in Wilson Harris's 'A Spectator's Notebook' (a column mirroring Kingsley Martin's 'London Diary') and in special contributions.

Leaders were normally written by the Editor or by his Assistant. From 1932 through 1936 almost all the foreign affairs leaders were written by

Wilson Harris himself; home affairs (usually second) leaders were left to the Assistant Editor. From the end of 1936, Wilson Harris gradually relinquished his monopoly of foreign affairs; by 1938 Rees was writing as many foreign affairs leaders as the Editor. But Wilson Harris remained in total control of policy; in writing leaders on European affairs, Rees exercised self-censorship.[20] Between 1932 and 1937 Wilson Harris wrote most of the leaders concerning the 'aerial situation' – air disarmament, air attack and defence, projected effects of bombing and hopes for its prohibition. During 1938 most leaders on these matters were written by Rees.

The weekly news-review paragraphs were penned by various staff-members, the Assistant Editor contributing the lion's share. They contained opinion and comment as well as straight news. 'A Spectator's Notebook', signed Janus, was usually completely written by Wilson Harris. He later said of the column that it gave him more satisfaction than writing leaders, for 'under cover of pseudonymity . . . [the writer] can permit himself an irresponsibility and freedom of comment not appropriate to articles with full editorial weight behind them . . . "Janus" had been permitted certain vagaries.'[21] Some of these will later be cited.

The Economist

Sir Walter Layton edited *The Economist* from 1922 until September 1938. A Cambridge-trained economist, he was a life-long Liberal Party supporter and a practising Nonconformist. In 1928 he was instrumental in organising the purchase of *The Economist* by the Financial Newspaper Proprietors Ltd. and a group of individuals. He was one of the journal's main shareholders in the thirties, and remained so until his death in 1966. In the reorganisation of 1928 a board of independent, non-shareholding trustees was created, vested with the power to veto the appointment or dismissal of the Editor by the proprietors. 'Thus the freedom of the Editor from the control of the financial interest was protected and his sole responsibility for the policy of the paper was preserved.'[22]

In the thirties, Layton became increasingly preoccupied with the management of the *News Chronicle*; he wrote few of the *Economist*'s leaders between 1933 and 1938. Most leading articles, however, were vetted by him before publication. Substantial revision was rare. But often he toned down leaders dealing with Nazi Germany and the European situation. He was generally averse to strong language. He preferred 'balanced' conclusions; usually, he did this by 'mutilating' the last paragraph of leaders 'to give the conclusion an "on the one hand" and "on the other" framework'.[23] The content and line of editorial articles was usually determined at editorial board meetings on Monday afternoons, with

Layton in the chair. Throughout these years he 'always had the first word and the last in deciding what to say and in deciding what to publish'.[24] On 1 October 1938 Geoffrey Crowther assumed the editorship. His tenure was also marked by the editor's total control over policy. Policy and leaders became firmer in their commitment against appeasement.[25]

The editorial staff of *The Economist* in the thirties, larger than that of any of its sister journals, consisted of some ten members. Of these, from 1933 Layton himself, Graham Hutton (until 1938), Douglas Jay (until the end of 1936) and Crowther concerned themselves with the paper's foreign policy. From October 1938, as Crowther's deputy, Donald Tyerman also took a hand in foreign affairs. Crowther, under Layton, normally wrote on economic subjects and on America. Jay contributed occasional leaders on European and German developments though he usually dealt with home affairs. Leaders on central and eastern European affairs were normally written by Hutton, though Arnold Toynbee contributed some, as he did most of those on League of Nations, Far Eastern and Mediterranean affairs. As in the *Spectator*, leaders were invariably unsigned.[26]

Foreign affairs coverage and comment was also contained in the journal's weekly news review paragraphs ('Notes of the Week'), in rare, signed full-length contributions, and in regular despatches from the journal's foreign correspondents. Luigi Einaudi wrote from Rome and F. Long from Berlin. Both were firm anti-Fascists though, of necessity, their articles were circumlocutory. These were usually sub-edited by Jay and Hutton. Their content was rarely amended in any substantive manner.[27]

The Monday afternoon editorial gatherings appear to have been characterised through 1933–39 by a virtual consensus on foreign affairs. Toynbee, a regular though non-staff leader writer, was an exception. From late 1935 he supported colonial appeasement of Germany and, until some time in 1937, believed in Hitler's sincere will to peace; *The Economist* never supported the former and, by and large, failed to believe in the latter. From Munich until the outbreak of the Second World War Toynbee reverted to an advocacy of appeasement, contrary to the journal's policy. Hence, Toynbee's editorial contributions in the journal between 1936 and 1939 were confined to Near and Far Eastern affairs.[28]

Layton's thinking in the 1930s was governed by a pervasive vision of British strategic and economic weakness and by an overriding concern for the safety of the mother country, the colonies and the Dominions. Before 1914, *The Economist* had posited that 'the economic, financial and social convulsions attendant upon a general European war appeared too evil to incur by any action or policy'.[29] This argument was more cogent still in the circumstances of the thirties. On the Munitions Council during the Great War, Layton had acquired a healthy appreciation of the enormous

17

costs of modern war. Britain had changed from a creditor to a debtor nation; the Empire's economic sinews had been severely tried. He envisaged a future war as yet more costly. To the latter-day Puritan conscience war appeared both immoral and infinitely wasteful.

Economic considerations aside, 1914–18 had demonstrated that the British Empire 'could not depend for its security, under modern conditions, on its own strength in isolation – any more than could the United States or other Great Powers'.[30] Security had henceforth to be 'collective' or not at all. The Empire was vast and fragile, an inviting target to would-be aggressors. In the course of the 1930s this vulnerability became increasingly stark. Successive assaults on weak states highlighted the condition of international 'anarchy'. Layton, Hutton and Toynbee were beset by the growing fear that Japan, Germany and Italy might eventually pounce in concert upon Britain and the Empire. 'Throwing the weak to the wolves' would serve only to 'whet the wolves' appetite' for the subsequent plunder of the Empire, wrote Toynbee.[31] As Hutton put it in 1936, 'the British Empire . . . would be quite indefensible if attacks were made on it from all the world's danger spots at once'.[32]

It was precisely because he recognised the fundamental weakness and vulnerability of the Empire that Layton was a staunch supporter of the League and of the Covenant during the 1920s and 1930s; only a collective system could assure the Empire's security. So,

> to the Editor of the paper after 1921, and to his associates, it was imperative that the British Government should see in the League the repository and instrument of this new collective security; and should put into that repository all the political and moral resources of which they were capable.[33]

Layton, between 1919 and 1921, had been instrumental in establishing the League's Economic and Financial Section; Toynbee, as a minor official in the British Delegation at the Paris Peace Conference, had also attended at the League's birth. Until 1936 at least, Layton, Hutton and Toynbee viewed the League as crucial to the maintenance of international law and order and as the sole institutional framework of collective security. Their view of the League was more muscular, and perhaps less moralistic, than Wilson Harris's. All three recoiled from war, but they looked with even greater trepidation upon the prospect of a war which Britain and the Empire could not win and might well lose. All three firmly repudiated pacifism.[34]

With the League's demise in 1935–36, proponents of collective security were hard-pressed to discover an alternative institutional framework. Layton was loath to plump for pre-Great War-type alliances. In the summer of 1936 he stated: 'We must never give the impression of endeavouring to build up a rival block against Germany.'[35] However, worsening world conditions and the growing strength and aggressiveness of the Dictator States eventually convinced Layton and Hutton that a reversion to old-style alliances was inescapable. With Churchill, *The Economist*, from September 1937, came out in favour of a grand, containing alliance with France and Russia, a course reluctantly adopted by most of the weeklies only some 18 months later.

The Economist found Communist theory and Bolshevist practice repellent. But it never ascribed aggressive intentions to Stalinist Russia. And, confronted by the choice of evil ideologies on the Continent, the journal never evinced uncertainty as to which was worse: 'If I had to choose between Communism and Fascism – which God forbid – I should choose Communism,'[36] declared Sir Walter Layton. However, like the *Spectator*, *The Economist* often predicted that an inevitable outcome of a new world war would be the subversion of social structures, paving the way for revolution.

Given its perception of British weakness and the economic woes of war, *The Economist* was engrossed with the problem of the Commonwealth and American connections. For most of the thirties there was, in practice, a frightening divide between maintaining the Anglo-Saxon connections and supporting the Covenant. On the one hand, Australia, Canada and South Africa were unwilling to commit themselves to League action against aggressors in far-away shores and were especially averse to participation in a further blood-letting on the Continent. Nor, it was understood, was an isolationist America poised on the brink of involvement against Germany, Japan or Italy. On the other hand, perversely, the great American public was known to look askance at any display of British weakness in confronting aggressors. And the Dominions and colonies, especially Australia, New Zealand and India looked to Britain for protection against possible Japanese encroachments. However, confronting Japan in the east, without American assistance, would denude Britain of power in the European theatre; and confrontation with Germany and/or Italy in Europe and the Mediterranean would fail to elicit Dominions aid. The latter might well bring about the dissolution of the Commonwealth.

To *The Economist*'s staff, the prospect of entering another great war without any assurance of ultimate American involvement was regarded with grave misgivings. Certainly this was a prominent consideration in Hutton's mind when, having outlined Germany's ineluctably aggressive intentions and having stressed the threat these presented to vital British interests, he advocated an inactive policy of rejecting all further

19

commitments. It was, he wrote in October 1936, 'axiomatic that America will not engage in a European war again to succour Britain until London lies well-nigh in ruins – and perhaps not then'.[37] Crowther, even before October 1938, believed war with Germany to be inevitable; and believed that 'the *only* way the war could be won and not lost was by (a) U.S. help and (b) U.S. participation; that was the *Economist*'s premise from 1938 through the bad days of 1940–1 to Pearl Harbour'.[38]

The usual dualism pervaded *The Economist* with regard to the Treaty of Versailles and its possible revision. Layton, Toynbee and Jay conceded, like most enlightened Englishmen during the 1920s and early 1930s, that the Peace Treaties had treated Germany unfairly, and that German grievances had ultimately to be assuaged if peace was to prosper. Collective security without the possibility of 'peaceful change', said Toynbee in 1935, would be like 'a boiler without a safety valve'.[39] Jay, however, while willing to see revision in favour of a democratic, unaggressive Germany, ruled against it once the Third Reich's expansionist credentials were irrevocably established.[40] Toynbee, differing from *The Economist*, from 1935 favoured colonial adjustments but was, before 1938, averse to the revision of eastern European frontiers.[41] Layton was a founder-member of the Anglo-German Group which, formed in the winter of 1933/4, espoused the abandonment of the Versailles settlement. But he was also a prominent supporter of collective security and an opponent of any Treaty revision in favour of an aggressive Germany.[42] The ambivalence with which many regarded the Versailles Treaty (and revision) in the wake of Hitler's assumption of power was perhaps epitomised in Hutton's survey of the European situation in 1936. In the volume *Is It Peace?* Hutton referred, on the one hand, to 'the error of a Carthaginian peace' and to 'the wind which the very small council of elder statesmen sowed in 1919', and, on the other, to 'the Peace of 1919–21 – the fairest territorial settlement of modern history, for it was drawn up by unimpassioned experts – [which] promised well for Europe'.[43]

Throughout the years 1933–39 *The Economist*, in leaders, news review paragraphs, foreign correspondence and signed articles, was unflagging and unreserved in its condemnation of Nazi Germany. The internal policies of the Reich were consistently vilified, and Hitlerism was usually portrayed as a standing threat to European peace. Reference to, let alone praise of, the social and economic achievements of the Third Reich (efficiency, standards of health, levels of employment) was extremely rare. Perhaps Layton failed to distinguish between the novel evil of Nazism and its Prussian-militarist precursor; but he rarely accepted Hitler's professions of peaceful intent at face value.[44]

Time & Tide

Time & Tide was founded in 1920 by Viscountess Rhondda (Margaret Haig Thomas), daughter and sole heir of Viscount Rhondda, the coal magnate and Liberal politician. She owned the journal until her death in 1958 and edited it from 1926. *Time & Tide*, wrote her successor, Anthony Lejeune, was 'shaped in every detail to her wishes, standing for the things in which she passionately believed: the infinite value of individuals, personal freedom, opposition to tyranny . . .'.[45]

Viscountess Rhondda in 1908 became a militant suffragette and a member of the Women's Social and Political Union. During the 1920s and early 1930s she was a left-wing Liberal though increasingly in later life (and especially after the Second World War) she found herself shifting towards the Right. An obsessive anti-Communism characterised *Time & Tide* in the late 1940s. In the thirties Lady Rhondda ran the journal with the aid of Veronica Wedgwood, Cicely Hamilton, Theodora Bosanquet (literary editor from 1935 until 1943) and Rebecca West, all of whom sat, at various times, on the board of directors.[46]

Through the thirties Norman Angell contributed a monthly four-page commentary on international affairs; his line usually, though not invariably, conformed to editorial policy. Leaders were normally unsigned. Major ones were written by Lady Rhondda; Cicely Hamilton, Norman Angell and Odette Keun occasionally contributed signed ones as did, on at least one occasion, F.A. Voigt.

As with the other weeklies, *Time & Tide*'s attitude to the Treaty of Versailles is revealing as to the origins and nature of appeasement in the thirties. Like most Liberals, Lady Rhondda, until 1933, strongly condemned the injustices of the Peace Treaties and consistently called for their revision. Hitler's assumption of power wrought a basic change. *Time & Tide* revealed an early understanding of the meaning of Nazism and of the foreign policy ambition of the Reich. Therefore, Lady Rhondda wrote in March 1933, 'another "peace" conference to unwrite the Versailles Treaty' would be due only 'as soon as the Royalist-Nazi revolution in Germany has got over its violent stage'.[47] And on 21 October 1933 the journal stated that while no 'self-righteous bullying' must be exercised against Germany, Britain must remain 'committed by honour and by common sense alike . . . to stand by the Treaties'.[48] Norman Angell at the time in fact dismissed the problem of the Treaty and its revision as secondary. Wars like 1914–18, he argued, arose not from grievances, feigned or legitimate, but out of fears by one side or another (or both) of an actual or developing imbalance of power to their detriment.[49]

But – and this applied to most of the weeklies, as will be shown – the events of 1935 undermined Lady Rhondda's convictions and political attitudes. In May of that year she called upon Britain

> to join with the Powers and prevent, in the last resort by force, any further violations of the Treaty . . . for there can be, in the view of responsible opinion, no greater danger to the peace of Europe that a continuation . . . [of] unilateral repudiations of the Treaty of Versailles.[50]

Yet six weeks later the journal enthusiastically welcomed the conclusion of the Anglo-German Naval Agreement with the observation that though it 'makes for a further breach in the Versailles Treaty . . . it is clear now that the time has come when the Treaty can no longer be regarded as sacrosanct'.[51]

From the summer of 1935 until the spring of 1938 *Time & Tide* reverted to its former, pre-Hitler advocacy of revision which, in the new context, meant the espousal of appeasement. On 21 November 1936 the journal resurrected the old lament: 'The whole world knows that the Treaty of Versailles was unjust', and called for a negotiated revision of its territorial clauses.[52] Of colonies *Time & Tide* wrote a month later: 'There seems no valid reason for refusing to Germany her share of the loot.'[53] 'Nothing', reiterated the journal a year later, 'that can be said about Hitler justifies us in refusing to recognise Germany's legitimate grievances.' If war must come, went the argument, Britain ought not to enter it with 'pockets bulging with swag'.[54] *Time & Tide*'s almost wholehearted support of positive appeasement, however, ceased in the spring of 1938, in advance of most of its peers. Henceforth, justification of Nazi policies and resuscitation of Versailles-based grievances were abruptly terminated.

Most of the journal's other assumptions followed a similar route. Through the twenties and thirties Lady Rhondda strongly supported the League of Nations and the Covenant. But from 1935 until 1938 this support was effectively circumscribed by the demands of expediency. Fear of war prompted the journal to drop its previous advocacy of a League blockade of the Suez Canal against Italian shipping *en route* to Eritrea in 1935. In 1936 *Time & Tide* questioned the necessity or utility of the League's condemnation of the Nazi re-militarisation of the Rhineland. After 1936, of course, the League was an irrelevance in the international arena. But *Time & Tide* refused to admit this. It persisted in offering lip-service to the ideal while advocating caution in practice; this, in turn, served to camouflage, justify and facilitate the journal's rejection of rearmament and alliances until 1938.

Antagonism in principle to 'great armaments' and to military alliances was a prejudice of Great War vintage. Until 1938 *Time & Tide* consistently opposed great armaments and only reluctantly endorsed small ones. Of the Defence White Paper and the Service Estimates of 1935 the journal wrote: 'The real criticism of these estimates is that they are framed on the basis of the world as it existed before . . . 1914.'[55] Such comment ran directly contrary to Lady Rhondda's (and Norman Angell's) perception of the threat to peace and to Britain posed by the militarism of Germany, Italy and Japan. Of the Conservative Party resolutions of 1935, calling for aerial and naval rearmament, she wrote:

> With none of these proposals . . . would any realist supporter of the League quarrel. It is useless to talk of pooled security unless Great Britain is prepared to put something effective into the pool . . . But though a measure of rearmament is necessary, it must be conceived within the framework of the League of Nations.[56]

There was no getting away from the time-worn thesis: arms make for wars. In the wake of the Rhineland coup, *Time & Tide* stated: 'Germany may be driven to war by the momentum of a gigantic armaments industry that cannot slow down.'[57] Yet, repeatedly since 1933, the journal had argued that Nazism meant war because of its racial philosophy, geo-political ambitions and general subscription to the tactics of gangsterism. The journal often asserted its objection to rearmament on the grounds that no amount of arms could 'ensure immunity from the European show-down which must inevitably come if the apostles of force are bent on challenging the apostles of order'; it omitted the crucial consideration that rearmament *would* influence the outcome of such a war if not assist in its prevention.[58]

If the League, and moral suasion, did not work, how could the dictators be stymied? *Time & Tide* 'confronted' the problem with lip-service to League principles, advocacy of revision – meaning appeasement – and a rejection of a policy of containment. This rejection, consistently maintained until 1938 (exclusive of the lapse of 1933–34), was based on the pre-Great War belief that military alliances spelt war. In September 1936 *Time & Tide* enumerated its objections to both 'popular front' and Churchillian thinking: It 'would reduce the League to a farce and could be guaranteed to bring the Second World War in the shortest possible time'.[59] To be sure, Lady Rhondda's repudiation of a 'grand alliance' owed something to her fervid anti-Communism. This did not, however, deter her (or many others) from advocating the self-same course in 1939.

Time & Tide, throughout 1933–39, consistently stressed the evil and peril of Nazism. It bitterly denounced the Reich's internal policies and usually deemed Nazi foreign policy to be unalterably aggressive. *Time & Tide* often warned of German designs in central and eastern Europe

23

and, as pre-figured in *Mein Kampf*, against Russia. Nor was the journal oblivious to the threat posed by Germany (and Italy and Japan) to the well-being and, indeed, the existence of Britain and the Empire. Like *The Economist*, Lady Rhondda argued that the British Empire represented the ultimate prey of the signatories of the anti-Comintern Pact.[60]

The New Statesman

The *New Statesman* was probably the most important of the serious weeklies of the 1930s; it was, at the time, the most widely read and the most widely quoted. One critical 'friend', Beatrice Webb, in 1938 thought the *New Statesman* 'the most influential of the political weeklies';[61] Douglas Woodruff, a Conservative antagonist, shared this view.[62] Many men, grown to prominence in the arts and in government, later recalled the journal as a formative influence in their adolescence. Perhaps Kingsley Martin offered a telling explanation when he wrote that the *New Statesman* 'was successful because it understood the perplexities of the pacifists, the Liberals, of Labour, the Communists and even of the Conservatives . . . We were a reflection of everyone's perplexities.'[63]

The *New Statesman* was launched by the Webbs, G. Bernard Shaw and Clifford Sharp, its first editor, in 1913, with the primary purpose of promoting social and economic reform according to the lights of Fabian socialism. Like *The Economist*, it initially opposed Britain's entry into the First World War. The journal reversed its posture with the German invasion of Belgium. But its support of the war effort was circumscribed by grave and consistent reservations: it adamantly opposed conscription and the persecution of conscientious objectors; and it viewed Tsarist Russia, in Sharp's eyes representing 'Eastern barbarism', as the great ultimate threat to civilisation. Almost from the start of the Great War, the *New Statesman* pressed for a negotiated, moderate and unvengeful peace; after the publication of the Peace Treaties, it campaigned vigorously for their revision.

During the 1930s the *New Statesman* absorbed two of its rivals, the Liberal *Nation* (1931) and the *Week-End Review* (1934), attaining a weekly circulation figure of 30,000. In large measure, this great leap forward was the product of the talents, policies and personality of one remarkable man, Basil Kingsley Martin, the *New Statesman*'s editor from 1931 until 1960. He was born in 1897, the son of an ex-Calvinist Unitarian minister. A pacifist, Kingsley Martin served in France during the Great War with the Friends' Ambulance Unit. Subsequently, he read History at Magdalene College, lectured at the L.S.E. and served, from 1927 until 1930, as a leader writer on the *Manchester Guardian*.

The policies advanced in the *New Statesman* during the 1930s are intelligible only in the light of the character as well as the mind-set of its editor; emotion was as fully represented as cogitation in its pages. Hugh Dalton, after a discussion of European war and peace prospects, described him as 'a most emotional, unstable person with little judgement'.[64] Beatrice Webb concurred, noting that Kingsley Martin was 'a somewhat neurotic type' and that 'his mind is a pendulum and moves from side to side over all issues in a rather tiresome fashion'. She believed him 'a typical specimen of a new type of mugwump'. She complained that he lacked 'any permanent scale of values . . . about men and affairs'. She allowed, however, that 'he means well'.[65] Though somewhat harsh, this view of the *New Statesman*'s editor was shared by most contemporaries who knew him. Perhaps Malcolm Muggeridge, a fellow leader writer on the *Manchester Guardian*, struck the nail most firmly on the head when he dubbed Kingsley Martin 'a man for all causes'.[66] Keynes apparently concurred for he once reproved Martin for his 'endless obsession with grievances . . .; you seem to love grievances and to love nothing else'.[67] Muggeridge added: 'He had a super-abundance of principles, enough and to spare for all possible eventualities', but 'indecision [was] the very heart and soul of him'.[68]

With rare lapses, Kingsley Martin alone determined and formulated *New Statesman* policy between 1931 and 1939. In all that concerned the Dictator States, that policy was meticulously inconsistent and confused. At the core of the confusion, aptly mirroring the soul of the editor, lay an almost ineffable abhorrence and fear of war. A single issue of the *New Statesman* carried articles variously and clamorously espousing British isolationism, pacifism, positive appeasement and military resistance to the aggressor states.[69]

Kingsley Martin was notoriously impressionable. Often, he echoed advice and suggestions most recently imbibed. Elizabeth Wiskemann, with ambiguous generosity, even ascribed Kingsley Martin's infamous piece of 27 August 1938, advocating Czech cession of the Sudeten fringes to Germany, 'to a last-minute caller . . . at the *New Statesman* office before the paper went to press'.[70] Of those who sat on the journal's board of directors, Keynes undoubtedly carried the most weight with the editor. For much of the decade – and particularly during crises – he was to reinforce Kingsley Martin's wavering acceptance of appeasement as a policy embodying 'wisdom and justice rather than fear and treachery'.[71] H.N. Brailsford and C.E.M. Joad, frequent contributors, also influenced the editor in the same direction. Brailsford was a life-long Germanophile and traducer of the Versailles settlement; Joad stuck through thick and thin to pacifism on moral and practical grounds.[72]

Unlike Joad, Kingsley Martin was never a systematic, 'philosophical' pacifist. While sharing man's normal abhorrence for conflict, his 'pacifism', if that is the correct term, boiled down to an acute, physical fear of war.[73] He was especially fearful of the projected devastation by air attack. His Nonconformist upbringing, his experiences in the war-zones in France over 1917–18 and his integration in the intellectual milieu of the 1920s undoubtedly also prompted him towards 'pacifism'. Through the 1930s he never cast doubt on the moral necessity of combating Fascism; but his fear of war and of air assault upon Britain consistently prevented him from advocating British involvement in that 'coming war' whose justice he never questioned. Like an unregenerate smoker who time and again 'breaks' the habit, Kingsley Martin repeatedly 'disavowed' his pacifist convictions. Later, he variously dated his rejection of pacifism from the Japanese assault on Manchuria in 1931, from 'the helplessness of the League of Nations in the face of the Italian invasion of Abyssinia' and from the first year of the Spanish Civil War.[74] But, ultimately, as he admitted to G.E.R. Gedye in September 1938: 'I am at heart a pacifist.'[75] Through the thirties he remained unable to face the prospect of a new world war, even if – as he often recognised – that were the only means of stemming aggression and destroying the dictators.

During the 1930s the *New Statesman* consistently espoused general disarmament, arms limitation agreements, and pacts prohibiting the use of certain weapons (gas, bombers and submarines). Until late in 1939 the journal refused to support or even condone limited British rearmament, which, in effect, meant the acceptance of gradual, unilateral British disarmament (given the rapid obsolescence of weapon types and the concomitant growth of the armed forces of potentially hostile powers). These too stemmed from vague pacifist convictions and a concrete fear of war.

According to Kingsley Martin, a rigid belief in the injustice of the Peace Treaties encumbered the *New Statesman* in its consideration of policy towards Nazi Germany in the 1930s. He wrote: 'Almost everyone, Conservatives, Liberals and Labour alike regarded the French notion of keeping Germany permanently as a second-class power as absurd, and agreed that the Versailles Treaty must be revised in Germany's favour.'[76] Hitler, soon after assuming power, replaced that Treaty (and armaments and French efforts to encircle Germany) as Kingsley Martin's *bête noire*. But the *New Statesman* continued to denounce the post-1918 settlement; anti-Versailles arguments were frequently trotted out in at least partial justification of German designs and actions, and in support of British acquiescence in them. German claims to the Sudetenland were upheld as late as August 1938 on this basis.

Yet clearly then and later Kingsley Martin recognised the fallaciousness and dishonesty of evoking 'Versailles' in defence of appeasement. From 1933 onwards the *New Statesman* often stressed that whatever the original sins of Versailles, concessions, by way of Treaty revision, should not in morality, and could not in safety, be vouchsafed an aggressive, expansionist Nazi regime. Keynes, Kingsley Martin later wrote, 'interpreted [Hitler's] objective as the end of the injustices of Versailles' whereas he himself never believed that Nazi aims were confined to Treaty revision.[77] It was, mainly, fear of war and not a desire to serve justice through Treaty revision which prompted the *New Statesman*'s frequently appeasing stance towards Nazi Germany.

Kingsley Martin's perception of Nazi internal policies as unmitigatedly evil was consistent and vocal. From 1933, the *New Statesman* continuously exposed and denounced them. Concerning Nazi foreign policy, the journal was somewhat less consistent and informative. Usually, though misleading as to its roots, the paper portrayed the thrust of Nazi policy as unalterably aggressive. In line with the thinking of Brailsford, John Strachey and other Marxist interpreters, Kingsley Martin viewed Nazism/Fascism as the final stage of crisis-ridden capitalism whose natural issue, for economic reasons, was aggression and war. Many years later he asserted that Elizabeth Wiskemann had opened his eyes to the fact that 'the Nazis represented a deep, nationalist force in Germany which appealed to something more primitive than class'.[78] As will be shown, such understanding failed to illuminate the *New Statesman*'s pages during most of the 1930s.

As intimated, Kingsley Martin was ambivalent towards collective security and the League of Nations. With justice, one might say that the editor and the majority of his colleagues were vocal supporters of the Covenant so long as that support was theoretical, unexacting and free of hazard (as was the case, with the exception of the Far East, before 1935). Following Hitler's declarations of rearmament and Mussolini's assault on Abyssinia, the *New Statesman* embarked on a course of vacillation. The journal blew hot and cold – hot and militant as the threat of war receded, cold and appeasing as the risk of war loomed large. With war in sight, the journal was wont to recall the iniquities of Versailles, pacifist inhibitions and the peril of aerial bombardment.

For Kingsley Martin, Brailsford and Keynes, 1935 revealed the terrible paradox at the heart of the Covenant. The League had been founded to stop aggression and war; until 1935, many viewed it as the great hope of humankind. But if, as in 1935, States flouted the Covenant, the League was committed to censure, sanctions and, *in extremis*, war. Collective security, if ineffective as a deterrent, compelled peace-lovers to resort to war; otherwise the concept was meaningless. 1935 unmasked the paradox, and the 'enlightened' were found wanting. Over Abyssinia Kingsley Martin privately even questioned the rightness of applying economic sanctions against Italy. In a letter to Konni Zilliacus he argued that such sanctions might precipitate a drift towards a 'regular imperialist war' which, in turn, would lead to a break-up of the Labour Party.[79]

After Abyssinia, collective security based on the League, as Kingsley Martin later acknowledged, became 'a mere slogan'.[80] But it was one regularly indulged in in the pages of the *New Statesman*. If anything, collective security after 1935 could only mean adhesion to a containing alliance between like-minded States directed *against* specific aggressive States and support of war against peace-breakers. But these things, through fear of the potential ravages of war, through Great War prejudices against military alliances and through pacifist sentiments, the *New Statesman* refused, in fact, to support.

Through the 1930s until the Molotov–Ribbentrop Pact, the *New Statesman* expressed a special regard for the internal development and well-being of the Soviet Union. It always believed that State to be Hitler's primary future target, and often condemned what it regarded as manifestations of support in Britain for a Nazi assault on the Socialist motherland. Late in the thirties, Kingsley Martin's pro-Soviet obsession prompted him to argue, in opposing British rearmament, 'that all the other threats of war were unlikely to be realised but that a combination against the Soviet Union was the probable upshot'.[81] Criticism of the internal policies of Stalinism was muted and infrequent. The editor often refused to publish reports, such as Orwell's on the suppression of the POUM in Catalonia, if their purport was anti-Communist.

Two other *New Statesman* figures are worth mentioning. Aylmer Vallance, *de facto* Assistant Editor from 1935, was a virulent detractor of the Peace Treaties. In 1937 he described Versailles as 'an abominable sowing' bred of wartime 'paranoia' and 'insanity', and asserted that it was responsible for 'the convulsing [of] the world to-day'.[82] Until 1939 Vallance remained a staunch supporter of appeasement. Of another cast of mind was R.H.S. Crossman, who joined the editorial staff in 1937. Speaking German and familiar with the Nazi reality at first hand – as Kingsley Martin was not – he was an early and usually firm anti-appeaser.[83] However, he too suffered lapses, perhaps in part due to exposure to Martin's influence. In October 1938, for example, he argued against holding staff talks with France and against entering into alliance with Russia for fear of a German pre-emptive air attack on Britain.[84]

Major foreign policy leaders in the 1930s were usually written by Kingsley Martin. Brailsford, Vallance from 1935, and Crossman from

1937 were frequent editorial contributors. The 'London Diary' column, which contained much political comment, was mostly written by Kingsley Martin. The weekly news review notes ('Comments') were written by the various staff members. G. Bernard Shaw, C.E.M. Joad and Keynes frequently contributed articles. The journal's foreign correspondents, Alexander Werth and Robert Dell in Paris, and Elizabeth Wiskemann in Central Europe, consistently sent in firm anti-Nazi, anti-appeasement articles.

Truth

Truth was the leading Conservative weekly review during the 1930s. In the previous decade it had attained a peak of influence and circulation under the editorship of Henry Labouchère. It had established a reputation as an exposer of frauds and commercial malpractice. In the thirties, under the editorship of Henry Newnham, the journal entered a period of decline. Its circulation levelled off at 7,000; its readership encompassed mostly elderly retired officers and civil servants, and parish vicars. It apparently had little if any political influence. Henry Brooke chaired the Board of Truth Publishing Company between 1937 and 1939; Joseph Ball, in the background, exercised control over the journal's policy.[85]

Before Hitler's rise to power *Truth* was vehemently revisionist and anti-French. In 1930 its editor stated: 'I for one would rejoice at [the overthrow of] ... some of the iniquitous injustices of Versailles and [at the removal] ... of the absurd frontiers and harassing tariff walls which now impede the financial rehabilitation of Europe.'[86] The journal called the Polish Corridor and the Silesian settlement 'monstrosities'.[87] It castigated British foreign policy as being 'all that the most ardent Parisian chauvinist could hope'.[88] *Truth*'s objections to the Versailles *status quo* were not mainly of a moral order; in the absence of revision it believed, simply, 'there will be another war'.[89] The journal's anti-French stance, which perhaps owed something also to the non-Conservative composition of successive French governments, even encompassed Locarno, which it deemed 'an act of lunacy'. Locarno bound Britain to France while Europe's eastern frontiers remained iniquitous and unchanged; France was bound to Poland which, 'like all parvenus, [was] touchy, provocative and quite reckless'; and without a solution to the problem of the Corridor, war between Germany and Poland was inevitable.[90]

A major if temporary change of heart affected *Truth* in the wake of Hitler's assumption of power. As the months passed, and the evidence mounted of Nazi barbarism, *Truth* perceived signs 'that the Hitlerite danger is not likely to be confined to Germany ... Germany is making ready to fall on her neighbours, and there is no shadow of doubt that nothing but her unreadiness is ever likely to deter her from her objective.' The journal therefore urged that Germany be unequivocally told 'that the Peace Treaty is going to stand, every word of it, until Hitler falls'.[91] Always anti-Communist, *Truth* by mid-1933 was pointedly comparing the real and imminent danger posed by Nazi Germany to Europe's States and peace with the lesser, and perhaps defunct, threat posed by the Soviet Union.[92] The journal welcomed Russia's return to active participation in European politics.

By the start of 1934, confronted by the dual spectacle of British infirmity and growing German might and militancy, *Truth* once again changed tack. It recommenced its pleas for Treaty revision and for British dissociation from France. Over disarmament, it affirmed: 'Germany has a cast-iron case.'[93] France, declared the journal, 'for a decade . . . went strutting and crowing over the rubbish heap of the last war'; rightly, this situation was about to end.[94] Contrary to its professions of a bare year before, *Truth*, in the wake of the Nazi murder of Dollfuss, wrote: 'The facts that Hitler is carrying on worse than Dillinger . . . or that Goering is a drug-sodden sadist are entirely irrelevant' to the need for revision of the Treaty whose maintenance 'is not a British concern'.[95]

Set on a course of appeasement, *Truth*, between 1934 and 1939, never looked back. It feared and distrusted Hitler; it loathed Nazism. But the safety and interests of Britain and its Empire, in its view, demanded the abandonment of friends and former allies. Austria, for whose territorial integrity the journal had in 1933 and early 1934 demanded a British commitment, it blandly consigned to its fate in 1938.[96] In 1934 *Truth* had called Czechoslovakia, despite the minorities problem, 'the most successful experiment in liberal democracy that has emerged from the post-war settlement' and 'a healthy example of democracy'.[97] In 1938 the journal affirmed that the Sudetendeutsch had 'a very real grievance' and that

> the exotic combination of consonants in 'Czechoslovakia' has always seemed to me a factor on the side of peace. There is a healthy prejudice in this country against going to war over what looks like printer's pie.[98]

Truth's *glissement* towards appeasement in 1934 was prompted by an appreciation of Britain's physical weakness and infirmity of purpose, and comparative German strength. Through the thirties it stressed the need for British rearmament. But through fear of repercussions (i.e. a pre-emptive attack by Germany) and through ideological aversions (to French liberalism and socialism and to Russian Bolshevism) it failed to advocate that other strength-producing course – the cementing of

30

military alliance. Often *Truth* chastised those who preached resistance to the Dictators while denying arms to the Government; never did it slap its own wrist for eschewing alliances, which were the necessary corollary to British power.

The Observer

The *Observer* in the 1930s was owned by Viscount (Waldorf) Astor who, with his wife Nancy, presided over the so-called 'Cliveden Set'. J.L. Garvin was never classified as a member of that clique, though himself a prominent appeaser in the late thirties. As the *Observer*'s editor, according to Gannon, he was left 'very much in unfettered charge of the paper, and its policy was his policy'.[99] There were, however, exceptions. In 1936, for example, Garvin wanted and nominated Douglas Woodruff as Deputy Editor. Astor demurred, suggesting other names. A stalemate ensued, and no Deputy Editor was ever appointed under Garvin.[100]

Garvin was born in Birkenhead in 1868. By upbringing a Catholic, in later life he gradually 'moved to a Christian mysticism outside any church'.[101] His formal education ended in his early teens. But he emerged from adolescence an immensely learned auto-didact. He served a lengthy journalistic apprenticeship in provincial newspapers before becoming, in 1899, a *Daily Telegraph* leader-writer. In 1908 Lord Northcliffe persuaded him to assume the editorship of the *Observer*, at which post he remained until 1942.

His thought before 1914 was dominated by two themes – the enormity of the 'German peril' and the need to counter it with a British–French–Russian alliance; and the desirability of Anglo-Saxon union.

His attitude towards Germany was marked by a not unusual ambivalence, atypical only in the depth of each of its components. Hatred and love intermingled, one or the other predominating at different points in time. His daughter Katharine later recalled that 'he had loved so much of what was best in Germany. He was steeped in German philosophy, in German thought and in German history. For years he read German newspapers daily.'[102] His other daughter, Ursula, recalls that he had 'a deep love for the German people'.[103] But he feared for Britain and loathed Prussianism. During the Great War he supported Lloyd George and Lord Milner in their espousal of a vigorous war policy.

His son Roland was killed on the Somme in 1916. 'Never Again' was to characterise his thinking in the wake of the First World War. He was among the first to denounce the Treaty of Versailles, less for alleged injustices towards Germany than for its inexpedience, which assured Europe of another 'round'. Through the twenties and early thirties

Garvin was a prominent supporter of Treaty revision. He repeatedly called upon the Powers to grant Germany 'equality' in armaments. He preferred an 'equality' based on mutual disarmament but, in its absence, upheld Germany's right to rearm up to the level of the victors.

Similarly, Garvin continuously called for territorial revision. But he rarely elaborated. An exception was his outspokenness on the Polish Corridor. He repeatedly named it the 'Achilles heel' of European peace. This stemmed, at least in part, from the great contempt with which he viewed the Poles. His daughter recalled him as saying that 'Poland will never be a Western nation . . . I doubt whether there is one serious work in Polish upon cricket.'[104] Another exception, at least in the early thirties, was the problem of Austria. In 1931 he supported the proposed Austro-German customs union, acknowledging that economic integration would lead to full political union. He deemed such a development both inevitable and just. Throughout the pre-Hitler period he castigated all French efforts to encircle and perpetually subdue Germany as unnatural and unlasting. He regarded German predominance in central Europe as 'an act of God'.[105]

But Garvin's denunciation of Versailles was not total or blind. Neither did he repudiate all its works. In 1932 the *Observer* saluted Dr Thomas Masaryk on his 82nd birthday with the words: 'He fashioned a State prosperous, respected, well-established. The records of human history have few better stories to tell.'[106] (Such words hardly conform to Gannon's description of Garvin as 'the British Press's most outspoken Czechophobe'.[107])

Garvin's enthusiasm for the League of Nations in the early 1930s was restrained and critical. He noted the League's theoretical uses. He hoped it would prove instrumental in the sane reconstruction of Europe's economic system, in achieving general disarmament and in implementing Treaty revision. But, in the twenties and early thirties he saw the League as essentially a tool of French hegemony and the Versailles *status quo*. To preserving that *status quo* Garvin refused to be a party: 'Never. Not a man, not a shilling shall we engage to stake again on Continental war in any contingency near or remote.'[108]

Ultimately, it was not in the League but in Imperial concord and in the American connection that Garvin vested his hopes for peace. The unity of a potent Empire and a firm alliance with the United States, in Garvin's view, assured Britain of security; none would dare challenge or attack her with such resources at her back. And none, he hoped, would dare incur the enmity of so potent a coalition by flagrantly embarking on a course of aggression. As Garvin wrote to Astor, Anglo-American friendship was the 'World's only real sheet-anchor'.[109]

32

Against the backdrop of the Great War, Garvin abhorred all thought of a repeated British military involvement in Continental conflict. Equally, however, he always recognised that isolation, if ever feasible, was certainly no longer so in 'the air age'. His concern about the 'air peril', as will be shown, was unbounded; it reached a decisive, humiliating climax at Munich-time. From 1932 Garvin was the most forceful advocate of British rearmament, especially in the air, in the serious press.

While abhorring Communism, Garvin, until 1935 (and again after Munich), stressed that Soviet Russia was not an aggressive or expansionist Power. Rather, as before 1914, he reiterated the need for a coalition of the 'peace-loving' States to deter Nazism from attack in Europe. Unlike many, he affirmed a belief in the military efficacy of the Soviet war-machine.[110]

In the light of these premises, Garvin's attitude to Hitlerite Germany was logical, explicable and shifting. Early in 1933 he recognised the menace of Nazism: 'Now it is too late to stop easily, or to stop at all, the mighty revival in the Reich of the old Prussian idea ... the nation in arms', he wrote on 5 February 1933.[111] He firmly set aside long-cherished hopes for Treaty revision: 'The very soul of the Nazi movement is an aggressive jingoism excited by the glorification of war memories. While these conditions remain, Treaty revision in every effective shape or form is rendered impossible',[112] he argued in May 1933. In August he wrote to Astor:

> This new barbarism in the centre of Europe *must* end by putting western civilisation in dire peril if allowed, and it already outrages every decent principle that people like you and me have lived for ... I am staggered here in this country by the utter want of comprehension ... blind!!![113]

He called for complete and immediate Anglo-French solidarity and implicitly posited alignment with the Soviet Union, 'a serious force on the side of peace'.[114] He denounced those who favoured giving Germany a free hand in eastern Europe. As he put it in June 1935, in an article entitled, in Litvinov's phrase, 'Peace is One': 'If ... Germany became an extended Power, over-shadowing the whole Continent, what would be the worth of Western security afterwards?'[115]

But in the course of 1935 Garvin's position shifted radically. In the light of the unwillingness of the Western democracies to unitedly confront the Nazi challenge and in view of Britain's military weakness, Garvin opted for appeasement. To Garvin's mind 1935 proved decisive on two major counts; he became convinced of the terrifying potency of German arms, especially in the air, and he lost hope, with Italy's estrangement and with the League's debasement over Abyssinia, of a coalescence of an effective, anti-Nazi united front. Thenceforth, until the occupation of Prague in March 1939, Garvin ruled out the adoption by Britain of 'confrontation politics'. He became an archetypal appeaser. (Garvin provides the prime though by no means only example in the British press of the demoralisation wrought by Baldwin's and Chamberlain's policies of passive and active appeasement of Germany.)

Between 1936 and 1939 Garvin professed to believe that Anglo-German accommodation, even at the expense of the Reich's neighbours, was both possible and desirable. He totally rejected alignment with France and Russia, deeming the Franco-Russian–Czech alliances 'as the gravest of all Continental entanglements'.[116] 'We must not', he wrote in March 1936, 'be dragged into war at the whistle of Bolshevism or at the beck of the Little Entente'.[117] He feared the precipitation of war by others at a time when Britain was still militarily and morally unready. His central concern in those years was to buy time for British rearmament for the war against Germany which he believed probable if not inevitable. This is not obvious from the articles that he published at the time, but is an inevitable conclusion from a reading of the *Observer* for 1933–5 and 1939. He was always convinced of the evil of Nazism and of the constancy of the threat it posed to British security and European peace. Gannon, I believe, is wrong when he states that Garvin, until Munich, 'was reasonably sure that Germany wanted peace', and in regarding him as a run-of-the-mill appeaser.[118]

Editorial opinion in the *Observer* was directly expressed in Garvin's weekly three or four columns of commentary and in regular leaders, usually written by others, such as George Glasgow, the Diplomatic Correspondent, but always bearing the Garvin stamp and policy. Indirectly, *Observer* policy was carried in the weekly news-review paragraphs and in the contributions of foreign correspondents. These latter were consistently anti-Nazi; but criticism of the Third Reich was less conspicuous and trenchant in 1936–38 than during 1933–35 and 1939. The *Observer's* correspondent in Berlin was P.B. Wadsworth.

The Sunday Times

In the 1930s the *Sunday Times* was owned by the Lords Camrose and Kemsley. As editor-in-chief, Lord Camrose (William Ewart Berry) exercised supervisory control of the paper and its policy until the start of 1937, when joint ownership ended and Lord Kemsley (James Gomer Berry) acquired his brother's shares and control. Both Kemsley and Camrose supported appeasement and the National Government. (In 1938, however, Camrose apparently switched to support of Churchill and 'the grand alliance', without, of course, effect on the policies of the

Sunday Times.[119]) Kemsley's conciliating posture withstood the tests of both Munich and the German occupation of Prague, and he continued to support the appeasement of Hitler well after Chamberlain's abandonment of any real hope of its success.[120]

William Waite Hadley, a Congregationalist by upbringing and a provincial and, later, London journalist by training, joined the *Sunday Times* in 1931. At Camrose's behest he became Editor in 1932, a position he occupied until his retirement in 1950 at the age of 84. According to H.V. Hodson, 'he believed strongly in the close partnership of editor and proprietor in the conduct of a newspaper . . . and admired and accepted Lord Kemsley's strong control of . . . general policy'.[121] Camrose's supervision of editorial policy, between 1932 and 1937, was, apparently, less rigid. Under both proprietors, pressures from above concerning policy towards Germany were superfluous as Hadley was himself, for the most part, convinced of the virtues of appeasement and was 'a friend and supporter of Neville Chamberlain'.[122]

In the thirties, Hadley wrote most of the *Sunday Times*'s major foreign policy leaders. An equally important outlet of editorial opinion were the full-length, leader-page articles contributed by Herbert Sidebotham, under the pseudonym of 'Scrutator'. Sidebotham, as shall be seen, was an appeaser of the most extreme order from 1933; to judge from his leaders, Hadley only gradually progressed to unqualified espousal of appeasement, attaining full 'parity' with 'Scrutator' only with Kemsley's advent in 1937. Until that time Hadley managed to affect a concoction based on lip-service to 'collective security' and practical placation of Nazi Germany.

Camrose, Kemsley, Hadley and Sidebotham all believed that an Anglo-German settlement was the first necessity of British foreign policy, and that it was attainable. The paper's news page, however, bore little resemblance in tone or content to Hadley's watery and Sidebotham's fervent outpourings. Reports from Germany, by E.B. Wareing and, later, Hugh Greene, and general analyses by Wickham Steed were consistently anti-Nazi and, openly or implicitly, called for British commitment against Nazi Germany. In 1937–39, however, under Kemsley, a degree of editorial censorship of the news-page is apparent. Reports critical of the Reich became rare; previously much space had been allotted to the persecution of minorities and dissidents in the Reich.

The *Sunday Times* rarely made a pretence of basing its foreign policy on anything save what it regarded as British self-interest. Certainly morality, as commonly understood, had no place in Sidebotham's perceptions and advocacy of foreign policy. In a memorable instance, in 1936, Sidebotham asserted:

> Perhaps the first and most welcome change of mind is to disabuse ourselves of the idea that we and our friends are better morally than other nations [for] in the domain of political morals all nations of western Europe [i.e. including Germany and Italy] are on much the same level.[123]

Moral relativism of this order, in pursuit of appeasement, would have made Chamberlain blush.

The assumptions underlying the foreign policy of the *Sunday Times* were few and simple. Fear of war, and especially of aerial devastation of Britain, suffused all. To a lesser extent, so did hostility towards the Versailles settlement. Before 1933, dualism pervaded the editorial pages of the *Sunday Times*. Leaders, especially in 1932 with militarism renascent in Germany, called consistently for Treaty revision. Beside them, the editorial-page articles, usually by Wickham Steed, supported 'collective security' and the territorial *status quo*, German disarmament, the League of Nations and the French alliance system in Eastern Europe. Alignment between the views in the leaders and in the leader-page articles was achieved in 1933, with Steed's usurpation by 'Scrutator'. Thenceforward Sidebotham exhibited remarkable consistency with regard to Versailles. German claims to 'equality' found no firmer advocate in the British press, Europe's eastern frontiers no severer a critic. Sidebotham was usually candid about his motives; British self-interest, meaning mainly avoidance of war with Germany, compelled massive territorial revision.[124] Occasionally, perhaps at Hadley's insistence, Sidebotham threw sops to those counselling British firmness in confronting what he believed to be the rising tide of neo-Prussianism: 'It is both our right and our duty', he wrote in May 1933, 'to maintain or relax Versailles's provisions in proportion as Germany convinces us that she has discarded the arch-heresy that might is right.'[125] But such reflections were uncommon. Having swiftly grasped the reluctance of the Western democracies effectively to inhibit German rearmament, Sidebotham turned his attentions to Eastern Europe, preaching the necessity of British indifference to the fate of everything lying east of the Rhine. On 27 May 1934 he summed up his views on Britain's vital interests: 'In peace and in coastlines we have an interest, but no conceivable territorial change in central Europe between the Rhine and the Dardanelles would be worth the death of a single British soldier.'[126]

Sidebotham's antagonism towards France's eastern alliances, un-bounded until 1939, was fired by two preconceptions: that military alliances in general were evil and war-breeding, and that Bolshevism was both fearful and despicable. Of alliances he wrote at the end of

1934: 'The prime cause of the last war was the belief in force and in a system of alliances to support it . . . The prime condition of avoiding a world war in the future is to avoid the system of opposing groups of alliances which made the last.'[127]

His condemnation of the Franco-Russian pact was absolute. He called it

> the shoal on which all the projects of a stable Europe run aground . . . All the subsequent complications – of Italy's intervention in Spain, of her imperial and naval ambitions in the Mediterranean, of the trouble that she is making with the Arabs, of Germany's demand for colonies and, perhaps, even of the war in the Far East – hinge on one cause, namely, that France and Russia will make war together to uphold the peace settlement in south-east Europe and that this country will be dragged in to support the Slav against the Teuton.[128]

Beside this 'Russian obsession', Sidebotham had an Imperial fixation which, in the circumstances of the 1930s, focused on the safety of 'the Middle Seas' (i.e., the North Sea and the Mediterranean). So long as neither Germany nor Italy entered into naval competition with Britain over supremacy in the Middle Seas, they could unmolestedly pursue their various ambitions in Europe and Africa. Hence, it was with misgivings that he viewed the German and Italian intervention in Spain and the assaults, in 1937, against shipping in the Mediterranean. Though a thorough-going appeaser, he never, as Garvin did, extended his support to France or turned a blind eye to the threat posed to Britain by the interventions in the Iberian Peninsula. However, he offered no objection to the Anglo-German Naval Agreement and persisted in supporting an Anglo-Italian accord throughout the thirties. Also somewhat inconsistent was his benign view of Japan's expansion in the Far East.

Throughout this period Sidebotham regarded the League, the Covenant and the concept of collective security as bulwarks of French domination and the Versailles *status quo* in Europe. In this, he differed from Hadley who, until 1936, paid continuous lip-service to all three.

SPECIAL INTEREST AND OTHER WEEKLIES

The Tablet

In 1923 Ernest Oldmeadow was installed as Editor of the *Tablet* by the Archbishop of Westminster, the journal's longstanding proprietor. Oldmeadow, a successful wine merchant, brought to the job limited journalistic experience and strident Roman Catholicism. Formerly a Wesleyan minister, his championship of Church interests and dogma was total and unquestioning. He regarded political affairs and the international situation almost solely in the light of their effect upon the Church or not at all. Policy in the *Tablet*, until Oldmeadow's departure in 1936, was laid down by the Archbishop whom the editor visited once a week to receive his ration of the 'Word'. Oldmeadow was assisted in the thirties by Eliot Anstruther. Editorials were normally written by one or the other in accordance with the Primate's directives.[129]

By the spring of 1936 the journal began to lose money. The archdiocese resolved upon a change of editor. Douglas Woodruff was approached but refused the editorship unless ownership, too, was transferred. The Archbishop agreed, and the *Tablet* changed hands. Woodruff henceforth edited the journal and determined its policy until his retirement in 1967.

Woodruff, born in 1897, read Greats and History at Oxford and was elected President of the Union in 1922. In 1926 he joined the staff of the *Times* as a leader-writer and Colonial Editor, in which capacities he served until taking over the *Tablet*. He continued, until Dawson's retirement in 1941, 'to remain in close touch with the *Times* people'.[130]

The assumptions underlying the *Tablet*'s policy towards Germany underwent a number of changes during the 1930s. However, always predominant were the interests of the Roman Catholic Church, in Oldmeadow's time as perceived by the Archbishop, and after, as perceived by Woodruff.

In the early thirties Oldmeadow and the *Tablet* were frankly (and unusually) anti-Revisionist. The overthrow of Versailles, the journal believed, would constitute a 'repudiation and [a] dishonouring of solemn covenants'.[131] 'Events have proved that not only Europe's interests but the whole world's demanded a halt in the matter of Equality of Armaments for the German Reich', stated the *Tablet* in the wake of Hitler's defiant withdrawal from the Disarmament Conference.[132] A degree of Germanophobia informed many of the journal's comments even after Hitler's assumption of power. It went out of its way to praise Wickham Steed's cautions concerning resurgent German militarism, and firmly rejected a policy of concessions which, it believed, would only elicit further demands.[133]

Oldmeadow matched his distaste for Germany, old and new, with a loathing for Nazism, which he believed to be a mutation of Teutonic paganism: 'Neo-paganism is too abundant and too lively an ingredient in it for this movement to expect a welcome from Christian men.'[134]

Over the second half of 1934 a gradual but major shift of policy occurred in the *Tablet*. Staunch anti-Communism had always characterised the journal. The imminence of a Franco-Russian pact, raising the spectre of ultimate British involvement in a war on the side of the Bolsheviks, the concurrent growth of German power and the evident failure of will in the Western democracies prompted a re-evaluation. If France were to align with the Soviets then Britain had better 'detach herself kindly but completely from a possible entanglement'. The journal went on to lament French opposition to treaty revision: 'revision, especially in Danubia, is essential to Europe's regeneration', stated the *Tablet* in December 1934.[135] This new-born sympathy for revisionism, however, was not loudly proclaimed under Oldmeadow; the completion of the *volte face* had to await Woodruff's advent in April 1936.

In the twenties, Woodruff had been an Asquithian Liberal, anti-French and a Treaty revisionist. He supported the League and believed in the virtues of the Commonwealth and in Anglo-Saxon union. In the course of the thirties Woodruff discarded both Liberalism and collective security. Over Abyssinia, the League and the Spanish Civil War he echoed Garvin. To his mind, the safety and interests of Britain and the Roman Catholic Church coalesced and compelled unflagging advocacy of appeasement towards Germany. Reversing Oldmeadow's policy, Woodruff through 1936–39 omitted almost all reference to persecutions within the Reich and constantly stressed the necessity and attainability of a German–British accord. He attacked criticisms of the Hitler regime as 'lamentable'.[136] Echoing Scrutator of the *Sunday Times*, the *Tablet* stated in 1937 that an impartial visitor from another Continent would find

> that both groups of nations [i.e., the Western democracies and the dictator States] stood on very much the same level of culture and live the same kind of life. It is only when he gets to Russia that he will find anything that can be called a different civilisation.[137]

Exponents of moral relativism in the service of practical political ends could not have bettered the *Tablet*'s pronouncement of 8 January 1938. Comparing the Western democracies and the Fascist and Nazi States, Woodruff observed:

> The difference is so very much less than it appears in the [British] papers . . . What matters for the soul of man is not whether there are elections or plebiscites, but whether there is among the people an essential respect for men as men. Plutocracy and authoritarianism have both their confessions to make.[138]

The British Weekly

The *British Weekly* was founded by the publishing firm of Hodder and Stoughton in 1886 as a mouthpiece for Liberalism, enlightened

Imperialism and the Nonconformist conscience. Ownership and direction of the journal in the thirties remained with the firm's heirs, Paul Hodder-Williams and John Attenborough.[139]

The Reverend Dr John A. Hutton edited the *British Weekly* from 1925 until 1946. A prolific writer of sermons, theological tracts and criticism on Browning, Hutton had no journalistic experience when he assumed the editorship at the age of 57. Hutton's Assistant Editor, until her retirement in 1937, was Jane T. Stoddart, whose association with the *British Weekly* dated from the 1880s. Stoddart was fluent in German and knowledgeable about the international situation. Among other things she contributed a weekly summary of the German Press to the journal's 'Notes of the Week' columns.

John Hutton was once described as 'a wonderful man for leading you up the avenue to a great house but he never reached the front door'.[140] A certain woolliness characterised the journal's foreign policy professions during the 1930s. Nonetheless, it was one of the more consistent anti-Nazi and anti-appeasement weeklies, despite a sincere subscription to pacifist values.

An undercurrent of Germanophobia is apparent in Hutton's thinking. Perhaps in consequence, Treaty revision, even before Hitler's assumption of power, was never explicitly propounded. For example, while thanking God for 'the peace and amnesty of Lausanne', the *British Weekly* commented: 'the extravagance of Versailles is easily understood, as the demand of sincerely anxious and still trembling peoples that such [Great War] horrors shall not be repeated in their day.' It went on to argue that 'the imputation of sole guilt to the defeated is a thing also for which all nations must nowadays be prepared. This very circumstance may yet become a safeguard against wars.'[141] After Hitler's assumption of power the *British Weekly* forbore from even implicit espousal of Treaty revision and never justified Germany's successive unilateral abrogations of Versailles. By mid-1938 the journal explicitly denounced the British detractors of Versailles.[142]

Over the League of Nations, that other pillar of the settlement of 1918–19, the *British Weekly* waxed enthusiastic. 'The unity of the human race under God is the truth of things which it is the main business of Christianity to achieve ... We cannot but support every movement, therefore, which looks that way', stated Hutton in April 1934.[143] Over a year later, he reiterated: 'A League of Nations is also the innermost and deepest intention of the Eternal Spirit in the Holy Scriptures ...'[144]

In the early thirties the *British Weekly* strongly supported Disarmament. Soon after Hitler's rise to power, however, and despite pacifist sentiments,

Hutton came out in support of the National Government's rearmament measures. But pacifist effusions continued to adorn the editorial pages in the mid-1930s. In May 1935 Hutton wrote:

> As a people, we have at the moment a horror of war. This horror of war ... might, in the event of an outbreak, give an even astonishing display of its depth and force ... Men and women ... have served notice that they will face any social consequence rather than aid and abet a war. Again and again during the last few years we ourselves have invited the Government of the day to omit from its forecast the likelihood that an enormous number of practising Christians will hold themselves aloof from war.[145]

Yet not half a year later, the journal adamantly supported the League against Italy over Abyssinia, enjoining British involvement 'whatever may prove to be the consequences'.[146]

The Listener

The *Listener*, the weekly journal of the British Broadcasting Corporation, was edited in the thirties by R.S. Lambert (1932–35) and J.R. Ackerley (1935–   ). It offered no direct comment on international affairs or British policy, but, on rare occasions, spoke out on politically significant matters related to broadcasting. Otherwise, opinion on international affairs was expressed only in its selection of articles.

In 1933 the *Listener*'s (and B.B.C.'s) main international affairs commentator was Vernon Bartlett. Intensely anti-Versailles, he was, at the time, an early and forceful exponent of appeasement towards Hitler. His ignorance of the nature of Nazism was profound, as is displayed in his book, *Nazi Germany Explained*, published in 1933. He was somewhat concerned about Hitler's bellicose statements but believed 'that there is nothing like responsibility for taking revolution out of a man'.[147] He even voiced hopes that Hitler 'might quite conceivably find himself in the unexpected role of defender of a radical and republican constitution against a very powerful reactionary and monarchist movement'.[148] Bartlett regarded Nazism in 1933 almost solely through the lens of his own revisionist convictions; for him, the overthrow of Versailles *was* Nazism. In Bartlett, at the time, the Nazis found a voluble apologist for almost every one of their actions.

Similar attitudes to Germany and Versailles also coloured the views of Sir J.Evelyn Wrench, Sir Arnold Wilson and Sir Arthur Salter, frequent contributors to the *Listener* in the early 1930s. 'A nation which has suffered greatly ... is trying to evolve a new kind of civilisation', wrote Wrench in April 1933.[149]

A more balanced approach towards Germany was introduced in the course of 1935. Contributions by outright Germanophiles like Wrench, Sir Arnold Wilson and H. Powys Greenwood were offset by those of anti-Nazis like R.H.S. Crossman and F.A. Voigt. From 1938 opponents of appeasement gained the upper hand in the *Listener*'s pages.

The Week-End Review

The *Week-End Review* had only a brief existence. Founded in the spring of 1930, it foundered and was absorbed by the *New Statesman* in January 1934. Its founder, owner and editor was Gerald Barry, former Royal Flying Corps pilot (1916–18) and editor of the *Saturday Review* (1924–30). Born in 1898, son of a church minister and educated at Marlborough and Corpus Christi, Barry was a Liberal, a Treaty revisionist and, until the mid-thirties, a pacifist. Through its brief life, the *Week-End Review* clamoured for European and world disarmament, seeing in it the *sine qua non* of future peace; the demise of the ambition coincided with the journal's expiry.

The journal was a vocal supporter of the League of Nations and the Covenant. It rejected all efforts to attain security through military alliances, and was unsympathetic towards France's eastern pacts. Even after 30 January 1933, it berated France's 'myopic' insistence on security. Rather, it advocated Treaty revision and granting Germany 'equality of rights' as the only assurances of real security.

In supporting 'a constructive policy of appeasement' towards Nazi Germany, Barry argued: 'Collective resistance to treaty breaking and collective insistence on treaty revision', taken together, were 'the essence of continued peace'.[150] He shut his eyes to the incompatibility of the two in the face of Nazi ambitions.

Barry's insistence on revision was not a function of ignorance of or indifference to the European situation and Hitler's real aims. In June 1933 Barry sympathetically conveyed the fears of Germany's neighbours: 'No one in this part of Europe [i.e., Vienna and Budapest] is the least bit deceived by Herr Hitler's recent show of moderation', he wrote. And he added, hyperbolically, that pan-Germany's ambitions apparently extended as far as Vladivostok.[151]

Such reflections failed to curb the ardour of Barry's revisionism. Like Bartlett, the withdrawal of Germany from the Disarmament Conference and the League of Nations served only to confirm his beliefs. 'To attempt to shame or bully' the Nazis he dismissed as 'dangerous'. Perversely, he argued that in refusing to meet German demands for arms equality there was 'not a risk but a certainty . . . of Germany's rearming'.[152] Barry continued to espouse Treaty revision until the journal's collapse. Later, he recanted. As Managing Editor of the *News Chronicle* (with a 'reformed' Bartlett as Diplomatic Correspondent), Barry was a leading anti-appeaser in the British press.

Like the *Sunday Times*, the *Observer* and the *New Statesman*, the *Week-End Review* blended advocacy of appeasement on its editorial page with virulent anti-Nazism in contributions from its foreign correspondents. Its Geneva correspondent, Robert Dell, and its Paris correspondent, Alexander Werth (both of whom later wrote for the *New Statesman*), persistently warned of the coming Nazi-engendered holocaust. On the other hand, Bartlett, G.E.G. Catlin and Sir Arthur Salter all contributed revisionist and pro-appeasement articles.

The New English Weekly

The *New English Weekly* was founded in 1932, and edited, until his death in 1934, by Alfred Richard Orage, formerly Editor of the *New Age*. To the *New English Weekly* he brought both literary eminence and an infatuation with the panacea of Social Credit. Everything the journal printed on economic, social, internal political and international affairs was coloured by this obsession with Major Douglas's doctrines. This usually made for a perverse appreciation of European realities, Nazism and British foreign policy.

Upon Orage's death in November 1934, Philip Mairet was appointed editor. Policy was decided in weekly meetings attended by Mairet, Mrs Orage, and Maurice B. Reckitt. Occasionally, T.S. Eliot, Will Dyson and Ezra Pound participated. The journal's literary eminence was thus assured; so was the reactionary, medieval flavour of its politics.[153]

At first, in 1932 and early 1933, the *New English Weekly* entertained hopes that Nazism would install the first social credit economy in Europe.[154] This hope dashed, Hitler's Germany too was consigned to that socio-economic pit dominated by the twin heresies of American liberal capitalism and Soviet State capitalism; henceforth, 'nothing distinguishes the new German dictatorship from the dictatorship of the Central Banks', stated the journal on 6 April 1933.[155] As Communists were often wont to lump together Western democratic and Fascist States as similarly evil emanations of malign capitalism, so the *New English Weekly* was prompted to print such unrealistic comparisons as:

> Despite the terrifying events occurring in Germany (with no greater domestic knowledge of them, in all probability, than our own people have of the sinister events now occurring in England: Fools can live in Hell and be duped into thinking it Heaven). . . .[156]

Both under Orage and under Mairet the journal regarded the

components of the Peace Settlement as the products of the manipulation of Big Business. The League it viewed as both the product and stamping-ground of 'the dictatorship of International Finance'.[157] Collective Security it regarded as 'exactly the pre-war treaty system, smelling just as explosive'.[158]

The *New English Weekly* regarded the Treaty of Versailles as another product of finance capitalism, ascribing to it all the ills of Europe in the 1930s. Occasionally, lucidity prevailed: 'The only thing the Germans fundamentally object to in the Versailles Treaty is that they weren't able to force it on their neighbours.'[159] Usually, however, everything was blamed on the Treaty's malignity – Hitler's rise, Europe's war fears and a variety of political murders and outbreaks. Under Mairet perceptiveness occasionally obtruded. In April 1935, for example, the *New English Weekly* made the distinction between the evils which confronted the world's enlightened:

> Nor is Germany merely one ambitious Power amongst others. She is something far more dangerous – a philosophy under arms . . . a great pagan collectivity . . . The totalitarian dragon is loose, and the feeble inheritors of a Christian civilisation, corrupted by avarice, have no name in which to challenge him.[160]

But while adhering to a belief in democracy as a dupe and a camouflage for the great evil of International Finance, the journal remained ill-equipped to understand events on the Continent or to espouse policies aiming at the defence of nations and interests thus perceived. Nothing appeared worth defending.

The Saturday Review

In 1930 Lady Houston, a wealthy ship-owner's widow and extreme Conservative, bought the *Saturday Review* and replaced Gerald Barry as its editor. Until her death in 1937 the journal obsessively preached rearmament and ever more rearmament. In so doing, it afforded lavish and sensational coverage to the threatened air peril; scenarios of a devastated London overshadowed all the review's foreign policy professions. Two other constants underlay Lady Houston's perceptions: hatred of Bolshevism and an unfaltering commitment to the existence and perpetuation of the British Empire.

Until the end of 1933, the *Saturday Review*, like the *Tablet*, was an anti-revisionist journal; like Oldmeadow, Lady Houston gave free rein to her Great War-vintage Germanophobia. In dealing with the 'Teuton', the lesson for the West was clear: 'Stand up to him, and he behaves himself; give him an inch . . . and he will take the whole measuring tape', she wrote in July 1932 at the spectacle of the Prussian Right resurgent in Germany.[161] In September she ruled: 'All legitimate concessions, and perhaps more than all, have already been made.'[162]

At first, Hitler's assumption of power introduced no change in Lady Houston's thinking. Rather, without calling it such, she reaffirmed commitment to 'collective security', calling for alliance with France. By the end of 1933, in view of British irresolution and weakness and Germany's growing power, the *Saturday Review* began to shift towards isolationism and appeasement. Always anti-Bolshevik, from 1934 the journal stressed its preference for Fascism and Nazism over Communism and consented to allowing Hitler a free hand in the east. Sympathy for the plight of Austria and Czechoslovakia, and support for the French connection, were swiftly dropped. As fear of Hitler grew, a note of admiration became increasingly evident. Perhaps a peak was reached with the Rhineland coup of March 1936. Versailles was condemned as 'harsh and irrational';[163] Germany was declared 'the greatest military power in the world';[164] an adulatory portrait of Hitler was published above the caption 'Heil Hitler!', and 'a pact between Germany, France, Italy, England and Japan' was advocated as a solution to the world's ills.[165] In one of a number of articles praising Hitler's action and person, the *Saturday Review* stated:

> It is the penalty of every great man that during his life-time he is criticised, misjudged and hated, as well as being admired ... For the sake of the future welfare of our Empire and of civilisation, let us recognise that the Führer has the power to dictate peace or war to the world. Let us acknowledge that in this man, whom we may hate or deride or admire, lies the only hope of world security and peace; let us remember that by his courage and determination he saved Europe from the spread of Bolshevik insurrection, that he and his armies stand like a bulwark between us and Soviet Russia [and that without him] England would be on the verge of ruin and chaos.[166]

The death of Lady Houston in January 1937 precipitated the return of the *Saturday Review* from the wilder fields of sensationalism and political reaction to the fold of a sedate conservatism. On 16 January 1937 the new editor proclaimed: 'Today the *Saturday Review* resumes its old position as the leading Conservative weekly. The dictatorship ... is over and we return to constitutional government.'[167] While retaining Lady Houston's commitment to Empire, the journal henceforth stressed that it was 'bound to be the spoil for which all the have-nots are eager'.[168] The journal returned to preaching the necessity of a French alliance and to voicing a conviction that 'a war in the east [of Europe] will inevitably involve the rest of the Continent'.[169] Contempt for the League and 'collective security' remained; belief in solid alliances was upheld. Nonetheless, the journal continued to support appeasement.

In April 1938 the *Saturday Review* collapsed; the damage done to its prestige and circulation under Lady Houston had proved irreparable.

Tribune

Tribune was launched in January 1937 by a group of Labour MPs, Aneurin Bevan, Ellen Wilkinson, Sir Stafford Cripps and George Strauss, the latter two providing the bulk of the necessary capital. The day-to-day management of the journal was vested in William Mellor, its first editor (1937–38), and policy was determined by all five at regular weekly meetings. Mellor was succeeded in the chair by R.J. Hartshorn, another well-known left-wing journalist. Hartshorn's editorship was even shorter than Mellor's. It terminated with the publication of an article by Palme Dutt which enjoined *Tribune* subscribers to cease reading the journal as it was insufficiently committed to Leftist ideals.

Tribune was founded for two specific purposes, to save the Spanish Republic and to promote the Unity Campaign launched by the Socialist League (to whom the journal's founders belonged), the I.L.P. and the British Communist Party. The founders hoped that the journal might succeed in converting Labour Party activists, agents and workers to support for a 'united front' against Fascism and, specifically, undermine the National Executive's allegedly 'weak' line on Spain as expressed in the Labour Party Conference's resolutions of October 1936. To counter Fascist successes and aims in Spain, *Tribune* advocated British diplomatic, financial and arms assistance to the Madrid Government.[170]

Tribune was caught on the horns of the usual Liberal–Socialist dilemma: It wished to stop Fascism's advance in Europe and to topple the aggressive regimes in Germany and Italy, but abjured the recourse to war on grounds of morality and fear. In espousing a 'united front', it thought in terms of avoiding and averting war rather than of fighting and winning one. It cherished the hope that the mere existence of such a front would in some manner suffice to both deter Fascist/Nazi aggression and prompt the allegedly pacific multitudes in Germany and Italy to overthrow their warlike masters.[171]

Though its owners and successive editors were all critics of Versailles, *Tribune* from 1937 to 1939 never argued that the injustices of the peace compelled concessions to Germany.

Through 1937–39 *Tribune* clamoured against the National Government for 'selling the pass' to the Fascists. Repeatedly, it hinted darkly at connivance and complicity between the Conservative establishment and Hitler's aims and policies in eastern Europe. It was particularly susceptible to all threats, real or imagined, to the Soviet Union.[172]

Tribune firmly and consistently repudiated British rearmament. It argued that any war entered into by the Chamberlain Government would of necessity be 'imperialist' in nature. As it phrased it in its maiden issue:

> For a workers' government, all the arms necessary *to safeguard its authority for socialism and peace.* For a capitalist government, not a man, not a ship, not a plane. We are not prepared for a new imperialist war. We do not trust our capitalist masters. [My italics.][173]

Tribune was unwilling to endorse rearmament even if specifically geared to combating Fascism.

None of the journal's founders were pacifists. Yet, despite its total verbal commitment to anti-Fascism, *Tribune* consistently shied away from forcing the issue with Germany, Japan or Italy. On three points it advocated policies which went beyond the calls of most of the Liberal and Socialist press: consistently, it supported arms for Spain, a military (though the word was not used) alliance of Britain, France and Russia, and, for a time, a British commitment to Czech territorial integrity. Like every other journal, however, it refrained during the Munich crisis from calling for British commitment to the threatened Republic. Like others, too, its vision of war was over-shadowed by 'air fear'.[174]

III

THE AIR FEAR

The terror that seized London during the Munich crisis was that dumb, chattering terror of beasts in a forest fire.
Louis MacNeice, *The Strings Are False*, p. 174

During the 1930s thinking about foreign policy in Britain was over-shadowed and, to a great extent, determined by an obsessional and, in retrospect, exaggerated fear of air attack. If the memory of the horrors of the Great War rendered a repetition of that experience unpalatable, the added dimension of the threat from the air made it unthinkable. Consciously and sub-consciously, the fear of air attack was a major factor in the adoption and promotion of the policy of appeasement.[1]

A taste of the potential of air attack had already been afforded during the Great War. Lloyd George and General Smuts had then predicted:

> The day may not be far off when aerial operations, with their devastation of enemy lands and the destruction of industrial and populous centres on a vast scale, may become the principal operations of war, to which the older forms of military and naval operations may become secondary and subordinate.[2]

Rapid advances in aerial technology during the 1920s seemed to confirm the forecast. By the early 1930s it was accepted that conflicting Powers would, in the course of future wars, unleash massive aerial attacks on each other's industrial and civilian centres. The concept of 'total war', partly realised in 1914–18, took firm root. Many of Britain's air experts even assumed that an attempted aerial 'knock-out blow' would replace the traditional declaration of war, and might well incapacitate the Power assailed before it managed to field its 'conventional' forces. The public, and most air experts, accepted until 1938 that such a 'first strike', and certainly a protracted bombing campaign, was likely to succeed. Air Marshall Sir John Slessor later recalled that 'in those years immediately before the war the possibility of what was referred to as the "knock-out blow" bore heavily on the minds of the Air Staff'.[3]

This belief was sustained by several factors. Until 1938 practically everyone concurred with Baldwin's dictum that 'the bomber will always get through'. The size of bombers and of their pay-loads had grown considerably since 1918. The 'quality' of the pay-loads, too, it was assumed, had vastly increased the potency and effectiveness of air attack. Fearful imaginings had it that a cocktail of high explosive, gas and incendiary devices would rain down on Britain's indefensible cities – if not blown to bits, the civilian was assured of asphyxiation by gas or immolation. Given the nature of the main prospective enemy from 1933, few doubted that, should it come to war, such means would be employed.

During the First World War passive defence measures had gone largely untested; for years their effectiveness remained in doubt. It was not until the end of 1937 that a public campaign was launched for large-scale shelter construction programmes and for the thorough organisation of the civil population against air attacks. The Spanish war experiences had demonstrated the effectiveness of passive defence measures in face of air assault. But the campaign was slow in achieving results. It took the apparent imminence of war during the Munich crisis to dispel the lethargy with which the problems of ARP were being handled.

The air fear was further enhanced in many minds by the belief that ships, like cities, were highly vulnerable to such assault; not only Britain's cities and ports, but its maritime life-lines and traditional bulwark, the Royal Navy, were thought to be perilously exposed. As Rothermere told Wrench in 1936: 'Warships cannot fight bombing planes.'[4]

The air fear held the British people in thrall until March 1939. Given the advances in all types of weaponry and given the threat from the air, it was commonly asserted that a new war would, 'at best', prove so devastating as to render the concept of 'victory' meaningless. As the phrase had it, such a war could only issue in 'the destruction of civilisation'.[5] Indeed, in retrospect many who lived through the thirties compared their fear of air attack and its potential devastation to latter-day fears of nuclear holocaust;[6] German Junkers and Italian Savoias were regarded in the thirties much as ICBMs and MIRVs are regarded today.

The air fear was born before Hitler's conquest of power, and came firmly to roost in the collective consciousness of Britain during 1935. It held sway for the following four years; Munich marked its zenith. Thereafter, its hold gradually declined. It was finally banished only with the successful conclusion of the Battle of Britain.

In the following pages I hope to trace the emergence, growth and dominion of the air fear as reflected in the columns of the weekly press in the course of the 1930s. In this matter the weeklies certainly reflected, and to some degree generated, public attitudes. Indeed, if anything, the bulk of the serious weeklies expressed their apprehensions of hostile air power in terms of greater moderation and caution than were rife among the mass of Britain's population. And, as will be intermittently shown, in this matter the weeklies substantially reflected government attitudes.

1930–1934

Fear of air attack already preoccupied major British weeklies before Hitler's rise to power. In a leader-page article in the *Sunday Times* in January 1930 Eduard Herriot, the former French premier, declared 'that no adequate protective means can be taken to preserve the civilian population against this new barbarism'.[7] By 1932 the paper stressed – a point unfailingly repeated in the following years – 'that of all the capitals of Europe London is the most exposed'; the problem of defending the capital against air attack was 'insoluble', asserted Sidebotham.[8]

As early as 1931 Garvin of the *Observer* clearly recognised the horrific potential of air attack: '. . . crowded towns have become the chief objective of bombing power – raining fire and poison, regardless of age or sex . . .'. Like Sidebotham, he was convinced of Britain's especial vulnerability to this form of assault, 'owing to the unique crowding of the vast majority of our population into dense industrial centres'. Simply put, 'a foreign air force could ravage half England and return within nine hours'.[9]

The *New Statesman* was even more fearful. In January 1932 it published two pieces on 'the next great war'. Geoffrey Weald, reviewing a publication entitled *What Would Be The Character of A New War* (An Inquiry Organised by the Inter-Parliamentary Union, Geneva), wrote: 'This is the most terrible book which has ever been written' (he was referring to the content of the work). It piled 'nightmare on nightmare' and suggested that 'the next war may well be won and lost before its professional land soldiers have ever fired a shot at each other'. Weald accepted the 'knock-out blow' premise and asserted that 'all air experts acknowledge the futility of air defence against bombing raids'.[10] Several weeks later V. Lefebvre unveiled a terrifying scenario of 'hundreds of thousands of people killed within a few hours by gases'. With great verve he described the projected effects of the new thermal and high explosive devices.[11]

Without doubt this sort of thinking was reinforced by Baldwin's famous declaration in the House of Commons in November 1932, that 'the bomber will always get through'.[12] If such was considered official opinion, could mere journalists demur? *Truth*, like the Air Chiefs and the Cabinet, was left only to assert the obvious in strategic thinking: the bombers could not be stopped; therefore, 'the most that can be done is to make it enormously costly to the invader by reprisals'.[13] In the absence of common disarmament, only Britain's possession of, and willingness to use, a powerful bomber fleet of its own could deter would-be attackers and avert war.

The air fear got into its stride with Hitler's assumption of power; thenceforth, the major potential enemy was clearly visible. Right-wing weeklies, especially Garvin's *Observer* and Lady Houston's *Saturday Review*, reacted to the air peril with the traditional reflex of supporting massive rearmament.[14] Lady Houston repeatedly and publicly offered the Government £200,000 towards bolstering London's air defences. Through 1933 the story of the offer and its rejection by Baldwin was splashed across the *Saturday Review*'s pages. Weekly, the journal carried descriptions and 'photographs' of what London would look like after an air assault. Usually the journal conceded that 'an effective air defence of England is not feasible'; but this, it argued, was no 'reason for shedding the true defence – our power to attack'.[15] Lady Houston through the years 1933–37 castigated the lack of British air defences and armaments as 'a crime against the State'.[16] The foreign policy implications of aerial defencelessness were never lost sight of. As the *Saturday Review*'s leading political commentator put it in mid-1934, Britain, for lack of air power, could not 'possibly engage in conflict' against another Power, whatever transpired on the Continent.[17]

The air peril similarly affected the *Sunday Times*'s perception of Britain's position in the world. As its air correspondent phrased it in 1934, 'our weakness as an Air Power reduces our voice in the council of nations to a feeble bleating'.[18] In the same year air fear even impelled Sidebotham – a long-standing detractor of France and its anti-revisionist policy – to propose an Anglo-French 'air alliance'. His concern was for Britain rather than France. The pact, he asserted, would have 'the specific object of laying the spectre of the terror in the air'.[19]

No one during the 1930s was more obsessed with the air peril than Garvin of the *Observer*. As he put it at the end of 1933: 'In case of conflict, the very entrails of each [country] would be devastated by the air arm.'[20] Garvin's initial solution was to advocate massive British rearmament, especially in the air. Without it, he wrote in January 1934, 'this island could be ravaged and shattered from end to end. The fate that would fall on London and its millions within twenty-four hours or less we shall not attempt to depict.'[21] Besides rearmament, Garvin in 1934 urged alliance with France: like Sidebotham, Garvin for years had opposed French foreign policy; unlike Sidebotham, he acknowledged that an Anglo-French alliance could not be restricted to mutual air support. Viscount Astor, the *Observer*'s proprietor, took issue with his editor: 'To go beyond Locarno and enter an alliance seems to me to be both provocative and dangerous.'[22] Garvin responded forcefully: 'This country is in most danger – not France . . . We must awake or perish.' Britain must catch up with Germany in the air race. But until then, 'we shall be dependent for air safety upon alliance with the air-power of France . . . And if we are not careful we shall seal our own doom by driving France the other way.'[23]

Among Liberals and on the Left the onset of Nazi rule also conjured up imaginings of aerial devastation. The *Week-End Review* reacted to the change of regime in Germany with a leading article significantly entitled 'War in the Air – or Disarmament'. War in Europe – from which Britain could not remain aloof – was, it stated, 'quite possible, if not probable, within the next five years'. It called upon statesmen to redouble their efforts to achieve disarmament, especially in the air.[24] Rearmament, the editor was convinced, would solve nothing. In mid-1934 he wrote of 'the present impossibility of effective defence against attack from the air. Build we ever so enormously, no tactics now known can prevent the arrival of enemy bombers over London and other key centres. We can retaliate but we cannot intercept.' Nothing, he asserted, 'would isolate us from an enemy's all-penetrating gases, his ubiquitous bacteria'.[25] Air fear increased the urgency of espousal of aerial disarmament in all the Liberal and left-wing weeklies during 1933–34.

The Economist, soon after Hitler's assumption of power, explicitly drew the connection between the air menace and British foreign policy. In March 1933 the journal accused Britain of 'wriggling out' of its obligations in the Far East during the Manchurian crisis and asked: would Britain, for fear of air attack on its home shores, similarly 'grovel' in face of aggression in Europe? The journal took note of the House of Commons air debate, and, concurring, alluded to A.S.C. Reid's statement that 'London could, within twenty minutes, be reduced to a collection of smouldering ruins over which hung a cloud of poisonous vapours'.[26] During 1933–34 *The Economist* usually attempted to retain a sense of proportion and to abjure the more panicky strains of 'air mania'. But its answers to what it regarded as the two central questions – 'Can aerial bombing be effective, and can it be parried?' and 'Is the capital ship at the mercy of air attack?' – left little room for optimism. In the main the journal accepted General Groves's thesis – that in air warfare the advantage lay with the attacker, that Britain was highly vulnerable to air assault, and that enemy fear of reprisals in kind was the only effective deterrent to such assault.[27]

During 1933–34 the *Spectator* also normally attempted to sound a cautious, moderate note regarding the air peril. In mid-1934 Wilson Harris discounted assertions that there was no defence against air attack but conceded that aerial invulnerability was beyond attainment.[28] Squadron-Commander P.R. Burchall similarly argued inconclusively in the journal's pages when commenting upon the results of a recent RAF exercise over London; but he stressed that attack was 'the only sound method of defending this country from air invasion'.[29] Occasionally, Wilson Harris forsook his usual restraint. In August 1934, for example, he endorsed the views of Fokker, that no defence against air attack existed and that an 'aerial knock-out blow' was to be expected at the start of a new war. In the same month he quoted Colonel Bons, another Continental air sage, to the effect that anti-aircraft guns were 'practically useless'; this was 'uncomfortable reading for those who like to think that London could be effectively defended'.[30]

Editorially, only *Time & Tide* consistently played down the air peril before 1935 though it remained aware of the interconnection between air power, its absence and British foreign policy. At the start of 1934 the journal attacked Garvin for using the Groves thesis in support of the *Observer*'s campaign for aerial rearmament. The thesis, contended *Time & Tide*, was 'one-sided' and 'ill-argued'; Britain was not 'weak' and was sufficiently well-equipped to fulfil her obligations under the Covenant; assertions to the contrary were 'preposterous'.[31] Nonetheless, some two months later the journal acknowledged that Britain, in its quest for a European settlement, had been 'stimulated' by 'an uneasy appreciation of the revolution wrought by the conquest of the air'.[32] Lady Rhondda counselled against succumbing to Europe's 'fear psychosis', and discounted Germany's alleged ability to launch a war, despite a capacity to field an air fleet of some '2,000–3,000' machines.[33] Sir Norman Angell, the journal's leading foreign affairs commentator, was, on the other hand, already in 1934 fully persuaded of the validity of the Groves thesis. He wrote that 'the coming war' would be 'a contest [not] between armies, but a contest in the destruction of civilian populations . . . a lingering torture by poison and disease of babies [etc.] . . .'. There could be no defence against air attack, he argued.[34]

1935

1935 – the year in which Hitler denounced the Versailles arms clauses and in which Mussolini 'got away with it' in Abyssinia – saw the British press, Government and public completely succumb to the air fear. Hitler's private announcement to Simon and Eden in March 1935 that the Luftwaffe had already attained first-line parity with the British metropolitan air force, and would shortly surpass it, 'created something like panic in the Cabinet'.[35] This panic was aptly echoed in Baldwin's 'appalling frankness' in the Commons on 22 May when he confessed that Germany's rate of aerial rearmament had substantially outstripped British expectations. In effect, he was proclaiming that Britain had already lost the 'air race'. Air Staff and Joint Planning Committee reports in the summer of 1935 confirmed for the Cabinet what the public already sensed – that Britain was defenceless in the air and that a new war was likely to begin with a successful German 'knock-out' blow against Britain's industrial and civilian centres.[36] Government and Services pessimism not unnaturally filtered down to the general public, where the tendency, if anything, was to over-state the problem.

In order to understand British policy from the spring of 1935 and reactions to it in the weeklies it is impossible to exaggerate the importance of one simple fact: Britain greeted Hitler's announcements of rearmament in March as statements of accomplishment as well as of intention. Hitler's deception of the visiting ministers in exaggerating German air strength only served to reinforce fears already acutely felt. The success of this deception was accurately reflected in the weeklies and immeasurably affected the conduct of British policy before the occupation of Prague.[37] In effect, the British Government and public began treating Germany as fully armed 3–4 years before this was remotely the case. Appeasement – as a policy born of and expressing fear – began in 1935, and it was primarily the spectre of the re-born Luftwaffe that conditioned the adoption and promotion of this policy.[38]

Even before March 1935 renascent German power was held in awe. In February 1935 the *New Statesman* noted 'a tendency on the part of [British] Ministers to be increasingly friendly in tone to Nazi Germany and to discuss concessions to threats which they refused to take seriously while Germany was weak'. And the nature of the threat was clear: 'The nightmare of a sudden air raid likely to settle a war in a night has dominated everything else . . .'. The fear engendered was not confined to members of the Cabinet; as Kingsley Martin urged, 'the true policy' should be 'to frankly recognise the menace of Nazi Germany' and 'to admit her right to equality of status and express readiness to open discussion of frontier adjustment . . .'.[39] The mechanism of appeasement could not have been more concisely encapsulated.

Before 1935 the *Sunday Times*, while accepting the conceptual moorings of the air fear, intermittently attempted to still the panic these engendered. In November 1934, for example, Sidebotham praised a correction, by Lord Mottistone, of 'the gross exaggerations that are current of the amount of slaughter that the most successful air raid could cause among civilians'.[40] By the spring of 1935, however, Hadley avowed that the Luftwaffe already outnumbered the RAF by a ratio of

2:1.[41] Sidebotham confirmed this and declared: 'Germany has given us a shock by the rapidity of her rearmament, especially in the air, where we are most vulnerable.'[42] In support of an 'Air Locarno' – the current panacea for air fear – Sidebotham stated in April 1935 that 'it appealed to the masses of our people who, while ready to die for their country for a sufficient cause, do not like the unheroic risk of being bombed in bed'.[43]

In 1934 Nigel Tangye, the *Observer*'s air correspondent, was wont, like Sidebotham, to denounce fear-instilling forecasts of the potency of air attacks.[44] In March 1935, however, he declared: 'Shelters or exodus could not be provided even for 10% of the people of London.'[45] Garvin needed no convincing. On 24 March he argued that Hitler's ability to challenge with impunity the rest of Europe was evidence that the Reich 'was already far stronger than is supposed in this country'.[46] In April the *Observer* stated that the Luftwaffe was already 'four times as strong as our own available squadrons at home'.[47] Such exaggerations were undoubtedly printed, in part, to promote the cause of rearmament; but they also substantively reflected their author's views and fears. A bare year later Garvin wrote to Astor: 'Germany is going to be relatively the strongest power Europe or the world has seen since Napoleon. The eventual disclosure of her astonishing combined resources will be a tremendous revelation.'[48] Oldmeadow in the *Tablet* was similarly convinced of German military prowess by the summer of 1935. He wrote: 'Germany's striking power with submarines must add a new terror to her already great air power. [Knock-out] blows from under the water and from over the clouds can be delivered in a single night.'[49]

'The sentence of death', thought Christopher Gay in the *New English Weekly*, could be carried out 'in a few hours on all inhabitants of big cities in all countries.'[50] *The Economist* abjured panic in reaction to Hitler's rearmament declarations. But it commended Baldwin's assertion that Britain should not have 'an air force inferior to any other within striking distance of our shores' and concurred with his emphasis on the 'fear-provoking potency of air power'.[51] However, the journal still refused to countenance substantial or 'massive' British rearmament.[52]

Air fear was given more explicit expression in the *Spectator* in 1935. In May Wilson Harris called upon Britain to respond immediately to Hitler's peace offers. Dwarfing all other problems, believed the editor, was that of air disarmament: There was 'no need to descant on the horrors of air warfare of the future. Its potentialities are unimaginable ... All odds are with the attack, none with the defence.' In the absence of aerial disarmament, he warned, 'the wholesale devastation of Europe' was not to be discounted.[53] Buttressing the editor's argument was an article in the same issue by Captain W.A. Powell ominously entitled 'Should London

Migrate?'. Powell answered his question in the affirmative. Those who scoffed at the perils of air attack were 'still living in the past', he asserted; in a future war London was likely to be rendered 'uninhabitable'. He concluded by calling upon the authorities to move all essential military and civilian services and HQs out of London in the event of crisis.[54] In June Air Commodore P.F.M. Fellowes, commenting in the *Spectator* on Jonathan Griffin's *Britain's Air Policy*, wrote that 'the power of air aggression even now – and it is rapidly becoming greater – is so drastic that it is conceivable that a nation may be so pulverised by the first [air] attack that it may be quite unable to recover sufficiently to readjust the balance'.[55]

Kingsley Martin was altogether obsessed by the air peril. Several months after the official rebirth of the Luftwaffe he ironically explained his interest in the matter as stemming from the likelihood that he would 'soon be mutilated, burnt to death, suffocated, disembowelled or blown into small bits'. He readily subscribed to General Groves's thesis that cities and ships were indefensible against air attack; he thanked the general for 'telling me the truth'. He rejected talk of a viable air defence as 'a cruel hoax'. Like Jonathan Griffin – whose pieces he occasionally published in the *New Statesman* – Kingsley Martin called for the internationalisation of air power.[56] A veritable imagery of air fear suffused the editorial pages of the *New Statesman* in 1935. For example, in July the journal criticised a projected visit to Berlin by a British Legion delegation: 'It is paradoxical that British regret for gallant Germans who died in Flanders should quicken only when the wings of German bombing planes are again audible over Europe.'[57] In August and October 1935, well in advance of any of its peers, the *New Statesman* devoted two leading articles to urging the Government to embark upon a massive air-raid-shelter construction programme. The alternative, of rearmament, was rejected on grounds of inexpediency as well as principle; Kingsley Martin was convinced that guns and planes could not 'save' London.[58]

1936–1937

The German re-occupation of the Rhineland in March 1936 heightened the air fear; the air peril, in fact, was summoned forth as a major reason for British inaction in face of the Hitlerite coup. Garvin dismissed any thought of an active British response because 'from a shattering air-war between the British and German peoples neither could recover'.[59] Sidebotham, in the *Sunday Times*, preferred to reflect not upon the march into the Rhineland but upon the peace proposals which had accompanied the action. He saw them as 'the best hope of delivering the people from their fear of the terror that flies by night'.[60]

By 1936 *Time & Tide* had come full circle, from designating Groves's thesis 'one-sided' to asserting, repeatedly, that 'today [London] is the most indefensible city in the world'.[61] Repercussions on the proper conduct of British foreign policy followed. With regard to the Spanish Civil War, for example, the journal declared that of the options open to Britain, that of 'intervention', open or semi-secret, must be ruled out because her 'aerial rearmament [was] too far in arrears to . . . risk a conflict with Germany and Italy'. Germany alone, contended *Time & Tide*, was superior to Britain in the air.[62] A year later, in November 1937, the journal reiterated its belief that London was defenceless and would remain so for at least another year.[63]

The *Spectator* was obsessed equally with German power and Britain's indefensibility and weakness. As early as 6 March 1936 it stated that 'Germany is today the strongest military power in Europe, with the possible exception of Russia . . .'.[64] In September Wilson Harris devoted a first leader to what he called 'The Shadow of Destruction'; it was a most revealing embodiment of war fear:

> Europe today, and this country as part of Europe, is living under the dominion of fear. In France there is fear of Germany. In Germany there is fear of . . . Russia. The fear that oppresses us here *is not the fear of any particular country* but the fear of war, and of a war that we shall have had no part in provoking . . . [All our activities are overshadowed by] the recurrent thought that all our building is for destruction . . . If war comes we shall suffer whatever may be in store for us, praying that it may be obliteration, not the torturing survival of maimed and crippled bodies. [My italics – B.M.]

As it disingenuously dismissed a fear of 'any particular country', so the leader even-handedly attributed the coming war to the culpable ideologies and ambitions of Russia and Germany. Bombers' wings palpably hovered over the expanse of this article.[65] Some months later the *Spectator* published a series of articles on 'Air War and the Civilian', the contents of which could not have served to promote public confidence.[66]

Throughout 1936–37 the *New Statesman* remained in the grip of air fear but refused, when it suited its editorial purposes, to acknowledge that this also underlay British foreign policy. Many years later Kingsley Martin wrote concerning Spain that 'though fear no doubt entered Chamberlain's mind, it was not that which prompted British policy'.[67] But soon after the outbreak of the Civil War the *New Statesman* argued that Britain's 'one-sided neutrality' had been 'conceived in fear'.[68] A month later, however, the journal 'flatly refuse[d] to believe' that Britain's deficient armaments were the cause of the nation's supine responses to Japanese and Italian aggression and to the outside interventions in the Spanish war.[69]

'Guernica', in 1937, came as no revelation to the *New Statesman*, long convinced both of the evil of Fascism and of the destructive power of air attack. Guernica, the journal stated on 8 May, was only a rehearsal 'for Oxford and London'. It called for the establishment of an anti-Fascist bloc but abjured rearmament on the oft-repeated grounds that 'no amount of rearmament will save English towns ... from the fate of Guernica'; it declined to explain, if war came, how the existence of an anti-Fascist bloc would do so.[70] The *New Statesman* wanted no part in war, even were that the sole means of stemming what it believed to be the world-wide Fascist offensive. As Kingsley Martin commented in November 1937 on the Halifax–Hitler talks, Britain had two alternatives, either to agree to concessions to Germany or 'to prepare to fight at once': the latter course he rejected out of hand as it would mean 'general suicide'.[71]

Through 1936 and most of 1937 the weeklies continued to espouse Groves's thesis – that Britain was virtually indefensible against air attack and that the only viable deterrent was counter-offensive capability. But left-wing and Liberal weeklies were loath, from principle, to support rearmament and in any case refused to believe that more arms would 'save' Britain's cities. Typically, *The Economist*, which until 1938 persistently refused to condone 'massive' rearmament, stated that 'the only effective aerial defence against aerial attack [was] the threat of overwhelming reprisals in kind';[72] but how credible was the threat of 'overwhelming reprisals in kind' without 'massive' rearmament?

1937 saw the beginning of a revolution in aerial thinking. It was prompted by the impact of the Spanish and Chinese war experiences; incidentally, it afforded an escape from the Liberal–Left-wing dilemma. Sole reliance upon counter-bombing capability was dropped. It was slowly perceived and acknowledged that passive and active defensive measures could be effectively brought to bear against the threat from the bombers. It was recognised that passive measures such as early warning systems, trenches, blast-proof shelters and gas-masks taken together with active measures, such as interception by fighters, anti-aircraft guns, searchlights, and a balloon barrage could limit, if not obviate, the consequences of air attack. Perhaps a premature and backhanded indicator of this shift in thinking was afforded in an article on Germany's air defence system by the *Sunday Times* air correspondent in January 1937. He wrote that it was 'certainly the most complete and best organised system that now exists' and that 'even modern bombers would fail to make much impression on the capital'.[73] In the short term, such praise of Germany's anti-aircraft defences served only to heighten British fears and reinforce support for appeasement; conceptually, however, the article revealed a novel recognition that effective defence against air attack was possible. A month later Sidebotham cast doubt on the omnipotence of the bomber from a different perspective. It would be 'mistaken', he wrote on the basis of what he saw as the lesson of the Spanish war, to believe

> that the most important use of aeroplanes in war will be to spread panic and terror by bombing raids on the civil population . . . the military uses of mere frightfulness have been grossly exaggerated. The moral effect diminishes with each repetition; in the Spanish civil war it is curious how indecisive have been the results of air raids on open towns.[74]

By October 1937 Sidebotham felt able to declare:

> The actual danger from air raids is probably diminishing rather than increasing. A year ago it was the correct thing to say that the only defence against air raids was the power to do as much (or more) to the attacker in his own country . . . That is still the best but not by any means the only defence.[75]

In the course of 1937 dissent from air dogmas began to appear also in the pages of the *Observer*. General Groves himself, in an editorial page article, argued in February 1937 that effective, though limited, defence against air attack was possible.[76] In September Nigel Tangye, the paper's air correspondent, contended that the Spanish Civil War demonstrated that (a) air attacks served to stiffen rather than subvert civilian morale, (b) the effectiveness of incendiaries had been vastly over-rated and (c) there had been few examples of ships being sunk or hit by aircraft.[77]

Towards the end of 1937 even Wilson Harris was beginning to question the conceptual bases of the air fear. In a leader in the *Spectator* he repeated the formula that a future war would 'take the trenches in its stride and descend in unimaginable devastation on the civilian populations beyond the frontiers'. But he hesitantly added the reflection that Baldwin's dictum – 'the bomber will always get through' – might no longer be as valid in 1937 as it had been when coined. It should not be assumed, stated Wilson Harris, that anti-aircraft defences were still 'useless'. The article concluded with a plea for more passive defence measures.[78]

1938

The hesitant and infrequent inconoclasm of 1937 was to issue, in the following eighteen months, in a virtual revolution in aerial thinking. This change, mirrored in the weeklies, drew sustenance from the shift in thinking in military and Government circles; this shift was expressed in the switch in emphasis in aircraft production programmes from bombers to fighters[79] and in the increased focus on ARP and on AA-gun and searchlight production. All implied that effective defence against air attack was possible.

Paradoxically, however, the latter months of 1938 saw the climactic submission of the British public and Government to air fear, as epitomised in Munich. For simultaneously with the realisation that effective defence against air attack was possible came the jolting revelation that the emperor had no clothes; that is, that before and during September 1938, despite the assurances and talk, Britain lacked adequate modern fighter aircraft, a balloon barrage, AA-gun and searchlight systems, and a full aircraft spotting and tracking network, and that the organisation and means of ARP were deficient. Thus, at the point when the conceptual moorings of the air fear were at last uprooted, the concomitant weakness and paralysis of British foreign policy were enthroned for a final, short-lived reign by dint of material inadequacies. So the air fear continued through 1938 to loom large and to influence British policy and public and press attitudes to European affairs.

Reflective of the new-found belief in the efficacy of passive defence measures was the insistent and vocal campaign launched in all the weeklies for more and better air raid precautions; of course, it also reflected the growing feeling during 1938 that war was imminent. The *Spectator, Tribune* and the *New Statesman* were particularly emphatic about ARP, perhaps because they abjured the path of rearmament. They had, as it were, to place all their eggs in one basket; other journals could, and did, press, in varying degrees, for both ARP and rearmament.

Indicative of the changed outlook on air defence was the *Spectator*'s first leader of 14 January 1938. W.J. Wells, a guest leader-writer, stated that although 'high explosive bombs remain[ed] an acknowledged and fearful menace', there was 'no evidence to justify fears of the annihilation of the population of London at one blow, or even from a series of blows'.[80] The author's emphasis on 'high explosives' as the primary source of danger is worth noting; this was typical of all the weeklies from the start of 1938. The major bogies of previous years – gas, bacteria and thermite bombs – were increasingly discounted as potent menaces and lost their stature as obsessions. In June Sidebotham in the *Sunday Times* contended that the threat posed by gas and incendiary devices was manageable if met by efficient ARP measures.[81] Perhaps the failure of either to be used or to make a mark in the Spanish and Chinese wars had led to this dismissal; perhaps, too, the provision of gas masks and fire-fighting equipment had decreased fears from those quarters. The second, and major, point made by the *Spectator* – the dismissal of the premise of the 'knock-out blow' – was equally revolutionary; it had always stood at the centre of the air fear. This iconoclasm was echoed in other journals in the course of 1938. In May Sidebotham wrote in the *Sunday Times*:

> The legitimate uses of aeroplanes in support of the military operations of armies are so important, especially in the opening phases of a war, that one takes leave to doubt whether war will begin as is so often supposed with an attempted 'knock-out' blow directed against the civilian population. We must be prepared against such an attempt; but it may be more likely later in the war.[82]

The *Observer*'s air correspondent declared on 25 September that 'expert opinion as to the relative powers of air attack and air defence has undergone noticeable modification during the past two or three years'.[83] In January 1939, recalling Munich, *The Economist* stated that 'three months ago the challenge of impending war showed that two years of preparation had failed to provide the crowded and vulnerable cities of Britain with any adequate protection against air raids'.[84] Implicit in this passage was the belief that active and passive measures would and could, together, provide a sufficient defence against the bombers. A similar understanding informed *Time & Tide*'s treatment of the problem in the course of 1938; effective defence against air attack was recognised as possible but the means to achieve it were known to be in short supply.[85] Hence *Time & Tide* and *The Economist*, and all the right-wing weeklies, campaigned vigorously for both increased production of fighter aircraft and AA-guns and the enhancement of passive defence measures.

Undoubtedly, the overthrow of the theoretical bases of the air fear in some minds owed much to the knowledge that Britain had invented and was producing efficient and novel tools of defence. The existence of the fast eight-gun fighters was, by 1938, common knowledge. Apparently, the existence of radar and the installation of a detection system based upon it was also known to some leading journalists, and was referred to, if not explicitly, in the pages of several weeklies. The air correspondent of the *Observer* hinted at the utilisation of radar in a major article on 7 August 1938. More explicitly, on 25 September he stated: 'It is now believed that the fighter, working with a full modern warning and indication system, could seriously hamper the bomber and might overcome it'; 'a good deal ha[d lately] been done' in this respect, he noted.[86] Kingsley Martin, according to Dalton, already knew of radar in April 1938.[87]

Yet the air fear continued to hold sway until 1939; indeed, 1938, and especially Munich, marked its zenith. In great measure this was due to the recognition of British unpreparedness and of German aerial potency. In addition, many people remained theoretically unconvinced of the possibility of effective anti-aircraft defence; the fear was too deeply rooted to be easily exorcised by inventions at home or practical demonstrations in remote war-zones. Kingsley Martin, for example, placed some value in passive defences such as shelters and gas-masks but remained unable to believe in the efficacy of fighters and anti-aircraft guns. (Counter-bombing he completely ruled out; it was an 'inefficient ... remedy for the menace of Fascism'.[88]) Britain's 'best' first line of defence, he argued, should be to 'counter-bomb' Germany with propaganda leaflets, explaining war's evils and Britain's goodwill. Passive defence measures he regarded as a second line of defence.[89]

Through 1938 air fear remained a major factor dictating policy in the weeklies. With regard to Spain Garvin declared in the *Observer*: 'The scenes in bombed Barcelona are hideous. Can they be mended by bringing on scenes a hundred times worse in a bombed London?'[90] He remained fearful of a 'knock-out blow' against Britain as the Czech crisis unfolded.[91] And in October he defended the Munich settlement by arguing: 'Germany holds a definite superiority of air-power over both Britain and France. This has been a dominant factor behind the ultimatum and the "squeeze".'[92] The same argument (among others) was used by Sidebotham in the *Sunday Times* in justifying Munich: 'Neither Great Britain nor France were sufficiently prepared in armaments or ARP for a great war.'[93] The *Saturday Review*, until its closure in July 1938, revealed a similar appreciation of the role played by the air peril in the determination of British foreign policy. The journal specifically opposed fresh British commitments on the Continent so long as it suffered from inferiority in the air.[94]

Among Liberal and left-wing weeklies the situation was no different; air fear roamed freely across party political lines. In June 1938 the assistant editor of the *Spectator*, Goronwy Rees, wrote a leader on Japanese and Fascist bombing atrocities in China and Spain. These were minor by comparison with what would befall Europe's major cities should world war break out, he declared. The *Spectator*, therefore, urged that Britain open talks with Hitler for 'it would appear that the German Government ... has still not disowned the proposals for the abolition of bombing of open towns and villages, and the dropping of poison gas or incendiary bombs which Herr Hitler definitely proposed in 1936'. The unreality of this recommendation was great, in view of the Condor Legion's ongoing devastation of Spanish towns, but the *Spectator*'s fears of air attack on England were, apparently, still greater. The journal suggested that Britain protest against the Japanese and Fascist air attacks but cautioned that it was 'not necessary to speak of sanctions or reprisals, or repeat ambitious phrases, long-forgotten, of "steady resistance to unprovoked aggression"'.[95] A week later, perhaps having drawn criticism, Rees confessed that German air attacks in Spain 'belie[d] her [previous] words' concerning a possible bombing limitation agreement, but urged the British Government to cease employing bombers on the North-West Frontier so as to give it the moral authority to condemn similar action by others.[96]

A fortnight later the *Spectator* declared that 'the immensity of the peril that threatens London and every great city has not penetrated the public mind', despite the Spanish and Chinese experiences. Death and destruction by aerial bombardment could be kept to a minimum but, given Britain's lack of the requisite defences, 'the complete annihilation [of Britain], the sudden and final "knock-out blow" . . . was possible at the present time'. Rees concluded the leader by calling for the immediate reorganisation of the civil air defence system. This could be shirked, he stated, only 'if this country is willing to accept the dictation of any Power that threatens'; the foreign policy implications of aerial defencelessness were clear.[97] Through the Munich crisis the *Spectator* reiterated its conviction that 'this country is still utterly unprepared for the greatest danger modern war implies – that of murderous attacks from the air, delivered with such efficiency as to break the morale of the population and destroy the great cities and those who live in them'.[98] Wilson Harris later justified the Munich settlement on the grounds of British and French unreadiness in the air; 'even the most desperate attempt to save the peace was worthwhile'.[99] At the time, the *Spectator* did not explicitly condone Munich on this basis; but, significantly, it devoted its second leading article of 7 October (and many leaders thereafter) to calling for massive rearmament, especially in the air.[100] *The Economist*, which opposed appeasement and the Munich settlement, throughout 1938 vigorously espoused the cause of civil defence reorganisation. Britain, it acknowledged, was 'in many ways . . . the most vulnerable of European nations'.[101] In general, *The Economist* did not allow its perception of the air peril to influence its foreign policy line. But most members of its editorial staff during 1938 were thoroughly aware of the air menace; Toynbee, for example, 'was very conscious of the "air peril"', recalled a colleague on the journal.[102] In other journals, such as the *Spectator* and the *New Statesman*, the air fear remained a pre-eminent consideration in the formulation and espousal of foreign policy. Years later, Kingsley Martin recalled that during the Munich crisis one 'factor frightening the Government into appeasement was the extremely successful propaganda of Colonel Lindburgh' concerning the omnipotence of German air power.[103] Without doubt, however, Kingsley Martin found Lindburgh's grim predictions as persuasive as did Chamberlain. On 17 September, for example, he calculated in a *New Statesman* leader that '500 aeroplanes each dropping two tons of bombs would, on average, kill 2,000 people'; he envisaged this as being England's daily casualty-toll should war erupt over Czechoslovakia.[104]

CONCLUSION

British attitudes to the European situation and 'the German problem' during the thirties were largely determined by air fear. To judge from the weeklies, the air fear, present from the early thirties, took firm root in public consciousness in the course of 1935. Its main stimulation was afforded by Germany's announcements of massive and open rearmament in the spring of that year. It was confirmed by the Government's contradictory statements in Parliament on the relative progress of German and British aerial rearmament, and by the generally and prematurely accepted view that air parity had been lost. The air fear was mainly a fear of German air power and its prospective devastation of England's civilian centres and maritime life-lines. From the end of 1935 onwards, Italian air power was joined to the Luftwaffe as a further source of anxiety, and the Mediterranean fleet, outposts and sea-routes to the East were cast in the role of additional potential targets. Underlying all, up to 1938, was the conviction that the bomber would always get through. The urban centres were seen as indefensible, and expectations of casualties from air attack ran into hundreds of thousands within weeks or months of the outbreak of hostilities. Immeasurable material destruction was anticipated. A final sting was added to the air fear by the belief that a new war would be inaugurated by a German 'knock-out blow' and that such an attack would in all likelihood succeed. The Air Staff usually subscribed to this belief and official views only confirmed the general public's fears.

A major dent was made in the air fear by the start of production of fast, eight-gun fighters, by the discovery of radar and its installation as a mainstay of an efficient, multi-faceted early warning system and by the revelation, in Spain, of the efficacy of passive defence measures, such as shelters, against bomber assault. Together, these introduced and sustained a belief that effective defence against air attack, including the 'knock-out blow', was possible. Given, however, Britain's known deficiency in all these, and Germany's equally obvious aerial prepon- derance, the air fear continued to reign well into 1939.

All the weeklies paid increasing attention to the air peril from the time of Hitler's assumption of power. The *New Statesman* and the *Observer* had succumbed to the air fear already in 1932. The other journals fell increasingly under its spell, some, like *The Economist* and *Time & Tide*, resistantly, between 1933 and 1935. During 1935 all came to accept the Baldwinian gospel that effective defence against air attack was not possible. In the weeklies, the controversy regarding the air question between 1935 and 1938 centred on the need for and acceptance of deterrent, counter-bombing capability. While the *Saturday Review* and the *Observer*, already from 1933, had fervidly advocated massive rearmament (especially with bombers), the *New Statesman*, *Tribune* and the *New English Weekly* condemned it on grounds of principle, ineffectiveness (killing Berliners would not resurrect pulverised Londoners) and cost (more arms meant less social benefits). *Truth*, *Time & Tide*, *The Economist* and the *Spectator* only reluctantly supported rearmament, and condemned any of a 'massive' variety. By the end of 1938 all the weeklies, excepting the *New Statesman*, *Tribune* and the *New English Weekly*, came to accept the need for 'massive' rearmament (while occasionally decrying the adjective), especially in the air and specifically in fighter aircraft, AA-guns and search-lights. This marked a shift from 1935–37, when advocacy of aerial rearmament focused on bombers. In the course of 1938 and early 1939 *Time & Tide*, the *Sunday Times*, the *Observer*, *Truth* and *The Economist* had come to believe that effective defence against air attack was possible; the *New Statesman* had not; the *Spectator* wavered between its pristine, gloom-laden convictions and the new-fangled, fighter-and-radar-based optimism.

It is impossible to avoid the conclusion that air fear was a major determinant of policy in the weeklies between 1935 and 1939. Admissions to this effect in the journals were infrequent and, when made, were usually indirect and allusive; no one readily admits to being motivated by fear. Nonetheless, the air fear figures prominently in almost all the journals' treatments of the crises of 1935–38, and always as an argument in favour of appeasement. Like background material, throughout and after the Munich crisis, most of the journals carried fear-promoting articles on the expected ravages from the air.

It was, primarily, the air fear which imbued many Britons during the thirties with a sense that a new world war would mark the end of civilisation. The fear engendered by the prospect of air attack was of colossal proportions; indeed it was likened by many who lived then and through the Cold War to the later fear of nuclear holocaust. In August 1938 Virginia Woolf noted in her diary that a new war would signify 'the complete ruin not only of civilisation in Europe, but of our last [hope]'.[105] A month later R. Bruce Lockhart concurred with Rex Leeper's feeling about the Czech crisis – 'a craven reluctance to see the end of the world'.[106] And Claud Cockburn, recalling the winter of 1938–39, wrote that 'the gas-mask was the expression of people's faith in the accepted apocalypse';[107] Heinkels, Stukkas and Junkers were seen as the harbingers of that apocalypse.

IV

FEBRUARY–JUNE 1935

February–June 1935 marked a turning point in Anglo-German relations. Appeasement, as a policy based on fear, was then inaugurated. It was pursued ineffectually and passively until Baldwin's resignation and thereafter with positive vigour until March 1939.

Against the backdrop of failure in disarmament negotiations and clandestine German rearmament, the British and French Governments issued a joint declaration on 4 February 1935, inviting Europe's powers to discuss and conclude a Western Air Pact and an 'Eastern Locarno'. (This proved to be the last major effort by the Western democracies to implement the concept of 'collective security' prior to the formation of the alliance against Germany in March 1939.) Hitler's response was vague and somewhat dampening. But an invitation was issued for British Ministers to come to Berlin and discuss the outstanding questions. The Simon–Eden visit was timed for 6 March.

A defence White Paper was issued in London on 4 March. It called for increased defence estimates in view of Germany's menacing rearmament. The Germans reacted with feigned anger and indefinitely postponed the British Ministers' visit. Hitler proceeded to set the stage for his long-contemplated coup. G. Ward Price, the *Daily Mail*'s special correspondent, was summoned to Berlin for a scoop. Goering blandly informed the journalist that Germany possessed a military air force. Reacting to the publication of this statement – announcing a blatant infringement of the Treaty of Versailles – Simon informed the House of Commons that it was still the Government's intention to proceed with the talks in Berlin. Having thus tested the water and finding it agreeable, Hitler, on 16 March, took the plunge. He proclaimed Germany's re-introduction of full-scale conscription, aiming at the establishment of a 36-division army; an official announcement of the rebirth of the Luftwaffe followed. The Versailles clauses pertaining to German strength on land and in the air were thus unilaterally repealed. The immediate British response was to inquire of Berlin whether it was still agreeable to the Ministers' visit. The talks between Simon and Eden and the Nazi hierarchs were duly held on 24 March. While no concrete advance was made towards agreement on the Air Pact or on the 'Eastern

Locarno' (to which, in fact, Hitler flatly objected), the British Ministers were informed by the Führer that Germany had already attained air parity in front-line machines with Britain's metropolitan air force and was rapidly advancing towards superiority.

British and French apprehensions of reborn German military power led to the convocation of a tripartite summit at Stresa on 11 April. On 14 April the two democracies and Italy declared continuing support for Austrian independence and condemned Germany's defiance of the Treaty of Versailles. The door was left open to some undefined measure of Treaty revision. It was hoped a 'front' designed to contain Germany had been established. Abyssinia was pointedly left unmentioned. France, desiring reinsurance, proceeded to cap Stresa with a Pact of Mutual Assistance with Russia on 2 May.

On 22 May Baldwin, eating his words of November 1934, told the Commons that German aircraft production had far exceeded British expectations. Though proposing an expansion of the RAF, his speech tended to confirm Churchill's belief that air parity had been lost and that the gap between German and British air strengths was rapidly growing.

On 21 May Hitler, pursuing his carrot-and-stick pattern, delivered a major pacific oration. Fervently, he denounced war, proposed bilateral non-aggression treaties with Germany's neighbours, offered agreements on arms limitation and the abolition of bombing and suggested the conclusion of a naval agreement with Britain based on a 35:100 ratio of tonnage in surface vessels, a suggestion already mooted in the Simon–Eden talks of March. Germany's defiant rearmament announcements of two months before and her dismissal of an 'Eastern Locarno' were quickly cast out of mind. Ribbentrop arrived in London at the beginning of June and on the 18th the Anglo-German Naval Agreement was concluded.

It is worth noting that prior to Hitler's speech, Germany had announced the construction of 12 submarines, adding the sea to its air and land repudiations of the Versailles arms clauses. This caused some alarm in Britain; the memory of submarine attacks during the Great War was still fresh. But doubts and fears were quickly dissipated by Hitler's pacific declarations.

This prelude prefigured the character of the Naval Agreement. Hitler's demand for 35 per cent in surface tonnage was met. In addition, Germany was allowed immediately to build up to 45 per cent of Britain's submarine fleet and to build up to a full 100 per cent in special circumstances. Critics of the Agreement argued that it condoned Germany's violations of Versailles, supported Hitler's predilection for bi-lateral pacts detrimental to collective security, divided Britain from France and, in fact, spurred on rather than limited German Naval ambitions.

The Liberal and left-wing weeklies unanimously acclaimed the Anglo-French démarche of 4 February. *The Economist* purported to believe that Germany merely desired 'equality' as France wished for 'security',[1] and hailed Hitler's mere willingness to consider the Anglo-French proposals as 'much to Germany's credit'. The journal invested high hopes in the Air Pact proposal.[2] But it looked askance at the rumoured German refusal to agree to an 'Eastern Locarno'. Germany's alleged fear of the Bolshevik menace, it believed, was sham; 'For our part, we do not believe that the Soviet Union has, or is likely to have, any intentions of military aggression', stated *The Economist*.[3] The contrary was true: 'It is . . . not Germany but Russia and the rest of Europe who look to the future with apprehension', for Germany was known to be intent on territorial changes 'of an uncertain extent'. But the German answer to the Anglo-French proposals, believed the journal, 'close[d] no doors', despite the silence concerning the proposed Air Pact and re-entry into the League of Nations, and despite the outright rejection of an 'Eastern Locarno'. Germany, asserted the journal, had 'a very strong [moral] case' behind her insistence on her right to rearm. Altogether, *The Economist* saw the new proposals as a laudable first step in Treaty revision.[4]

The *Spectator* went one better in its optimism. Germany, believed Wilson Harris, should at least be interested in the conclusion of an Air Pact. For 'Herr Hitler . . . was a realist, and in foreign affairs had exhibited . . . sanity and restraint . . .'.[5] On the whole, the journal thought the German reply to the Anglo-French proposals 'favourable', and believed that too much stress should not be laid on the absence of references to disarmament, to a return to the League or to the conclusion of an 'Eastern Locarno'.[6] At first, the *New Statesman*, too, was hopeful that the Anglo-French proposals were 'being examined seriously in Berlin'. The journal admitted that there was 'a section of opinion' in Germany which wished that country 'to go on her own defiant and independent way'; but 'this does not seem to be the view of Herr Hitler and his Government'. There were, it was true, fears in Czechoslovakia and Russia that a Western accord would free Germany for eastern expansion. But, apparently, it was not clear 'that Germany is so bitten with Herr Rosenberg's doctrines as to be spoiling for a fight with Russia'.[7]

Two weeks later disappointment set in. Germany had flatly rejected an 'Eastern Locarno'; and an Air Pact by itself could not guarantee European security, believed the *New Statesman*. The journal was now 'inclined to accept Hitler's word in *Mein Kampf*, that war against France is to follow ... expansion in the East ... and [that] when he says Germany has no expansionist aims, we remain sceptical'; the theory of the 'evil counsellors' was thus for a time laid to rest. The *New Statesman* berated those who wished to direct German aggression eastwards and criticised the 'tendency on the part of British Ministers to be increasingly friendly in tone to Nazi Germany and to discuss concessions to threats which they refused to take seriously while Germany was weak'. But, in view of its own fear of 'a sudden air-raid likely to settle a war in a night', the journal concluded that 'the true policy' should be frankly to recognise the menace of Nazi Germany, admit her right to equality of status and 'express readiness to open discussion of frontier adjustment'. To these the journal tacked on conditions: that Germany return to the League, that it cease to flirt with Japan and that it subscribe to 'the obligations of League membership'. Specific mention of the need for German participation in an Eastern Locarno was pointedly omitted.[8]

Time & Tide of 9 February considered the Air Pact proposal by Britain and France 'the most significant development of international relations since the signing of the Covenant'. It was more circumspect with regard to the reason behind the Anglo-French overture: the Air Pact was being proposed because the Western democracies possessed a dossier 'showing that German rearmament would give Berlin, by the middle of 1936, the same preponderance in striking efficiency it had in 1914'. Unfortunately, 'nobody knows whether Germany wants equality and peace, or is driving towards preponderance and war', stated the journal.[9]

The right-wing weeklies remained divided on the merits of the Anglo-French proposals as on the 'German problem' itself. In the *Observer* on 3 February, Garvin signalled the coming reversal of his views on the European situation. Germany, in his eyes, was already a major military power. Hence, he wrote, 'nothing more must be heard or suggested of compulsion upon the Nazi Reich' and the Western powers must concede to Germany the right to 'absolute equality' in armaments and otherwise.[10] For a time, however, this remained a temporary aberration. On 17 and 24 February Garvin came out strongly in favour of both the proposed Western Air Pact and the Eastern Locarno. And, indicative of his persisting belief in a policy of anti-German containment, he warned that Russia must on no account be left out of any future European peace system. He warned that a Western Air Pact, on its own, might prove perilous to Britain's security: 'All the political anxieties and uncertainties would remain unsolved and unabated', he wrote; any agreement confined to Western Europe 'would be a delusion'; 'it is idle to think that you can segregate "western" and "eastern" questions'.[11] Britain and France, he declared on 3 March, could never countenance the wholesale mutilation of Russia as prescribed in *Mein Kampf*.[12]

The *Sunday Times*, on the other hand, continued to advocate British non-intervention in eastern Europe. Sidebotham flatly rejected the proposed Eastern Locarno as 'a dangerous entanglement' while clamouring relentlessly for the conclusion of a Western Air Pact.[13] He believed, in fact, that talk of an Eastern Locarno endangered the conclusion of the coveted Western settlement. Britain must look to the security of its own people. And in any case, he contended, 'what conceivable injury can this Air Locarno do to the States of eastern Europe?' His solution to the problems of eastern Europe was clear: 'May not some sort of federation with State autonomy, even under German hegemony, be the best issue?'[14]

Truth and the *Saturday Review* rejected both proposed pacts. *Truth*, above all, desired Treaty revision. The Air Pact, believed the journal, was a complete waste of everybody's time unless Versailles was first revised. The *Saturday Review*, abjuring revision, asserted that the Air Pact, like all pacts, was 'humbug'; all treaties and pacts were 'scraps of paper', violated by all upon convenience.[15] Moreover, thought *Truth*, taking an isolationist tack, all new pacts imperilled British security inasmuch as they involved further commitments.[16] Pacts and plans aside, 'the fundamental fact' of the European situation continued 'to be the great rearmament of Germany', contended the *Saturday Review*. Simon's mooted visit to Berlin would be of use only if, while there, he could 'draw aside the veil ... over German rearmament'; 'otherwise Sir John had better stay at home'.[17] *Truth* also objected to Simon's visit, and not merely on grounds of distaste for the Air Pact and Eastern Locarno proposals. Hitler, argued the journal, had been strengthened by the Saar plebiscite results. The visit would therefore be interpreted as a concession to a victorious Germany:

> The strengthening of the Nazi Government might be a cheap price [to pay] for the peace of Europe. But whether that peace can ultimately be secured by encouraging Germany to believe that her enemies are more tractable to force than to reason is a different question altogether.

Concessions to Germany, such as it believed the projected visit to be, might result in a 'stiffening' of German demands and attitudes.[18] The other weeklies, left-wing, Liberal and right-wing, offered no objection to the Simon–Eden visit.

This visit was set for 6 March. But, on 4 March 1935, a Defence White Paper, unusually initialled by MacDonald, was presented to Parliament. Its publication was greeted in the weeklies by a wave of indignation, criticism and protest. Hitler postponed the imminent ministerial visit. *The Economist* of 9 March called the *Statement Relating to Defence* a 'Black Paper'. Its hopes had been high for the Simon–Eden visit: 'Today these hopes lie shattered.' The Government had been 'guilty of a grave blunder in psychology and in tactics'; it was responsible for the unfortunate postponement. For 15 years Britain had supported 'a system of military supremacy on the Continent which left a great nation disarmed and resentful'; though Germany was rearming, to publicly arraign her as a menace was to cast her in the role of a 'scapegoat' and was 'in no sense a fair apportionment of the blame'. *The Economist* called upon the Government to make clear 'that this is not a case of giving judgement against Germany' and 'that there are two points of view – and both legitimate points of view – to be reconciled . . .'.[19] A week later the journal condemned the arms race and stated: 'Great Britain does not believe in the encirclement of Germany or in the building-up of a military alliance that would make it too dangerous for Germany to break the peace.' Even-handedly, it questioned whether Nazi Germany and Communist Russia really desired peace.[20]

The *Spectator* viewed the White Paper's attempt 'to pillory Germany as the guilty cause of the world's rearmament' as 'grossly inexpedient'. The journal thought it 'unfair' and 'indiscreet' to 'reproach Germany alone for the present situation in Europe'. Blame, it thought, certainly attached also to France. R.A. Scott-James, the journal's Assistant Editor, feared that the White Paper heralded the adoption by Britain of a new policy of 'peace by enforcement' in place of the previous one grounded on 'peace by persuasion'. He feared, too, that this would encourage the 'warlike spirit . . . being organised in Germany'.[21] There was still ground, thought the *Spectator*, 'for believing that Hitler's own inclinations are pacific, but that is by no means true of a section of his advisers . . .'.[22]

Time & Tide was more critical still. The Commons had received the rearmament proposals with 'alarm'. The White Paper had been 'very clumsily worded' and mis-timed, in view of the impending Simon–Eden 'Peace Mission', and had definitely worsened the international situation. Not arms but allies were the touchstone of a nation's security; the White Paper constituted a 'repudiation' of the League of Nations and of collective security.[23] The *New Statesman* also thought the White Paper and the increased defence estimates 'deplorable'. Like *Time & Tide*, it saw arms as the negation of 'collective security'; the White Paper meant an arms race which portended 'bankruptcy or war – or both'. The journal objected to the 'threatening language' of the anti-German passages, and thought it 'a bad blunder' in view of the postponement of the Simon–Eden visit: 'the hope of conciliating Germany . . . had been indefinitely postponed.'[24] Perversely, it argued: 'We do not deny that the appeal to force is the most likely to affect the minds of the present rulers of Germany. But whether Britain's increases in arms will have the kind of effect Mr Baldwin hopes for is open to doubt.' Now, as always, until 1939, the *New Statesman* flatly objected to any and all British rearmament.[25]

The *New English Weekly* struck an important nail squarely on the head in its reaction to the White Paper and the defence increases. It pointed to the contradiction implicit in at once running 'with the pacific hare' (i.e. the Simon–Eden visit and peace proposals) and hunting with 'the armament hounds' (i.e. increased estimates). The journal offered no objection to MacDonald's 'calling attention to those theories and practices of Nazism which are turning Germany into a drill-ground and may end by turning Europe into a wilderness'. But 'neither denunciation nor conciliation can be effective if they are to be indulged in simultaneously'.[26]

For the right-wing weeklies the publication of the Defence White Paper of 4 March posed a problem. On the one hand, they were unanimous in their clamour for British rearmament; in this sense, the move was seen as a major step in the right direction. On the other hand, all were nonplussed by the timing of the White Paper and some, such as the *Sunday Times*, by its condemnation of Germany; it obviously threw a spanner in the works of appeasement.

Truth took exception to the timing of the warning to Hitler, in view of the impending Simon visit. But it agreed that the time had come for Britain to rearm.[27] The *Sunday Times*, still pushing the Western Air Pact proposal and British rearmament, offered somewhat milder criticism of the timing and anti-German phraseology of the White Paper.[28] Garvin, on the other hand, waxed enthusiastic at the Government's move. He called the White Paper 'a searching document' and 'for the most part an admirable elucidation'; hyperbolically, the *Observer*'s first leader of 10 March designated the document 'one of the great State Papers of our time'.[29]

Germany's rearmament proclamations of 16 March were the first public unilateral repudiation of articles of the Treaty of Versailles. The response of the British Government, with which the bulk of the weeklies concurred, was to inaugurate the era of appeasement; fear, based on a feeling of aerial vulnerability, on an assumed general military weakness and on a profound aversion to war, dictated the adoption of a policy of concessions. Previously, concessions to Germany had been envisaged on the basis of a moral impulse to right Treaty wrongs and from a position and feeling of strength.

73

Goering's revelation of the rebirth of the Luftwaffe drew little comment in the weeklies. When mentioned, as in the *Spectator* of 15 March, it was buried among reports of the 'similar' rearmament of other States.[30] Germany's official proclamations of rearmament were something altogether different. *The Economist* divined that the German declarations marked 'the termination of the post-war chapter of European history'. The Treaty of Versailles was 'now defunct'. The journal wondered what was left for Simon to talk about in Berlin but failed to recommend the cancellation of the visit. It made light of Hitler's pacific assurance and called upon Germany to declare the sum total of her objectives and to renounce the use of force and enter the collective system. Should Germany refuse to meet these conditions, 'the rest of us', declared the journal, 'would be compelled to conclude that she was re-assuming military power ... as a means to military predominance'. Rather lamely, the journal predicted the re-emergence of armed alliances and the ultimate irruption of war.[31]

The Simon and Eden talks in Berlin, on 24 March, afforded *The Economist* little ground for optimism. It drew crumbs of comfort from Hitler's reiterated willingness to discuss arms limitation and the abolition of 'offensive weapons'. But on the main issue, wrote the journal, 'while casting no doubt on Herr Hitler's desire for peace, what we most regret is that the Führer appears to have made no serious attempt to meet and to allay the real preoccupation of his neighbours'. Germany still opposed multi-lateral pacts, indicating '"Rosenbergian" Eastern aspirations'. And it still claimed the right to attain 'air parity' with France and preponderance on land.[32]

The *Spectator* preferred to interpret reality in brighter shades. 'Germany', Wilson Harris conceded, 'may ... be contemplating war, not to-day or tomorrow, but as the ultimate instrument of a national policy whose ends can be attained by no other means.' If that were the case, then a world alliance against her was the only answer. But, he argued, 'there is little hope that way; peace by compulsion is a poor substitute for peace by consent'. And, in any case, it was 'not essential to put the worst construction' on Germany's declarations of rearmament: Germany had 'broken the Treaty of Versailles, but it is little to the purpose to split legal hairs about that now ... Germany has all too much justification for her action in other Powers' unfulfilled pledges' (i.e. of disarmament). The *Spectator* upheld the Government's decision to proceed with the Simon–Eden visit. It suggested that Germany declare her willingness to return to the League of Nations; 'If she refuses that, no credence will be placed in her *bona fides* anywhere.'[33]

The inconclusive, not to say dismal, results of the Eden–Simon visit to Berlin left the *Spectator* in an appeasing frame of mind. In an aside, it urged Britain to protest against Lithuania's treatment of Nazi subversives in Memel.[34] On the main issue it preferred to put the 'best construction' on German intentions; that is, to believe that Germany's fear of Russia was sincere and that her desire for great armaments stemmed from this fear rather than from dreams of expansion. In either case, Wilson Harris recommended that Britain adhere to 'collective security' rather than enter into commitment-laden alliances.[35] To reinforce these recommendations Wilson Harris, in the following week, stated that the Russian regime was no less criminal – and possibly more so – than that of Germany; he conceded, however, that Russian foreign policy was consonant with the principle of collective security whereas Germany still refused to re-enter the League.[36]

Time & Tide's reactions to Germany's declarations of rearmament were numerous and contradictory. The journal believed Britain had been 'right' to protest against Germany's repudiation of Versailles and 'right', also, to enquire if the Simon visit was still on. Like the *Spectator*, it believed that Hitler's proclamations had 'cleared the air'. The journal hoped that in Berlin Simon would succeed in divining whether Germany was willing to join the collective security system. Implicitly contrary, however, was the journal's first leading article by Norman Angell. He took as a matter of course Germany's (and Japan's) desire to crush Russia – which should have ruled out any hopes of German enlistment in the collective system.[37] (Adding to the confusion was Wyndham Lewis's 'Notes on the Way' contribution in the same issue, fully endorsing Hitler's actions.)[38]

Following the Simon visit, *Time & Tide* clearly spelt out the dangers posed to Britain by the twin menace of Germany and Japan. It took to task Britain's isolationists and stated bluntly that retreat from collective security would ensure the destruction of Western civilisation.[39] A guest contribution from Robert Dell, the *Manchester Guardian*'s Berlin correspondent, went further. Before 1933 Dell had been a fanatical revisionist; with Hitler in power appeasement had no greater critic. He chastised the Government and Press in Britain for sowing illusions about the Hitler regime. Talk of Germany rejoining the League, or adhering to the concept of collective security, was nonsense. Germany aimed at European hegemony; all else was illusion, he argued. Only the formation of an all-powerful 'combination' would deter Hitler from his contemplated course.[40]

The *New Statesman* declared itself unsurprised by the German declaration of rearmament. It had been 'precipitated' by the White

Paper and by France's increase of its conscript service. 'On the general issue of Germany's rearmament, any show of moral indignation is absurd', stated the journal: it was the direct result 'of the dishonesty and blindness' of the Great War's victors. The *New Statesman*, for one, 'shed no tears' over this further emasculation of the Versailles Treaty. It, too, thought Hitler's action had somewhat clarified matters. It was open to two interpretations: either 'Hitler means to go on from impudence to impudence', for which there were foundations 'in the history of the man and the temper of his people'; or it meant 'no more ... than the supreme assertion of Germany's demand for equality'. Implicit was the journal's preference for the second possibility. The journal criticised France's intention of denouncing Germany in the League of Nations as 'a most unfortunate course to take': it would effect nothing, and while Germany's 'armaments are doubtless excessive ... so are those of the rest of us'. The 'sensible course', according to the *New Statesman*, was to ascertain 'whether Hitler is now content' and ready to return to the League and sign an 'Eastern Locarno'. The journal concluded by calling upon Britain to reaffirm support of collective security – without rearmament; if Germany then refused to subscribe, she would have only herself to blame for her 'encirclement'.[41]

Of the Simon talks in Berlin the *New Statesman* thought that 'nobody but an armaments manufacturer can draw any comfort from them'. Hitler had flatly rejected an 'Eastern Locarno' and any accommodation with Russia.[42] Despite, or possibly because of German belligerency, the journal now advocated Treaty revision in the case of Memel.[43] Yet, contradictorily, in the same issue, the *New Statesman*, revealing that Hitler had told Simon that Germany was still bent upon the incorporation of the Corridor, Austria and Memel, commented: 'Thus bluntly to announce that *Mein Kampf* still represents his policy is to alienate even those who have earnestly pleaded the injustice of Germany's past treatment.' But the leader went on to caution against the establishment at Stresa of an 'encircling' alliance against Germany. The way to negotiated revision regarding the Corridor, Memel and the colonies should not be barred to Germany. Following the revelations about German air power and the rearmament proclamations, what Hitler claimed the *New Statesman* was now eager to deliver, despite its oft-asserted appreciation of *Mein Kampf*'s gospel.[44]

The German rearmament challenge moved the *Sunday Times* not at all. In its strongest reaction Hadley stated: 'Though [Hitler's] action in re-introducing conscription was most provocative, the deed has been accompanied by words strongly expressive of peace.'[45] And words, as all appeasers knew, were more telling than deeds. Therefore, argued

Sidebotham: 'It seems a mistake for France to talk of arraigning Germany's action before the League when one of Sir John Simon's objects in his visit to Berlin is to bring Germany into the League.' It was no real matter that Germany would 'once again [have] the most powerful army in Europe' for German ambitions were now 'less over-leaping' than in 1914; simply put, Germany desired changes and, perhaps, expansion in eastern Europe but intended to leave the West in peace and British naval supremacy unchallenged. The maintenance of the eastern European *status quo* was no concern of Britain; and the establishment of the formidable land army with which Germany was to subdue recalcitrant eastern Europeans was similarly no grounds for apprehension in the West. Sidebotham was convinced that peace in the West could be secured by the sacrifice of others (including French allies) in the East.[46] As to the threat from the air, Sidebotham was still hopeful that the conclusion of a Western Air Pact and an agreement prohibiting bombardment would provide the solution.

Garvin in the *Observer*, despite his previous support for German 'equality' in armaments, was far less sanguine. With the rearmament declarations, Hitler had drawn off 'the velvet glove' and extended 'his gauntlet' to Britain, he declared; in this he divined proof that Germany was 'already far stronger than is supposed'. 'The resolve to restore the military supremacy of the German race in Europe has been the foundation of [Hitler's] movement', he warned; and he called upon Simon to display firmness as well as courtesy in Berlin.[47] But the outcome of the Simon–Eden visit confirmed Garvin in his perceptions and gloom. 'The British and German peoples today', he declared, 'differ as fundamentally in their ideas of world-policy as in their domestic systems'; at heart there was here 'an antithesis of two conceptions of political civilisation'. He called upon the Government to reaffirm its commitments to collective security and to the Covenant, and to abjure isolation 'as suicide as well as sin'.[48] There was no future in 'limited liability'; the West could not be secured at the price of sacrificing eastern Europe, for France's safety depended upon its eastern alliances and Britain's upon France.[49]

Truth and the *Saturday Review* also refused to indulge in self-delusion or to advocate placating Germany in the wake of Hitler's rearmament challenge. Unlike the *Observer*, the *Saturday Review* called for the cancellation of the Simon visit: 'The only result that can be expected is another snub for our wretched Government.' The journal found Britain's position *vis-à-vis* Germany 'odiously humiliating'.[50] *Truth* was less sensitive to considerations of British honour. It upheld the Government's decision to proceed with the Simon–Eden visit despite Hitler's repudiation of Versailles; cancellation 'would have meant the virtual breaking of contacts between Great Britain and Germany. That could only have led to a period of strain and mutual mistrust.' But *Truth* remained pessimistic for it could discern no basis for negotiation in Berlin.[51] On the wider issues *Truth*, the *Observer* and the *Saturday Review* were in gloomy accord. *Truth* had long advocated revision. But revision of the defiant and unilateral kind à la Hitler it found totally unacceptable and ominous:

> The outlook and philosophy behind Hitlerism – of which the concentration camps, the victimisation of the pastors, the baiting of the Jews and the military execution of the dissidents are manifestations – are such that civilisation cannot suffer it to obtain the moral victory of achieving its ends. A success that we might welcome in the Weimar Republic, and that we might tolerate in a restored Empire, we can never suffer in a Nazi dictatorship. If we do, we might ultimately find ourselves as badly off as the German Socialists and the German Jews.

Peace in Europe was impossible without 'loyal co-operation from Germany' and a Hitlerite Germany would never proffer that co-operation. *Truth* called upon the Western democracies to 'administer a sharp rebuff' to the Nazi regime falling short only of 'preventive war'. The journal expected Germany to proceed in its treaty-breaking to territorial issues – Austria, the Corridor, Memel and Malmedy.[52] The *Saturday Review* foresaw a similar development but looked to the Demilitarised Zone of the Rhineland.[53]

Truth, however, shortly reverted to a more balanced and conciliatory stance. It noted the 'ardent desire for mutual understanding among peoples' and again upheld the Simon–Eden visit, 'notwithstanding the curious [sic] behaviour of Germany's rulers' (i.e. the rearmament pronouncements). The journal, curiously, went on to voice its antipathy for 'Rumanians and Russians and other outlandish folk whom ... we would sooner not see off musical comedy stages', and declared itself 'most at home' in the company of 'our ex-enemies, Hungarians, Austrians and Turks'; the journal was 'anxious to extend the same feeling to Germany'. The British, it affirmed, had a natural and keen sympathy for the defeated.[54] The journal continued to reject any dealings or friendship with Russia, a state it viewed as bent upon murder and the export of revolution.[55]

April and May 1935 saw the creation of the 'Stresa front' and the signing of the Franco-Russian Pact, tokens of the fear instilled in the Powers by the resurgence of Germany. An anti-French note, mostly dormant since

78

Hitler's advent, crept back into the pages of *The Economist*: 'France has committed the crime of creating a Germany in the jaundiced image of French fears and hatreds' and Britain had 'obligingly ploughed the furrows in which France sowed her seed of dragon's teeth'. *The Economist* rejected military alliances but avowed that Britain could not permit the domination of Europe by 'a single aggressive military power'. It therefore urged Britain to adopt the golden mean – to wholeheartedly uphold collective security while accepting the need for Treaty revision.[56] In April the journal recommended a colonial settlement with Germany,[57] and declared itself happy with the results of the Stresa Conference; the world, thought *The Economist*, had just drawn back from the 'precipice'.[58] It was also satisfied with the Franco-Russian Pact, regarding it as 'strictly and exclusively defensive' and compatible with League principles, unlike the malign pre-war alliances.[59]

Delusion and appeasement mixed in equal measure in the *Spectator*'s admonitions about and reactions to Stresa. With the Conference in session, the journal stated: 'There must be no suggestion of a security pact aimed directly or indirectly against Germany . . .'. Germany's desire for weapons possessed by others was not 'unreasonable'. Nor were her claims to 35 per cent of British naval tonnage and to air parity with France. 'In personnel on land', thought the *Spectator*, 'the claim is for a maximum of 550,000 men, a high figure, which may be put forward as a useful datum-line [sic] for future disarmament discussion. For Herr Hitler talks seriously about an agreement on arms limitation . . .'.[60]

The *Spectator* was obviously relieved by the non-extension of Britain's commitments at the Stresa Conference. Locarno and the Covenant were sufficient. (It is worth noting, in the light of its later reaction to the Rhineland coup, that Wilson Harris felt it 'worth noting that an armed occupation by Germany of the Demilitarised Zone on France's frontier would rank as an attack'.[61]) The journal thought the League Council's condemnation of Germany's rearmament somewhat extreme and condemned a castigation of Germany by Ramsay McDonald in the National Labour Party's *News Letter* as 'a blunder that verges on a crime'.[62] Revision, now that reparations and armaments were out of the way, was reducible to two questions: Austria and the Colonies. The *Spectator* favoured Austro-German union, but not of a coerced variety, and advocated colonial readjustment, despite Nazi race theories.[63]

Like *The Economist*, the *New Statesman* drew a careful line between the (impending) Franco-Soviet Pact and old-world alliances. But it cautioned Britain against joining 'a super-alliance designed to encircle Germany'. The *New Statesman* continued to espouse revision even while, in the same article, defining Germany's aims as expansion and domination.

The journal opposed 'token' revisionism; Austria, the Polish Corridor, Memel, Colonies – all had to be tackled. The contradiction implied in all this was not lost upon Kingsley Martin. Soul-searchingly, he asked: 'If you yield to bluster and military power, are you not putting a premium on their use? . . . Do you seriously believe that this barbarian movement . . . can ever be tamed . . . within the Geneva family?' And answered, begging the question: 'The condition of revision must be that both sides abandon the principle of power' and that 'before one asks a wronged nation to abandon its reliance on power, one must first show it that a peaceful road to justice lies open'. At Stresa, hoped the *New Statesman*, 'genuine equality and effective revision' would be enthroned.[64]

With the Stresa Conference over, the *New Statesman* commented approvingly that Britain had at least given a limited affirmation of the principle of collective security and that the word 'revision' had at last appeared in a document signed by the ex-Allies.[65]

Time & Tide, with Stresa in session, was also prompted to uphold commitment to collective security. But it envisaged that commitment as entailing wider obligations than Locarno and the vague Covenant of the League. The journal, however, did not specify what additional commitments it wished Britain to enter into.[66] After Stresa it noted, and criticised, the British Government's unwillingness 'to assume further responsibilities in Europe'.[67]

The *New English Weekly*, after Stresa, was also critical of British conceptions of collective security, but from another angle. The collective system, as embodied in the League, the Stresa front and the Franco-Russian Pact, was simply a camouflaged means of keeping Germany at bay; it was 'exactly the pre-War treaty system', and just as explosive. Even-handedly, the journal asserted that the policies of 'the terrorists' (i.e., Germany and Japan) were in 'no degree' different from those of 'the terrified' (i.e., England and France); both were based on rival commercial aspirations and interests.[68]

Truth was unhappy with the creation of the 'Stresa front' to the extent that it involved Britain with France which, in turn, was committed in eastern Europe and on the verge of concluding an alliance with Russia. The journal argued that Britain could commit itself to nothing in eastern Europe, even if it wished to, because the Dominions would object; Britain should not subvert the Empire to save Russia or to soothe France. *Truth* agreed with the *New English Weekly* in its view of the League and collective security as new names for an old and reprehensible system. The journal upheld the need for territorial revision.[69]

Stresa found the *Observer* and the *Sunday Times* still advancing along divergent routes. Britain, stressed Garvin, must not abandon France and must commit herself to the cause of continued Austrian independence.[70] The *Sunday Times*, on the other hand, expressed hostility towards the creation of the Stresa Front; world wars sprang from 'a system of alliances and counter-alliances', asserted the paper. In any case, thought Sidebotham, 'to try to frighten Germany into moderation is too great a concession to the spirit against which we fought the last war' and it held out little prospect of success.[71]

On 18 June the Anglo-German Naval Agreement was signed. Its content had been indicated in Hitler's proposals of 21 May. Wishful credulity marked the weeklies' reception of that speech; satisfaction, enthusiasm and facile optimism marked their reception of the Naval Agreement. The two must be taken together to understand the acceptance by the journals of the first major act of positive appeasement.

In view of what followed, the reactions of the weeklies to Germany's announcement in April of the construction of 12 submarines served as an instructive (and dissonant) prelude. The *Spectator* greeted the announcement as 'provocative'; it tempted 'the average Englishman to despair of any understanding between the two countries'.[72] *Truth* deemed it unsurprising.[73] The *Saturday Review* thought Britain was being wilfully blind, and called for more rearmament.[74] Only *The Economist, Time & Tide* and the *Sunday Times* thought the matter worthy of leader comment. *The Economist* stated that in past months German actions, capped by the submarines, had more than sufficed 'to account for the alienation of English opinion'. It compared Hitler's bellicosity to that of the Kaiser.[75] *Time & Tide* opined that the submarine announcement had 'caused more alarm in Parliament than any single item of news that has come from Germany since the Nazis took control . . .'. But the journal cautioned against using the German submarines as an excuse for massive rearmament.[76] Even Hadley and Sidebotham of the *Sunday Times* regarded the news as ominous; a raw nerve had been touched. Hadley wrote: 'If the current course of German policy is persisted in, it is bound to have a disastrous effect.' Sidebotham echoed him: 'The tradition of the old German diplomacy which seriously thought that threats were a means of persuasion seems as strong as ever.'[77]

Reactions to the German submarine announcements had been unequivocal; so, too, was the reception in the weeklies of Hitler's speech of 21 May. Enthusiasm reigned. The *Spectator* sounded its wonted note. Wilson Harris thought that to regard the speech as fundamentally insincere 'leads straight to disaster'. It was preferable to believe in Hitler's goodwill.[78] The journal went so far as to recommend that 'it is essential in the interests of humanity and sanity to base Great Britain's air policy on the assumption that Herr Hitler means what he says [i.e. regarding prohibition of bombing] and will stand by his word'.[79]

The Economist thought that the speech had 'brought us to the parting of the ways in our dealings with the present master of Germany's destinies'. Upon the editor's mind, as 'upon the great majority of English minds, the speech makes an overwhelming impression of sincerity'. The speech bore the hallmarks of 'the sincerity of "the ex-service man" who has seen war and its aftermath ... Herr Hitler is speaking with the sane and simple voice of the common man'. *The Economist* thought the German proposals should be taken as the basis for an over-all European settlement.[80] But unlike the *Spectator*, *The Economist* preferred, at all events, that Britain keep her powder dry: 'lamentable' as were the Government's contemplated air increases, the journal considered opposition to them untenable.[81] The *New Statesman* expressed satisfaction with the Government's resolve to give Hitler's speech due consideration; it condemned Baldwin's decision to treble the RAF.[82]

Time & Tide, like the *Spectator* and *The Economist*, thought the speech had ended 'the deadlock in which the Powers have been standing'; 'to fail to take advantage of this new German declaration would be disastrous folly.' The Commons, admitted *Time & Tide*, was divided; some thought the speech insincere, an 'evasive subterfuge of an astute and ruthless despot'. But, declared the journal, 'the more informed and responsible members ... do not share this view'. Like these last, the journal was 'impressed' and 'particularly delighted' by Hitler's reference to the Demilitarised Zone, by his disarmament proposals, and by his offer concerning the abolition of bombing.[83] Here then was a bizarre spectacle. Left-wing and Liberal journals, which had for years warned against innate Nazi barbarism and duplicity, acclaimed Hitler as an apostle of peace. Here, in fact, was liberalism in play: the irrational and frightful must not be real; a fleeting image of a 'reformed' Hitler sufficed to launch a wave of forgetful optimism.

The right-wing weeklies were by and large more sceptical. Sidebotham confined himself to lauding Germany's 'resignation ... of naval ambition' as embodied in the 35 per cent demand.[84]

Truth argued that Hitler's word could no more be trusted than that of a lunatic with a six-shooter. But that was not the question. The journal believed that Germany desired peace, if only because the German people desired it, and Hitler's popularity would decline were he to embark on a course of war. Peace suited Hitler: 'So I think we should accept Hitler's gesture and try to negotiate upon his offer.' The unacceptable alternative was war.[85]

The *New English Weekly* offered the only substantially discordant voice to the acclamation of the speech by the weeklies. Tersely it commented that it was all very well to praise the moderation of Hitler's words. But he had done nothing to revoke conscription or to halt Germany's rapid aerial rearmament.[86]

In June the Anglo-German Naval Agreement was negotiated and concluded. In substance, it reflected Hitler's demands of March and May. Germany was allowed to build up to 35 per cent of the British Empire's surface tonnage; in submarines it was allowed 45 per cent, and 100 per cent under special circumstances. The *Spectator* 'wholeheartedly' welcomed the conclusion of the Agreement. Had Hitler's offer been disregarded, the Germans would probably have raised their claim to 50 per cent or more of British surface tonnage: 'British Ministers would have been guilty of criminal negligence if they had not taken Herr Hitler at his word and tested his sincerity. They have done so, and the result is eminently satisfactory.'[87] In the following week the *Spectator* wrote that Sir B. Eyres-Monsell had told the Commons that Germany had 'renounced resort to unrestricted submarine warfare'. The journal thought that it was 'foolish to disparage such an understanding by the argument that nations at war do not abide by conventions. That . . . means a policy of despair.'[88]

The Economist, too, thought the Naval Agreement 'an . . . auspicious event', 'heartily to be welcomed'. The 35 per cent was a 'very moderate' basis 'from the German point of view'. Back-tracking on its previous comparison between Hitler and the Kaiser, the journal now counterposed them, to Hitler's 'great credit'. As its main argument in support of the Agreement, the journal stated that it was better to conclude minor (and bi-lateral) pacts than to wait for a far-off and uncertain overall settlement.[89]

Likewise, *Time & Tide* thought the Agreement could not 'be regarded as anything but satisfactory'. It successfully limited naval competition. True, it had made a further breach in the Treaty of Versailles. But that Treaty could no longer be regarded as 'sacrosanct'. The journal admonished France for vainly protesting and advised it to attempt to reach agreement with Germany on army ratios.[90]

While the naval talks were proceeding in London, the *New Statesman* commented that only 'innocents' accepted the German claim to 35 per cent of British surface tonnage as 'relatively modest'. As Britain's navy was normally dispersed over five seas, 35 per cent would give Germany parity in home waters. As well, Germany's new navy would be composed of modern vessels; many of Britain's were obsolescent.[91] With the signing of the Agreement, the *New Statesman* wrote that Germany had 'got away with her big navy plans far more easily than she could have expected';

'The British Government's complaisance to Hitler looks ominous to many people here as well as [in Europe].' But the journal added the all-important rider that the Agreement could be justified on the grounds that the alternative, of unrestricted naval competition, was worse.[92]

On 1 May 1935 *Truth* had pointed out that were Germany's claim to a 35 per cent navy granted, she would have a marked advantage over Britain in home waters.[93] Nonetheless, once signed, *Truth* claimed that the Agreement put 'an end to Anglo-German rivalry at sea' and delivered Britain 'from the nightmare race in armaments'. The journal deemed French objections 'incomprehensible' and 'illogical', Russian criticism as 'unbalanced' and 'hysterical': 'There must be limits even to the sane man's hatred of Hitler.' With satisfaction, *Truth* noted that the Agreement would give Germany eventual command of the Baltic, putting her in a position to 'check Russia', 'the most fundamentally implacable antagonist of the British Empire'.[94]

The other Conservative weeklies were less enthusiastic. The *Sunday Times* restricted itself to calling the Agreement 'a useful stepping-stone to general agreement'.[95] Garvin, after declaring the Agreement 'commendable on mere balance and no more', unleashed a scathing criticism of British policy. The Agreement, he thought, had 'markedly facilitated the rise of Germany to a massive preponderance in the combined arms'; it marked a shift from 'collective' to 'selective' security.[96] On 30 June the *Observer* concluded that 'creeping British weakness' had characterised policy from Simon's visit to Berlin until the signing of the Agreement. He called upon Britain, 'in concert' with France, Russia, Italy and Poland, 'to safeguard the present *status quo* with all its defects ... against violent and arbitrary disruption'; Western security could not be preserved by 'promoting in effect the insecurity of others in central and eastern Europe'.[97]

The *Saturday Review*, mindful of the German menace to British security, remained consistent. With British assistance, argued the journal, Germany had succeeded in burying a further segment of the Treaty of Versailles. The Agreement would not help limit naval rearmament; on the contrary, it could only promote a naval race.[98]

CONCLUSION

February–June 1935, as reflected in the weeklies, was a crucial period in Anglo-German relations. Early optimism, bred on Air Pact and Eastern Locarno prospects, gave way, with the trumpet-blast of German rearmament declarations, to depression and fear. These were shortly replaced by a cautious and appeasing buoyancy based on Hitler's pacific oration and embodied in the Anglo-German Naval Agreement. The shift in mood was paralleled in most of the weeklies by a shift in emphases and policies regarding Nazi Germany.

During February and the first half of March all the weeklies focused their attention on the possible conclusion of pan-European peace pacts; most strongly supported the Air Pact and the Eastern Locarno proposals, viewing them as the ultimate embodiments of 'collective security'.

To be sure, Treaty revision was not ruled out. But its espousal was definitely muted. Most of the weeklies thought that European security had first to be assured; negotiated revision could follow. Unilateral German revision was firmly and unanimously opposed. *Truth*, an exception, advocated 'revision first', believing that the pacts would be meaningless and dangerous if not preceded by the settlement of German grievances. The *Saturday Review*, another exception, opposed both the projected pacts and Treaty revision. In all the weeklies save the *Sunday Times* – which pressed for the Western Air Pact but opposed the Eastern Locarno – air fear was apparent but subdued.

The German declaration of rearmament on 16 March 1935 proved decisive. In its wake, panic beset the weeklies; priorities and policies changed. The *New Statesman* (and, to a lesser degree, *The Economist*), which had long warned that Hitler's ambitions far exceeded the rectification of Versailles's injustices, now pressed for immediate, wholesale and, even, uncontingent revision. The *Spectator*, with air fear uppermost in its mind, followed suit. *Truth*, which at first (after 16 March) refused concessions to a Germany 'arrogant and armed', rapidly reversed its judgement, coming down strongly in support of the Naval Agreement.

Depression and fear were miraculously dissipated by Hitler's peace-mongering oration of 21 May. There was nothing really new in it, as the *New Statesman* pointed out. Bi-lateral non-aggression pacts (excluding Russia), arms limitation offers, the abolition of bombing, a naval agreement with Britain – all had been heard before. Yet the weeklies, excepting the *Observer*, the *New English Weekly* and, to a degree, *Truth*, jumped like alcoholics unexpectedly offered a much-missed bottle. Journals like *The Economist* and *Time & Tide*, long aware of the evil and duplicity of Nazi techniques, came out in praise of the Führer's pacific sincerity. The *Spectator* went so far as to advise that Britain base her defence requirements on Hitler's word. The *New Statesman* and, reluctantly, *Truth*, recommended that the Government seek the solution to Europe's problems on the basis of Hitler's offers.

Before 16 March, most of the journals had consistently opposed Hitler-style bilateral pacts and arrangements. *The Economist*, the *Spectator*, the *New Statesman*, *Time & Tide* and the *New English Weekly* regarded such pacts with Germany as inimical to the principle of collective security; as subversive, in fact, of all League principles. Yet after 16 March, at the first chance of 'a separate peace', almost all more or less jumped at the dangled bait. *The Economist* (with some late misgivings), the *Spectator* and *Time & Tide* enthusiastically acclaimed the conclusion of the Anglo-German Naval Agreement; the *New Statesman* and the *New English Weekly*, while offering reservations, did not oppose it. *Truth*, which had before 18 June pointed out the danger of allowing Germany 35 per cent of British surface tonnage, also came out in wholehearted support. Sheep-like, all the journals save the *Saturday Review* and the *Observer* took the Government's cue.

Hitler's rearmament proclamations and the Government's confused and alarming statements on British defences boosted and enthroned the air fear. Only the *New Statesman* and the *Spectator* more or less explicitly pointed to the air peril or the general fear of war as having determined this change of posture between February and June 1935. Nonetheless, the menacing shadow of Germany resurgent darkened the pages of all the journals following the 16th of March. Strident 'revisionism' took hold, ill-concealing an appeasing zeal. In the wake of Hitler's pacific speech the weeklies hastily abandoned their advocacy of collective security and multilateral pacts, and effusively welcomed a bilateral, revisionist, Anglo-German accord. Despite the fourteen or so days of haggling which preceded the Anglo-German Naval Agreement, it was not even a 'negotiated' revision in that what had been demanded was, *in toto*, delivered; and delivered by Britain without real consultation with Versailles's other signatories. No reciprocity was seriously demanded or extracted. And the '35 per cent' constraint was fictitious as Germany, at the time, had no sizable navy to limit; had, in fact, no 'big navy' plans (stressing the air and armour in its rearmament efforts); and was, under Nazi rule, generally considered a dubious proposition as far as abiding by international agreements was concerned.

The great hopes illusorily vested in the Naval Agreement, as a first step in achieving a firm Anglo-German rapprochement or as the initial move in a pan-European settlement, quickly faded. The weeklies soon reverted to advocacy of 'collective security'; some ostensibly held to it while espousing an insular Anglo-German accord. Nevertheless, the Naval Agreement shook the Stresa front and undermined French (and Russian) trust in the sincerity of Britain's commitment to collective security. The spectre or, alternatively, enticement of a separate peace hovered over European affairs for the ensuing four years, subverting alliances and all thought of resistance to Nazi designs.

V

ABYSSINIA, THE RHINELAND AND SPAIN

In the weekly press, the consensus supporting appeasement which evolved in the spring of 1935 was, within a year and a half, put to three successive (and, in part, overlapping) tests – the Italian invasion of Abyssinia, the re-militarisation of the Rhineland and the German–Italian intervention in the Spanish Civil War. The consensus survived, and indeed was reinforced by, these crises, thus setting the pattern of perception of European affairs until March 1939. In June 1935 there were still deviants, such as the *Observer*; by February–March 1936 the consensus was complete and Garvin too was running with the pack.

The Rhineland coup is obviously relevant to a study of appeasement. Indeed some historians see in British and French reactions in March 1936 the first instance of that policy. Abyssinia and Spain are also relevant. Western reactions to the Italian assault on Abyssinia were, above all, governed by fear of Germany. In March 1935 Hitler had demonstrated that the democracies could be flouted with impunity. With a fearful eye on Germany, French and British leaders speaking with Mussolini in April 1935 pointedly refrained from mention or condemnation of Italy's Abyssinian designs; much, if not all, would be condoned to obtain Italian adhesion to an anti-German coalition. Thus, when a policy of sanctions was forced upon the British Government by public opinion, it was pursued with great reluctance and without effect. British fears for the fate of its Mediterranean fleet also played a part in the adoption of a policy which produced maximum ill-will and minimum success. Where Germany, and fear of Germany, had sown, Italy reaped.

Germany's turn soon followed. Hitler ventured into the Rhineland in the knowledge that German rearmament had been 'countered' only by the Naval Agreement and that the assault on Abyssinia had elicited only token Western resistance. In consequence, Locarno was overthrown, Belgium withdrew into neutrality and demoralisation took hold in France and its eastern allies.

What could be done singly could certainly be embarked upon in concert. Following Franco's revolt, Italian and German arms, soldiers and airmen poured into Spain. Though many regarded this as a peril to vital interests, Britain and France adopted, and persisted in, a policy of non-intervention. A German, or pro-German, presence on France's southern frontier and threats to Gibraltar and British Imperial communications in the Mediterranean counted for nothing as compared with the fear of involvement in war against Germany and Italy in Spain and, by extension, elsewhere in Europe. Non-intervention proved vigorous and long-lived.

ABYSSINIA

By and large, the weeklies viewed the Italian aggression against Abyssinia with hostility. The issue between Italy and Abyssinia was complex, involving colonial rights, commercial concessions and territorial disputes. As an element in international relations, however, the issue was seen as simple: 'Abyssinia' was a challenge to world order, to the League and to the concept of collective security. If the League was successfully defied, collective security would perish; future aggressors could expect to proceed, and win, unmolested. The bulk of the weeklies wished to see Mussolini, a minor miscreant, chastened if only to serve effective warning to that more potent malefactor, Herr Hitler. Some journals, such as *The Economist*, also stressed the direct threat posed by Mussolini's attack to British maritime and African interests.

If such were the considerations prompting resistance to the Italian adventure, there were others which directed otherwise. Incurring Italian hostility would shatter the Stresa Front and might well throw an alienated Italy into Germany's arms. War against Italy might well leave the British fleet severely damaged. The problem, then, was how to block Italy in Abyssinia without producing an Italian–German alliance and without shattering the League and the British Mediterranean fleet.

Italian intentions towards Abyssinia became clear in the early summer of 1935; Mussolini's pronouncements and the massive deployment of Italian troops in Eritrea and Somaliland supplied a surfeit of evidence. An attack on Abyssinia was imminent, declared the *Sunday Times* on 30 June; Abyssinia, declared the *New Statesman*, had become 'the hub of the universe' and Europe's 'centre of gravity'.[1] With the exceptions of the *Saturday Review* and the *Observer*, the weekly press was unanimous in its condemnation of the impending assault. The Liberal and left-wing press stressed arguments of morality and the threat posed to world order, the Covenant and collective security. The *Sunday Times*, while aware of the general problem, laid emphasis on the traditional threat to Imperial routes and possessions. Normally, this was also a major concern of the *Observer*, the *Tablet* and the *Saturday Review*; but not in the case of Abyssinia. Above

88

all they desired the retention of Italian friendship.

The Economist tellingly stated the danger posed to world order and collective security. It was true, argued the journal on 31 August 1935, that the sea-route to India would be imperilled by the fulfilment of Italy's African ambitions. But 'the heart of the matter' lay elsewhere. Vital to Britain was the 'preservation, confirmation and extension' of the reign of law in international affairs. Successful Italian aggression would unleash 'anarchy' in the relations between all States. Britain and its over-extended Empire would then become the focus of the designs of all 'hungry' Powers. Fears of Germany and of an aggressive Japan loomed uppermost.[2] The *New Statesman* and *Time & Tide* pursued similar arguments. The *New Statesman* cared little for Imperial well-being or trade-routes. But were the League to fail over Abyssinia, it argued, Hitler would undoubtedly venture forth on the Continent. The 'Stresa Front' was dead whether or no the League acted; at all events, a German–Italian deal, or 'axis', was on the cards. But failure to curb Italian designs would mark the end of collective security in Europe. The same point was made repeatedly in *Time & Tide*[3] before the Italian attack. Germany, the *Spectator* assured its readers before the Italian attack, was hoping that 'Abyssinia' would lead to 'the breakdown of the League'. Even taken alone, this consideration 'should assure the hesitant of the vital necessity of defending that system'. But fear issued in wishful not to say perverse thinking: 'Herr Hitler can have little sympathy with Signor Mussolini's methods', wrote Wilson Harris on 23 August.[4]

Truth, surprisingly, subscribed to the Liberal–Left viewpoint on the nature of the threat to Britain and to Europe posed by Mussolini's proposed attack on Abyssinia. Britain could not remain indifferent to the danger to its sea-routes and to the waters of the Upper Nile. But even more ominous, believed the journal, was the threat Mussolini posed to 'the entire system of the League of Nations and Collective Security'. The threat was not so much to Abyssinia as to Europe. Upholding collective security against that 'dangerous lunatic', Mussolini, would deter Hitler from indulging in similar ventures.[5]

In principle, the *Sunday Times* cared little for collective security or for the League's good name; imperial concerns predominated.[6] Sidebotham, however, feared that Hitler might exploit an Italian–League dispute to further his Continental ambitions. He forecast that League action would prove ineffectual. Hence, his initial instinct was to let Mussolini have his way while acknowledging that the assault on Abyssinia was immoral. Nevertheless, as shall be seen, for some weeks he allowed himself to be caught up in the compelling current of opinion and, for a time, preached limited sanctions.

From the start, three weeklies came out in opposition to the Conservative–Liberal–Left consensus concerning the Abyssinian problem: the *Saturday Review*, the *Observer* and the *Tablet*. Lady Houston's line in the *Saturday Review* was clear and simple. Long enamoured of Mussolini and the alleged efficacy of authoritarian government, she regarded the Italian adventure in Africa as a mission of civilisation. Upon the successful conclusion of the Italian campaign, the journal stated: 'Mussolini has proved to the world what Italy can do to-day . . . Italy to-day has found her soul . . . [and is] a Great Power whose friendship and support is well worth cultivating.'[7] Lady Houston's fear of Germany no doubt had much to do with this quest for an Italian alliance. Her attitude to Abyssinia was also influenced by her unbounded hatred of the League, which she viewed as largely an instrument of Bolshevik intrigue. On 13 December 1935 she wrote to Baldwin: 'To get out of and to destroy the League is the only short cut out of the fear of war which is now looming blacker and blacker day by day on the horizon. The League of Nations (meaning Litvinoff – never forget that) wants war – *and will surely bring War*.'[8]

Garvin shared Lady Houston's desire to retain Italian goodwill. He still, at this time, opposed appeasement. He believed that war with Hitler was probable and coalition with Italy desirable. A personal consideration obtruded; his daughter and son-in-law lived in Italy. Always a lover of Italy and things Italian, he pursued the mirage of Anglo-Italian *entente* remorselessly through the thirties. 'For me (and for private reasons as well as a lifelong political motive)', he wrote to Sir Samuel Hoare three years later, 'the great *détente* with Italy lifts a weight from mind and heart.'[9] Like Sidebotham, but with unflagging consistency, from the summer of 1935 Garvin argued in the *Observer* that League action against Italy would only serve to 'incur the ridicule and odium of impotence', 'aggravating every complication in Europe'.[10] Hence he argued that Abyssinia was a barbarous, slave-ridden country, unworthy of League membership or sustenance; that the Amharic spirit was akin to the inflamed nationalisms of Germany and Japan; and that Italian fears for the safety of Eritrea and Somaliland were understandable. He feared that the alienation of Italy would expose Austria to *Anschluss* and he advocated British pressure on Addis Ababa to compel the Negus to compromise with Mussolini. Above all, in view of the danger from Germany, he believed that Britain could not afford the added enmity of Italy which would expose her Imperial life-lines to hostile assault.[11]

Though it deemed Italian designs upon Abyssinia immoral, the *Tablet*, throughout July 1935, repeatedly emphasised the issue of slavery in Abyssinia, underpinning its rejection of League action against Italy. 'As

Christians ... we say that if Liberty ... has to be taken away from Abyssinia in order that the slavery ... of poor negroes shall cease, then common humanity will have got the best of the bargain', it stated on 27 July. The journal dreaded the prospect of an Anglo-Italian war in the Mediterranean. Though never made explicit, Oldmeadow's attitude towards Abyssinia conformed to the needs of the Vatican, a political entity hardly in a position to incur Mussolini's wrath.[12]

If an Italian attack upon Abyssinia was immoral and jeopardised the foundations of collective security, and if the peril of alienating Italy was minor by comparison with the precedent and temptation an Italian success would present to Hitler, then Britain and the League had to act. But in what manner? 'Sanctions' was the obvious answer: The League was empowered to impose them and, from the autumn of 1935, Britain subscribed to their imposition.

The *Observer* and the *Saturday Review*, for the reasons already alluded to, rejected outright any thought of sanctions against Italy. They pursued this line through the Abyssinian crisis. The *Tablet* remained uneasy, the Vatican pulling one way, Oldmeadow's conscience the other. Between July and October the journal pointedly refrained from even using the word 'sanctions'. Silence was broken on 12 October:

> While hardly anybody in this country of ours approves the Italian campaign in East Africa, almost everybody dreads the prospect of military conflict between Italy and Great Britain. Therefore, it is by other means [than sanctions] that pressure must be applied to the aggressor in this ugly affair.

Perhaps a non-official boycott of Italian goods would suffice, it suggested.[13] On 14 December the *Tablet* came out in support of a territorial compromise between Abyssinia and Italy. But a week later Oldmeadow bowed to the pressure of public indignation and joined the outcry against the Hoare–Laval cession of chunks of Abyssinian territory.[14]

This curious performance was matched, if not outdone, by Sidebotham in the *Sunday Times*. His tortuous arguments appeared bereft of conviction. In June he condemned the Italian design as immoral and as a challenge to the League. In July, however, he stated that League action would prove ineffectual and that 'all talk of active constraint on Italy, whether economic or military, would at best be bluff'. Rather, he urged territorial compromise, in line with Eden's offers to Italy. He argued that were the Italian invasion to proceed and be met by League opposition, Hitler would swoop upon Austria; previously, Sidebotham had never supported Austrian independence, nor did he thereafter.[15]

In September the *Sunday Times* fell back into line with public opinion and Government policy. It supported the Government's affirmation of the Covenant but asserted that 'sanctions must begin quietly with those penalties that general agreement will consent to enforce'.[16] Sidebotham firmly ruled out a British or League blockade of the Canal as 'even if we had been prepared to accept its risks, [it] could not have been taken without offering violence to the very principles of the League which we proposed to be defending'.[17] Hadley, the editor, struck a firmer note. On 24 November 1935 he called for the imposition of the oil sanction.[18] But three weeks later Sidebotham declared for the Hoare-Laval proposals. He memorably phrased it: 'Surely . . . to try to find a settlement now is not to put a spoke in the wheel of Sanctions. It is only to anticipate what you will have to do some day even when Sanctions have ideally succeeded.'[19] Sanctions remained decidedly unattractive to Sidebotham.[20]

The *New English Weekly* always entertained a weak spot for Mussolini. Ezra Pound frequently contributed pieces and advice from his adopted homeland. Nonetheless, from the start the journal condemned Mussolini's designs. It loathed imperialisms and big-business ventures impartially. But support sanctions it could not. Britain, in view of its imperial domains, had not the right to prescribe that 'moral castor oil be forcibly administered', it asserted on 10 October 1935. The same issue carried a feature article by C.H. Norman in which he condemned sanctions as 'punitive' and 'worthy of the human statesmanship of the King of the Cannibal Islands'. The real thrust of his argument, however, was inserted at the end: 'Nothing could be more insane than to involve the whole of Europe in war to attempt to stop a war in Africa.'[21] Some weeks later a sense of balance was restored, perhaps due to pressure from its readers or to reports of the barbarism of the Italian armies. While offering no explicit support for sanctions, the *New English Weekly* spoke out against 'those who urge us to take no notice of Italy's stark infraction of [civilised behaviour]; to allow a ruthless and calculated war to "burn itself out" . . . rather than trouble the waters of European diplomacy – such people are no good friends of the causes to which even Social Credit is but instrumental'. The journal went on to identify itself once more 'with the principles of collective security, while fully aware of the hypocrisies from which that phrase is inseparable'. It condemned 'Communist adventurers' and those who 'would divide Europe into two camps with the final prospect of the Third International lurking among the ruins', and called for 'moral and intellectual rearmament'.[22]

In company with the *Sunday Times*, *Truth* followed a tortuous and half-hearted road to sanctions. At the end of August 1935, the journal cautioned that sanctions would involve great difficulties: boycotters as well as boycotted would suffer, universal support would not be forthcoming and it was 'idle to suppose that [Mussolini] would submit to any form of sanctions – especially to the closing of the Suez Canal, which in itself would be flagrant breach of treaty – without military retaliation'. 'Sanctions', concluded the leading article, 'would mean war.'[23] A fortnight after the start of the Italian invasion *Truth* came out in support of economic sanctions and condemned Rothermere and Garvin for 'giving comfort' to the enemy. In November *Truth* condemned *The Economist* and the *News Chronicle* for supporting a unilateral British imposition of the oil sanction but, later, itself supported a League application of the same sanction, even if this prompted 'the mad dog of Europe' to 'an act of lunacy'.[24] But support of sanctions, any sanctions, sat ill with *Truth*. On 6 January 1936, the journal revealingly called upon Britain to turn over a new leaf in relations with Italy: 'The edifice of peace must be built up again. To imperil that task by quibbling now over the *fait accompli* in Africa would be the act of a crank.'[25]

Support of sanctions in the Conservative journals was at most lackadaisical; in the Liberal and left-wing weeklies it was far from whole-hearted and, in essentials, conformed to official Government policy. The *New Statesman, Time & Tide* and the *Spectator*, ostensibly supporters of collective security and the Covenant, rarely ventured beyond the bounds of consensus and invariably shunned anything remotely interpretable as advocacy of confrontation with Italy. Only *The Economist*, to a substantial degree, displayed consistency and the courage of its convictions.

Good-weather militancy – matched by infirmity when crisis was reached – was nowhere better exemplified than in the *New Statesman*. In contrast with the *Observer*, the *New Statesman* in August 1935 urged Britain to press Italy, rather than Abyssinia, for concessions to avert the impending conflict. Failing this, the journal saw no escape from the imposition of sanctions against the aggressor, including, 'in the last resort, even some form of military action'. But the journal failed to call for the repeal of the embargo on arms for Abyssinia though it was 'in defiance of the most elementary justice'.[26]

But as the crisis neared the boil, vacillation prevailed in editorial comment. In September, Hugh Dalton chided Kingsley Martin over this: 'I agree with much of what you say, but much the most important thing to stress at this moment is that the Labour Party demands that the Covenant shall be applied with whatever degree of vigour that circumstances may require.'[27] On 7 September Kingsley Martin had called upon the League to apply 'the whole weight of its sanctions, at least in the economic field', against Italy. On 21 September he had reverted to calling for a blockade of the Canal should economic sanctions prove insufficient. But on 28 September he cast doubt on the wisdom of blocking the Canal or applying an embargo on non-military goods; both, or either, he feared, might provoke war.[28]

With the outbreak of hostilities, the *New Statesman* called for the immediate application of economic sanctions but ruled out the imposition of any of a military variety.[29] While privately questioning the wisdom even of economic sanctions,[30] Kingsley Martin set a high standard of double-talk when, on 26 October, he took the Government to task for ruling out military sanctions. Nor did he reject the idea of treating with Mussolini in an endeavour to reach a compromise at the territorial expense of Abyssinia.[31] Throughout the war, the *New Statesman* continued to rule out, 'under present circumstances', the imposition of military sanctions. In essentials, it conformed with Government policy. On 30 November the *New Statesman* diagnosed that British policy towards Italy turned upon, and was constrained by, fear of Germany.[32]

A similar pattern was followed in *Time & Tide*. For Lady Rhondda, the crisis was not so much about Abyssinia as about the future of collective security. On 28 September, therefore, the journal urged the immediate application of 'the most drastic economic sanctions' against Italy. A week later it reiterated this call adding that, if necessary, a naval blockade of Italy should be imposed as well. In a significant innovation, *Time & Tide* even reconciled itself to a measure of British rearmament. When sanctions were at last applied, the journal urged the inclusion of oil among them; it noted, however, that a naval blockade of the type it had previously urged had not been instituted because of 'the obvious dangers its application would provoke'.[33] Blockade and military sanctions were never again mentioned in Lady Rhondda's editorials or in Norman Angell's monthly foreign affairs commentaries. Yet previously, Angell had been quite clear on this point. In a letter to Edward Behrens he had written that it was Britain's obligation

> to use her strategic points and power for international purposes, as in the Italo-Abyssinian dispute. Britain holds all the keys in the Mediterranean and by an entirely peaceful sanction – that of closing the Suez Canal – could put a stopper on the Italian war against Abyssinia. If the Empire really understood these obligations, she would as an instrument of the League exercise these powers for that purpose.[34]

Fear of war with Italy, and fear of what Germany might do, quickly reduced *Time & Tide*'s vigorous support for the League and heartfelt sympathy for Abyssinia to mere lip-service to the Covenant.

Nowhere was the disparity between the espousal of principles and the espousal of policies greater than in the *Spectator*. Concerning Abyssinia, Wrench and Angus Watson appear to have been of a firmer persuasion than Wilson Harris. On 15 September 1935 Wrench jotted down in his diary: 'I read Sir Samual Hoare's speech and was glad to see that the Government has spoken in no uncertain way as to its support of the League of Nations.'[35] And in January 1936 Rothermere rebuked Wrench for his seeming intrepidity: 'Warships cannot fight bombing planes. In view of the fact [that] Italy is known to have an air fleet of nearly 4,000 up-to-date aeroplanes, how can you advocate that a disarmed country such as ours ... should apply if necessary military sanctions to that country?'[36] Watson, for his part, stated on 8 October that Britain must discharge her Covenant obligations 'whatever that may cost her'. For Britain could not, 'without national dishonour and humiliation, fail to recognise her pledges ... To accept any alternative is to repudiate the validity of all that the Church stands for.' He did not believe that war would necessarily follow, but 'whatever the price', it had to be paid.[37]

But the views of its proprietors notwithstanding, the *Spectator* between July and September 1935 moved only with marked reluctance towards acceptance of the national consensus and endorsement of sanctions. On 11 October Wilson Harris argued that if economic sanctions had to be imposed, then they had better not be weak ones; somewhat in advance of the majority of his countrymen, he called for the imposition of the oil sanction. However, this call for the oil sanction reappeared in the *Spectator*'s pages only on 29 November, when it was common coin in most of the weeklies. On 25 October the *Spectator* explicitly endorsed Hoare's arguments against the advocates of a closure of the Canal to Italian shipping.[38] The thrust of Wilson Harris's views was embodied in his reaction to a lecture by Toynbee in Chatham House in December 1935. Germany and Italy shared a real 'sense of injustice' over their lost colonies, Wilson Harris stated. It would be best, he suggested, 'somehow to associate Germany and Italy and conceivably Japan with the administration of territories at present under mandate'.[39] The phraseology was cautious, the thinking, in the van of appeasement.

The Economist was easily the firmest of the weeklies with regard to Abyssinia. On 29 February 1936 the journal asserted that Britain should have imposed a blockade on Italian shores or on the Canal 'months ago'; that would have put paid to the Abyssinian adventure. Six months earlier the journal had condemned the British arms embargo on Abyssinia and called for sanctions potent enough 'to prevent or arrest' aggression completely.[40] With the war a week old, the journal stated that the proposed League sanctions were 'if not innocuous at least mild'. It urged the League to immediately impose the 'decisive' sanction, 'a blockade and the severance of communications between Italy and Africa'; it was the only weekly to so argue once the crisis had been reached. *The Economist* contended: 'In contrast with the method of slow pressure, which is likely to combine the minimum of effectiveness with the maximum of ill-will, this step will establish the prestige of the League and ensure the maintenance of peace more decisively than any other [action].'[41] In the following issues, the journal refrained from re-issuing this call but persisted in demanding, in language unusually forceful for Layton, the most severe economic measures against Italy. It is probable (and it was implicit) that *The Economist* still desired 'military' sanctions. But Layton perhaps realised that to call for them would lessen, rather than enhance, *The Economist*'s leverage on public opinion and Government policy.[42] In December *The Economist* made clear, in no uncertain terms, its willingness to contemplate war with Italy. The journal assailed those who allowed the fear of an Italian attack on the Mediterranean fleet and bases to govern policy towards Italy. This stance was 'suicidal': 'We are living in a world in which the chance of an Italian attack on us . . . is one of the smallest of the many possible dangers that we may be called upon to face. By showing weakness now, we should be plainly inviting a coalition of the predatory powers to fall jointly upon the British lion.'[43] A week later *The Economist* added: 'The man who flinches from the risk of having to fight for his honour will assuredly be forced before long to fight for his skin.'[44] Of the Liberal and left-wing weeklies, only *The Economist* matched professions of principles and of policy during the Abyssinian crisis.

THE RHINELAND

The Treaty of Versailles had prescribed that, after the withdrawal of the Allied armies of occupation, the Rhineland should remain a de-militarised zone. Germany consented to this stipulation in the Locarno agreements of 1925. Between 1933 and 1935 Hitler repeatedly pledged to abide by the de-militarisation, most notably in his 'peace' speech of 21 May 1935. On 7 March 1936 several battalions of the Wehrmacht demonstratively marched into the Rhineland; the de-militarisation was at an end.

The coup did not come as a total surprise. The debate over ratification of the Franco-Russian Pact in the French Chamber was accompanied by continuous denunciation from official and unofficial German sources. The German press in the early months of 1936 argued that the Pact subverted the 'Locarno spirit' and was but a further Gallic attempt at encirclement. The British weeklies took heed. Some predicted where a 'retaliatory' German blow might fall. In fact, a re-militarisation of the Rhineland had been recurrently mooted ever since Hitler's assumption of power. Surveying the possibilities open to Germany after her repudiation of the Versailles arms clauses, the *Saturday Review* in March 1935 predicted that the next blow would fall in the Rhineland.[45] More immediately, the drift of German intentions was clearly grasped by *The Economist* at the end of February 1936:

> The German contentions [against the Franco-Russian Pact] have raised the fear that Herr Hitler and his advisers intend to seize upon the ratification . . . as a pretext for one of those stirring gestures of the new Germany's national independence . . . The French think that the remilitarisation of the Rhineland, in flat contravention of the Versailles and Locarno treaties, is planned.

The journal went on to demolish the Nazi argument: The proposed Pact was purely defensive and, in any case, Germany had long been invited to join an 'Eastern Locarno', an offer she had persistently rejected.[46]

Time & Tide entertained similar apprehensions and reacted in a like manner. France, Russia and Czechoslovakia were fully justified in entering into pacts of mutual assistance, it believed, so long as Germany refused to endorse an 'Eastern Locarno'. And Britain would view the re-militarisation of the Rhineland as 'a clear violation of Versailles and Locarno'. But the journal correctly predicted that Britain would do nothing: 'The British will await the French lead, and the French will do nothing but talk.'[47] The *Spectator*, too, rebutted the German denunciation of the Franco-Russian Pact but remained unmoved by French fears over the Rhineland. The *New Statesman*, equally aware of the direction events were taking, on 8 February 1936 stressed the compatibility of the Franco-Russian Pact with Locarno. But as he was often to do later, Kingsley Martin deflected attention from one unpleasant crisis or contingency by referring to another less immediate and explosive. The uncertainty of British policy, he noted, prompted many abroad to 'prepare for the worst'. What would Britain do if Germany attacked Russia, seized Austria or re-militarised the Rhineland? He replied: Britain should 'convey to Germany the certain knowledge that in the event of a deliberate attack on Russia, she must reckon with the active hostility of this country'. Not a word was said about the necessary or desirable reaction to an Anschluss or a coup in the Rhineland.[48]

All the Liberal and left-wing weeklies condemned in advance a re-militarisation of the Rhineland; all avoided mention of military commitments or of the possible British reaction to this decreasingly hypothetical contingency. The attitude of the Conservative weeklies to the forthcoming event was predictable. The *Tablet* echoed the German press. It attacked the impending ratification of the Franco-Russian Pact without specifically endorsing a German coup in the Rhineland.[49] Between 1933 and 1935 the *Observer* had flatly rejected piecemeal concessions or Treaty revision in favour of Germany. In February 1936 Garvin still pointed to Hitler as the primary cause of insecurity in Europe and sympathetically noted the general quest 'for collective security against a potential German danger'.[50] But on 1 March he wrote:

> Germany's intentions in the Rhineland are an increasingly disturbing speculation . . . [But we must distinguish between] right and wrong. The Rhineland is German territory. She must have the sovereign right to do as she pleases with her own territory. To give Germany a legitimate grievance might be a fatal disservice to Europe.[51]

Motivated by anti-Communism and fears of the consequences of 'eastern entanglements', *Truth* also regarded the Franco-Russian Pact with hostility. Like the *Observer* and the *Tablet*, it too, for a time, had rejected Treaty revision in favour of a Nazi Germany. Yet on 5 February 1936 the journal stated that the re-militarisation of the Rhineland was 'merely a matter of time and cannot be indefinitely prevented'. Three weeks later *Truth* argued its case in more forthright terms:

> It must be conceded that the [German] claim to be released from [Locarno] obligations by the Franco-Russian Pact . . . is at any rate understandable. Germans might well ask what they are getting in return for leaving their western frontier unguarded. So long as there was no fear of an attack from that quarter they could afford to make such a gesture, but if the first move of Hitlerism against the Communist east . . . is to be the signal for a French irruption into the Rhineland, can any German Government afford to leave the Rhineland undefended? If France chooses to enter into close engagements with the Soviets, can other countries be expected to observe engagements undertaken before such new complications came about . . .? This is a method of reasoning which will not, I imagine, be confined to Germany.[52]

In the weeks before 7 March 1936 totally discrepant views were proffered in the *Sunday Times*. As usual, Hadley was firmer than Sidebotham. On 9 February Hadley asserted that 'the independence of Austria [was] a cardinal necessity for the peace of Europe', and that 'there [could] be nothing but friendliness in this country towards' France's eastern alliances. Sidebotham was clearly of another persuasion. He wrote: 'If Locarno fails as a guarantee of peace, the cause will be that France is bent on forming a Latin–Slav block against what she calls German aggression.' He added: 'There should be a hard and fast frontier between the areas of Eastern and Western pacts.'[53]

Through January–February 1936 the weeklies displayed awareness of the probability of a German march into the Rhineland. The Liberal and left-wing journals condemned, a priori, the contemplated Nazi move. But pessimistic forecast apart, they omitted any call for a firm British commitment to buttress the Locarno (and Versailles) stipulations. The right-wing press (with the exception of Hadley in the Sunday Times) restricted itself to echoing and endorsing the German arguments offered in advance of the coup. Here were the two faces of appeasement: condemnation of a breach of treaties coupled with a passive acceptance of British inaction, and outright justification of the aggression in advance.

Fear palpably governed the reactions of the weeklies to the march into the Rhineland. From the start, all the weeklies reluctantly or willingly fell into line behind the Government's policy of verbal protest and physical inactivity. In most of them, stress was laid on Hitler's accompanying peace proposals, on the German-ness of the Rhineland and on the injustice of the status quo ante. Few regarded the coup as a fundamental upheaval in European affairs, as a subversion of the French security system, as a test-case for the future of collective security or as a stone in the mosaic of Nazi ambitions of expansion. In its wake, the Government refused to contemplate a course of compulsion to obtain a German withdrawal; neither did any weekly propose or endorse such a course. Fear dominated all reactions; above all, war must be averted. The weeklies accurately reflected what Harold Nicolson perceived to be the reaction of those in power: 'General mood of the House is one of fear. Anything to keep out of war', he noted on 9 March. And on 23 March: 'The feeling of the House is terribly "pro-German"; which means afraid of war.'[54]

The nature of Time & Tide's reaction is indicated in a laudatory letter sent by Lady Rhondda to Baldwin some three months after the coup. Perhaps with Churchill in mind, she wrote: 'I happen to be one of those people who believe that it might mean national – and more than national – disaster for you to leave the helm at this moment.'[55] Time & Tide's initial attitude was plaintive and conciliatory: 'Whatever Herr Hitler's "rights", they could have been better secured by negotiation. Germany has not acted in a way which will inspire confidence in her "freely contracted obligations" in future.' But what Britain must do was clear: 'Negotiation is in the very marrow of this country, and it has yet to be proved that this method will be less successful than taking an attitude which may lead to a world conflagration.'[56]

Once the immediate threat of war had receded, *Time & Tide* sounded a bolder note. Such a disparity between initial infirmity and, later, more bellicose reflection was to characterise most of the Liberal and left-wing reviews in this and later crises. On 21 March 1936 *Time & Tide* lamented that Britain, France and Russia, apparently, would fight only to defend themselves and the Low Countries. 'Does this mean that Hitler can get away with anything?' asked Lady Rhondda. The journal placed no trust in Hitler's peace proposals and promises: 'peace talk is an enveloping fog', it stated, quoting a German General Staff manual. But the employment of force against Germany was as far from Lady Rhondda's mind as from Baldwin's. The journal warned that 'those nervous and no doubt well-meaning people who are urging Britain to add threats to overwhelming power are playing the most dangerous game of all – and some are even doing it in the name of the rule of law and the principles of the League'.[57]

Rejecting the path of resistance while dismissing Hitler's professions of peace inevitably meant the perpetuation of inconsistency. Despite its talk of 'an enveloping fog', *Time & Tide* continued to insist that the door to discussion must be left open; without discussion, 'an explosion will be inevitable'. The journal reflected: 'Nazi-ism and all that it means has to be taken in the flank – not by military means, but by a firm insistence that the real Peace Conference should take place before the [next] war and not after [it].' The journal put its faith in 'the sound heart of Germany'.[58]

The *Spectator* also preferred to focus on Hitler's peace proposals rather than on his actions. In its issue of 13 March, a news report item covered the march into the Rhineland while the first leader concentrated on the peace offers. Wilson Harris reproved France, Russia and the Little Entente for contemplating war or economic sanctions against Germany, and warned against the formation of a British–French–Belgian alliance. 'The essential thing is to get discussion started on Herr Hitler's positive proposals', he wrote. The strategic significance of the Rhineland coup apparently eluded Wilson Harris and Wrench: 'That the Rhineland should no longer be de-militarised is a small thing in itself ... Nor is anyone disposed to moralise over-much about Germany's repeated breaches of the Treaty of Versailles.'[59]

A week later, the *Spectator* exhibited somewhat greater boldness. Wilson Harris condemned Germany's action as 'a flagrant violation of the Locarno Treaty'. But he diagnosed 'two very good reasons' for Britain's inability to 'even contemplate armed intervention': the thrust of popular feeling against war and the tendency, in Britain, to 'rebel against France's exigencies and condone Germany's treaty-breaking'.[60]

'British opinion', stated the *New Statesman* on 14 March, 'deplores the violence of Hitler's methods but accepts his moral right to occupy the Rhineland.' Previously, Kingsley Martin had never supported a re-militarisation of the Rhineland nor mentioned the inequity of Versailles in this connection. But now he declared: 'We all have bad consciences about Germany's treatment since the war.' In the same breath he acknowledged that Hitler's aims went beyond the mere rectification of Versailles; to crush France was not the least of *Mein Kampf*'s exhortations. However, he argued, Britain and France must not miss the opportunity of discussion afforded by Hitler's peace proposals. He concluded: 'Great Britain will not regard the occupation of the Rhineland as a *casus belli*; nor are economic sanctions a practical policy against Germany.'[61]

A firmer note prevailed in the *New Statesman* in the following weeks; the threat of war had receded. The British public, the journal lamented, had failed to understand the demands of 'collective security'; had failed, too, to 'realise the facts about the Hitler regime'. Many in Britain had tried 'to persuade themselves that once the injustices of Versailles were removed, Hitler will settle down in the European comity of nations'. This was not so. Nazism, by nature, was incompatible with peace: 'The French [therefore] are right, and Britain should stand by them in insisting that the unilateral and violent breach of treaties should be condemned and that Hitler must either withdraw from the Rhineland or submit his case to the High Court.' Beside high-sounding declarations, however, the *New Statesman* suggested nothing save offering Germany some colonial concessions.[62]

The Economist reacted to the Rhineland coup with a great deal of soul-searching, resignation and self-delusion. Outside the journal's pages, Layton evinced sympathy for the French, and focused on the fact of the *coup* rather than on Hitler's pacific proposals.[63] On the other hand, Toynbee, an *Economist* leader-writer, was 'convinced of [Hitler's] sincerity in desiring peace in Europe and a close friendship with England'. Like Kingsley Martin, he supported colonial concessions to Germany.[64] On 18 March Toynbee declared: 'It was because France had made a treaty with Russia that Hitler had gone into the Rhineland.'[65] Later in the year, Graham Hutton dismissed the German justification of the *coup* as 'a mere excuse'.[66] In *The Economist*, Layton's and Hutton's views prevailed, but traces of Toynbee's attitude were also visible.

The Economist condemned the *coup* as a 'lawless' defiance of both Versailles and Locarno. But its objection stressed the manner and timing rather than the substance of the *coup*. Unlike the other Liberal and left-wing weeklies, it faced the problem squarely and candidly. Hitler could be evicted from the Rhineland only by 'the threat of force'; a will to sustain it must underlie the threat, if made. In short, war would have to be risked: 'Is this a risk which it is right and wise to make?', asked the journal. If the Führer's word was worthless and further aggression his aim, then

101

Britain and France confronted 'the choice between a risk of war now, at our time, and a certainty of war later, at Hitler's time. Logic would counsel us that this was the moment to put our fortunes to the touch.' Hitler's words pointed to a desire for 'European appeasement', his actions to a will for 'German military domination over Europe'. With the problem thus eminently stated, *The Economist* proceeded to abjure the dictates of its own reasoning. 'The need for handling the Italians firmly in Africa is one among the many strong reasons for doing our utmost to arrive at a settlement with Herr Hitler in Europe,' it stated. Logic dictated war; fear, and perhaps a desire not to appear 'warlike', directed otherwise.[67]

Alone among the serious weeklies, *The Economist* quickly noted the repercussions of the Rhineland *coup* upon the strategic balance. Britain must end its silence concerning the fate of the Succession States: 'the domination of the Continent by a single Power' would spell 'the end of British independence'. It was possible that Hitler had renounced his ambitions in eastern Europe. But this, implied *The Economist*, was barely credible. It therefore called upon Britain to do her 'duty' by Czechoslovakia, as she clearly meant 'to fulfil it towards Belgium'.[68] Layton, however, refrained from calling for British adherence to the Franco-Russian alliance system.[69]

As a result of French prevarication over Abyssinia during March and April 1936, Layton was in a blatantly anti-French mood. The Rhineland *coup* only partially blunted it. On 11 April *The Economist* accused France of playing 'fast and loose with the Covenant, the collective system [and] the sanctity of treaties'.[70] But the reality of German intentions was not lost sight of: Germany had 'scarcely yet begun the course of violence to which she is being invited by the present French sabotaging of the Covenant and the present British acquiescence in it'; Germany was a far 'stronger, grimmer power on the warpath' than Italy.[71]

The *British Weekly* reacted to the Rhineland coup with the usual blend of conciliation and high-minded affirmations of collective security. Though Germany had 'taken the law into its own hands', it stated on 12 March, the action could not be regarded as 'a warlike measure'. It asserted ambiguously that 'our country is prepared to reaffirm in the strongest way the Locarno guarantees'.[72]

Predictably the *New English Weekly* offered nothing constructive to the debate on the Rhineland. Fear assailed proponents of Social Credit as it did most others. Hence, it wrote on 12 March, 'little profit, indeed much loss to all mankind would be the inevitable result' of the imposition of economic or military sanctions on Germany. It was 'stupid' to assume that Germany would for longer suffer the shackles of Versailles. On the other hand, whatever interpretation was put on the character and aims of Herr Hitler, the man boded ill for Europe. But then, apparently, so did every prominent statesman: 'On the subject of faith in strong right arms, Goebbels and Eden speak the same idiocy', stated the *New English Weekly*.[73]

A note of lucidity and reason was introduced in the journal with the publication of a number of articles surveying world affairs by A.S. Elwell-Sutton. Of the Rhineland *coup* and German policy in general, this special contributor wrote:

> A passionate consideration of these events can lead to only one conclusion. It is no use yielding to any of Germany's claims in the expectation that it will be the last. The contrary is the truth. Each point gained opens up the way to something else, and the final goal of romantic militarism is well nigh illimitable. Megalomania would feed on success, until the world-empire of the Reich has become a reality.[74]

Needless to say, this line in no way reflected editorial thinking on the *New English Weekly*.

Truth mixed rebukes to Germany with abuse of France; confusion dominated its pages during March 1936. Having previously justified the impending *coup* on the basis of the Franco-Russian Pact, its editor's emphasis on the warm applause which greeted the Wehrmacht's entry into the Rhineland was predictable: 'If this is an act of aggression under the Covenant ... then it is certainly time the Covenant were changed.' The British people 'will very definitely not fight to stop Germans from seizing Germany'. Nonetheless, *Truth* considered the action 'a pointless display of bad manners'; Nazi methods were upbraided.[75] The journal, however, categorically rejected sanctions against Germany or the formation of a Franco-British alliance: 'That way lies war ... Englishmen will join no alliance less comprehensive than the League of Nations. If Germany must learn her duties as a member of a world community, so too must France.' Presumably, *Truth* was alluding to such French 'sins' as the occupation of the Ruhr and the Franco-Russian Pact; it was certainly not criticism of French policy over Abyssinia.[76] *Truth* welcomed Hitler's peace proposals and called for the convocation of a peace conference. At the same time, however, the journal thought that to be rid of Hitler 'would be an excellent thing', that his solemn word was meaningless and that he was a 'dangerous lunatic'. The journal concluded that 'there cannot be real peace in Europe as long as there is a Nazi Government at the centre of it'.[77] But any thought of resistance to Germany was nowhere in evidence.

The *Tablet*, still under Oldmeadow in March 1936, condemned France's 'damnable policy' of friendship with Russia but argued that 7 March would be remembered for the Rhineland's re-militarisation rather than for Hitler's peace offers. It completely dismissed the silken cloak which had accompanied the mailed fist: 'How can we trust the promise-breakers of today to become the promise-keepers of tomorrow?' Only 'simpletons' would be deceived. The problem was clear but, given the fear of war, insoluble: 'War is too terrible a prospect; yet Germany must not break pacts with impunity.'[78] With Woodruff's assumption of the editorship in April 1936 the *Tablet* abruptly reversed its line. Christopher Dawson, in a major policy article, wrote of 'Hitler's call for a fresh start' as an 'appeal to sanity'. Reconciliation was as necessary as ever. Sympathetically, Dawson wrote: 'A rearmed and remilitarised Germany is preparing to recover her place in the world by force if no other way is open.'[79]

Over the Rhineland the *Sunday Times* swam with the Conservative tide. In its strongest comment, Hadley wrote that Hitler had acted in accordance with 'the principle of Prussian militarism' and had 'dealt a severe blow' to his own credibility in western eyes; but it was not 'necessarily a fatal one'. Sidebotham was more conciliatory: 'An injury to the Treaty is not necessarily an injury to France, still less an aggression on the soil of France', he argued. He preferred to discern fresh possibilities for 'a new and better Locarno': 'Uneasiness and hope are balanced against each other, and on our present knowledge it is impossible to say in which scale is the greater substance', he concluded. At all events, one option was unthinkable: 'the problem is one of law and politics, and it would be a sin to think of it in terms of association with war.'[80]

In the course of March the gap between Hadley and Sidebotham widened. Sidebotham dismissed the view that Hitler 'really had horns and a tail' and that his peace proposals were camouflage and deception. Even-handedly, he admitted that his sympathies were 'divided'. French ideals, of tolerance, democracy and legality, were attractive; but so, too, were Hitler's proposals. So 'British statesmen should be neither pro-French nor pro-German; their duty is to their own country'. Britain must abjure a French alliance. Even staff conversations he found suspect for 'it [was] dangerously true', he argued, that they tended 'to harden into military alliance'. Above all Sidebotham worried about a war stemming from France's eastern entanglements; Europe west of the Rhine must look to and after itself alone.[81]

Hadley, on the other hand, demanded of Germany proof of her peaceful intentions (in east and west) through acts rather than words. If such proofs proved unforthcoming, he ventured, 'the Powers wedded to peace will have to consolidate their joint action for defending it. To stand firmly together may for Great Britain, Belgium, France,

Russia or Czechoslovakia be the only alternative to their being shot at singly.'[82] Hadley's brief sojourn beyond the pale of appeasement proved short-lived. But, apparently, existing policy occasionally discomfited him; Sidebotham never displayed such sensibilities.

In the weeks following the Rhineland *coup* the *Sunday Times*, like *Truth*, hammered away at the need for British rearmament. Garvin gave this theme the highest priority in the *Observer*. As he wrote on 8 March: 'The first need for Britain is to repair her defences. The second, to consider Herr Hitler's proposals in a spirit of sympathy and goodwill.' The need to keep one's powder dry, and to increase its stock-pile, was to characterise the three years of Garvin's espousal of appeasement; unlike Chamberlain, he always considered appeasement as mainly a policy designed to buy time before a probably unavoidable conflict. But, between 1936 and 1939, an appeaser he was. He called Hitler's peace proposals 'brilliant and timely' and agreed with the need to detach the Covenant from the Treaty of Versailles: 'There can be no peace without elementary justice and common sense.' Nor did he omit mention of the reason underlying his pursuit of appeasement: 'From a shattering air-war between the British and German peoples neither could recover', he wrote on 15 March. Like Sidebotham, he flatly rejected British involvement in war for anything east of the Rhine.[83] At the same time, however, he argued that concessions to Germany must be made only within the context of a final, total settlement: 'Any sort of mere piecemeal surrender is unthinkable.' But if war for anything east of the Rhine was rejected out of hand, what impediment did Germany face in its projected piecemeal *Drang nach Osten?* Garvin resolved this contradiction, as did Britain, only in March 1939 with the rejection of appeasement.

By and large, the right-wing weeklies condoned the German re-militarisation of the Rhineland both before and after the event. Liberal and left-wing journals, while strongly condemning it in forecasts, moderated their tone in its wake. All rejected any attempt to reverse the German *coup* through either sanctions or military threats and measures. In most of the weeklies emphasis was laid on Hitler's peace proposals rather than on the *coup* itself, and, with regard to the *coup*, on its manner rather than its substance. Appreciations of the detrimental effects of the remilitarisation on the strategic posture of the western democracies were, except in *The Economist*, either muted or non-existent. The right-wing journals reacted to the *coup* by increasing the virulence of their advocacy of British rearmament. They continued to reject the conclusion of a military alliance with France and/or Russia. The Liberal and left-wing weeklies persisted in rejecting both massive rearmament and alliances. A persistent feature of the treatment of the Rhineland coup in these weeklies was a moderation of the tone of their anti-Nazi pronouncements while the crisis was on the boil. As soon as the threat of war receded, a degree of militancy crept back into their pages.

SPAIN

'Probably not since the French Revolution had a "foreign event" so bitterly divided the British people', wrote K.W. Watkins in his study of British attitudes to the Spanish Civil War.[84] Certainly, the war resulted in a division of sympathies. However, pro-Republicanism was probably not as fervid as many later accounts of politicians and intellectuals make out; few, at the time, desired the translation of that sympathy into a more intrepid British policy. The consensus supporting appeasement, which had developed during 1935–36, continued to hold sway in British minds, if not hearts, with respect to and for the duration of the Spanish conflict. The persistence, and pertinacity, of this consensus was reflected in the weekly press.

The German and Italian interventions in the Spanish Civil War permit and perhaps compel treatment of that conflict, and British reactions to it, within the context of a study of appeasement. Mussolini's successful defiance of the League and Hitler's successes over rearmament and the Rhineland undoubtedly paved the way for their forthright involvement in Spain. British reactions to these previous crises established a pattern of behaviour which was repeated in the new context, even in typical details. For example, the effectively one-sided arms embargo against Italy and Abyssinia was repeated in relation to Spain.

Few observers at the time questioned the proposition that vital British interests were involved in the Spanish conflict. Gibraltar and western Mediterranean waters were thought to be at the mercy of whatever power dominated the Peninsula. In a future war, Spanish iron ore and other minerals were as important to the Axis as to Britain. For French military planners the threatened emergence of a hostile State on the Pyrenees portended the nightmare of a three-front war; that a Franco Spain would join the German–Italian Axis in the event of European war appeared more than probable during the Spanish conflict. And what imperilled France, threatened Britain. Many believed that a world-wide 'Fascist' offensive was in progress and that it was a British interest to support democratic government wherever it flourished.

The failure of Britain and France to come to the aid of the assaulted Republic stemmed from a variety of causes. Ideological antipathies between a Conservative British establishment and a Liberal–Left Republican Government undoubtedly played a part. So, too, did fears of Comintern intrigues and Communist penetration of Iberia. Undoubtedly, however, the determining factor in British and French calculations was the fear that involvement in Spain would entail confrontation with Germany and Italy, and that a wider European war would result. Hence, the democracies resolved upon, and persisted in, 'Non-Intervention', while Italy, Germany and, eventually, Russia actively participated in the Spanish Civil War.

The weeklies divided along distinct lines of sympathy. The Liberal and left-wing journals, with varying degrees of fervour, from August 1936 came out in support of the Republic and maintained this partiality for the duration of the Civil War. The Conservative and Catholic journals, like the *Observer* and the *Tablet*, favoured the Nationalist cause and a Franco victory. At first *Truth* attempted to adhere to a strict neutrality towards the Spanish antagonists; eventually, however, it evinced greater 'understanding' for the insurgents than for the Madrid Government. Only the *Sunday Times* achieved a thorough and consistent impartiality for the first year of the conflict; Kemsley's acquisition of the paper in 1937 introduced a pro-Nationalist tilt into its pages.

'The Spanish Civil War loomed very large in the *Tablet* between 1936 and 1939.'[85] The journal's unremitting interest in the conflict in part stemmed from a desire to counter the contrary commitment of the Left.[86] Catholicism, anti-Communism and unflagging advocacy of appeasement in general prompted Woodruff unequivocally to support Franco from the outset of the war. Catholicism and anti-Communism determined his views on the merits of the Spanish antagonists; support of appeasement accounted for his attitude towards the German and Italian interventions, and to British reactions to them.

'From a Catholic point of view the Spanish Civil War was fundamentally about religion', Woodruff later recalled.[87] The revolt of the generals was viewed favourably because 'the present [Republican] regime was rapidly bringing the country to demoralisation and Red ruin'; at last, 'law and order' were being restored.[88] Social and political considerations were shunted aside by the demands of faith: 'All those Spaniards who wish to see the Church survive . . . will have had to side with the insurgents.' Clearly, the devil's disciples were massed in Madrid and Catalonia; the Moors investing the capital were apparently seconded, for the duration, to the heavenly host. 'Already there is scarcely a church standing in Barcelona', Woodruff stated, with questionable accuracy, on 1 August 1936.[89]

If the character of the internal struggle was beyond dispute, so too were the war's European implications. Woodruff initially hoped that 'the chief powers shall agree to the principle of Non-Intervention'. Open foreign involvement, he feared, would serve to 'spread the conflict . . . beyond the Pyrenees.'[90] Yet Italy, Germany, Portugal and, increasingly, Russia were intervening. At first, Woodruff maintained that charges of German and Italian intervention were unsubstantiated; besides, France, Mexico and Russia were equally at fault. Nor was it certain that all these involvements were 'connived [at] by the Governments in question', he stated as late as 10 October 1936.[91] By February of the following year such arguments were no longer tenable, even in Woodruff's eyes. He therefore argued: 'What brought the help, first of Italy and then of Germany, for Nationalist Spain was the proof which the Nationalists adduce that there was already the most formidable Communist intervention in the Peninsula.'[92]

But support of British (and French) 'Non-Intervention', as Woodruff early admitted, bore little relation to the extent or character of the aid being offered from abroad to the antagonists. 'The purpose of the Non-Intervention agreement', he wrote in October 1936, 'was less to prevent help going to the different groups in Spain than to prevent the spread of the Spanish issue to the rest of Europe.' Fear of British embroilment in war against Germany and Italy sustained Woodruff's support of non-intervention through the Spanish war. An appreciation that an Italian- and German-backed Franco victory might imperil British interests in the Mediterranean was no deterrent. For he still hoped for an Anglo-Italian *entente*. Besides, he argued, 'the truth has long been known that the Mediterranean is no longer the safe place it was when neither aeroplanes nor submarines' were around.[93]

Anti-Communism and Catholic origins certainly played a part in Garvin's espousal of the Nationalist cause in the *Observer*. The desire to avoid war with Germany and Italy, even more palpably, underlay his commitment to British non-intervention.

For Garvin, the conflict was clearly between 'the soul of the old Spain' (the Nationalists) and 'the new deliberate godlessness that calls itself Communism and destroys the very foundations of fellowship and even of pity'; opposing the 'Red Camarilla of Madrid' was General Franco, 'an intelligent and anything but reactionary statesman'.[94] Through the war the *Observer* published unequivocally partisan reports from the Peninsula. Nigel Tangye's contribution of 10 January 1937 was representative. He wrote: 'At the risk of being charged with bias [I] must say that wanton torture and murder is confined to the Reds . . . The scum of the Red population were armed and indulged in orgies of torture.'[95] 'Guernica' and similar Fascist atrocities evoked the response that the 'Reds' had 'butchered' 350,000 men, women and children in the first eleven months of the conflict.[96]

Like the *Tablet*, the *Observer* at first denied the facts of German, Italian and Portuguese intervention and then, in justification, ascribed them to the prior intervention of Russia. 'To assert that foreign intervention in Spain was started by Germany and Italy is a rank untruth ... That interference was started ... by the Soviet Power and the Comintern ... The action of Germany and Italy has been a reply to the flagrant aggression of Communism in western Europe', wrote Garvin on 3 January 1937.[97] The British commitment to non-intervention was never questioned; 'intervention on which side?' Garvin might well have asked. The foreign interventions apparently cancelled each other out: 'Russian and French volunteers on the one side, German and Italian on the other, are the backbone of the conflict.'[98] The Italian depredation of commercial shipping in the Mediterranean in 1937 was dismissed by the *Observer* as 'likely' to have been due to 'Red' provocations. The Nyon Conference, called to end it, was condemned by the *Observer* as dividing Europe into two camps, with Britain wrongly ranged against Germany and Italy.[99]

The *Saturday Review*, under Lady Houston, reacted to the Spanish Civil War with similar, unreserved support for General Franco. Anti-Communism supplied the keynote; Spain had to be saved from 'the curse of Bolshevism'; 'Communist usurpers ... were indulging in every form of excess and cruelty'.[100] At first, the change of ownership and editorship following Lady Houston's death in January 1937 failed to alter the journal's attitude to Spain. The *Saturday Review* accused France and Russia of unnecessarily prolonging that country's agony.[101] But Fascist atrocities and the spectacle of Britain enduring humiliation led to a dampening of its pro-Franco ardour. In April the journal contrasted 'Potato Jones', the anti-Franco blockade-runner at Bilbao, with a weak-kneed British Government; significantly, the article was entitled 'Franco's Armada'. By November 1937 however, the *Saturday Review* had agilely leapt back on to the Franco band-wagon; it criticised the Government for its anti-Nationalist 'neutrality' and called for belligerent rights to be conferred on the Nationalists.[102]

Unlike its Conservative peers, *Truth* found the Spanish conflict a conscience-tormenting episode: espousal of appeasement towards Germany and Italy clashed with its appreciation of Britain's interests in the Mediterranean, fear of Communism with abhorrence of Fascist mores and ideals, compassion for an embattled democracy with a desire to support the Conservative Government. Implicit sympathy for the

Republic pervaded its pages for the first six months of the war, muted support for Franco afterwards.

Henry Newnham, *Truth*'s editor, at first attempted to display impartiality towards the Spanish combatants. On 29 July 1936 he declared that there was nothing to choose between the sides. But a marginal preference for the Republicans soon became apparent. In August he took the *Daily Mail* to task for its 'hysterical' anti-Republicanism and called Azana's Government 'moderate', though he criticised it for failing to curb its extremist supporters.[103] Covert sympathy for the Republic vanished, however, in the course of 1937; Russian intervention, the increasing strength of the Communists in the Republican coalition and a rekindled affirmation of support for appeasement in general came to bear.

From the start, *Truth* supported non-intervention. On 12 August 1936 it praised France's 'wisdom' in denying arms to the Republic. For most of 1936 *Truth* played down German–Italian intervention.[104] By December, however, the journal had seemingly had enough of the 'grim joke' of non-intervention; massive intervention was obviously taking place, and Britain was being visibly humiliated. 'Many Englishmen', wrote the editor, 'are beginning to wonder whether their Government's attitude of masterly inactivity and studied zeal to give no offence to General Franco may not perhaps have gone a little too far.' The arms embargo was understandable. But the proposed legislation prohibiting British vessels from carrying arms to Spain went 'beyond the point consonant with the dignity of world power'. If Madrid was now dominated by the Communists, the fault lay with Britain for standing by while Russia alone sustained the Republic.[105] Non-intervention had clearly failed. Two courses were now open to Britain: to stand completely aloof from the conflict or to impose a total blockade of Iberian coastlines 'against all comers'. The latter course, argued the journal, could either prevent or precipitate European war. There was, therefore, 'a case for complete inaction as well as for decisive action'; the public, *Truth* declared, would support the Government 'in either course'. But the country would not tolerate 'a policy vigorously proclaimed and then abandoned in the face of danger'.[106]

This ambivalent advocacy of British firmness proved short-lived; it died with the signing in Rome of the Anglo-Italian Declaration of Mutual Assurance at the beginning of 1937. The journal welcomed the spurious 'ban on volunteers' and declared that the problem in Spain was the restoration of law and order and not which side won.[107] Several months later *Truth* opposed the granting of British protection to food-vessels running the blockade around Bilbao; this would be to 'take sides', and 'it [was] . . . pertinent to inquire which side we should take'.[108] In subsequent months *Truth* refrained from pointing an accusing finger at Germany over Guernica and was not especially disturbed by the German shelling of Almeria. It did, however, offer heartfelt condolences to Germany over the loss of life on the bombed battleship *Deutschland*.[109] This line prevailed in *Truth* until the fall of the Republic.

As regards the merits of the internal struggle in Spain the *Sunday Times* clung to a strict neutrality. Once the Army of Morocco had revolted, the issue was between 'a dull copy of German and Italian political models' and a Communist-inclined Republican Government.[110] Neither found favour in the eyes of Sidebotham and Hadley. Both sides, the paper assured its readers, were equally guilty of atrocities. Unlike the *Observer* and the *Tablet*, the *Sunday Times* persisted from 1936 to 1939 in referring to the Nationalists as 'rebels' or 'insurgents'.

From the start, Sidebotham was acutely aware of the implications of the conflict for the rest of Europe. The absorption of Spain by the Nazi–Fascist coalition, he believed, would vitally threaten British interests. As he cautiously phrased it in October 1936, 'a militantly Fascist Spain would introduce a new and disturbing factor into the politics of Europe'.[111] But the *Sunday Times* was bent on accommodation with Germany and Italy. For months, it closed its eyes to the facts of foreign intervention in Spain. It usually spoke of 'charges of intervention' rather than of 'intervention'.[112] By December–January, this myopia was no longer tenable. In late December the paper admitted that large units of the German armed forces were participating in the conflict; in January, that 'Italy assisted General Franco at such an early stage of his enterprise as to suggest to some minds that she must have been privy to it beforehand'.[113]

Despite its awareness of imperilled interests and foreign involvement, the *Sunday Times* unwaveringly supported British 'Non-Intervention'. As Hadley explained in October 1936, 'the need for saving the peace of Europe must obviously remain the dominant consideration with British statesmanship'; he objected to any reversal or mitigation of the arms embargo on the Republic.[114] At the start of the war, Sidebotham praised France's 'coolness and clear vision' in not arming Madrid. To Sidebotham's ears, criticism of British policy rang 'strange', for 'neutrality' was 'the most practical form that love of peace can take'.[115] He took atrocities in his stride, condemning both sides with enviable impartiality. For example, he unequivocally condemned the bombing of Guernica, but added: 'No one has more strongly condemned air raids on open towns than Hitler himself.'[116] The pursuit of appeasement demanded heavy tribute in the coin of naïveté or hypocrisy.

For the Liberal and left-wing weeklies Spain was a prolonged agony. At peace, the Republic enjoyed their sympathy; in war, assailed by Spanish clerics, generals and gentry, and by Italian and German soldiers and airmen, it elicited their support and devotion. Despite the Communist presence in Spain, never were the merits of an issue clearer: ideological kinship, morality and politics combined, for socialists, democrats, liberals and supporters of the Covenant and collective security, to dictate one policy – 'Help the Republic'. Yet, beyond expressions of sympathy and good-will, the Republic received no real help from Britain's Liberal and left-wing weeklies. Not once did any journal call for British and French intervention in support of the Spanish Government; rarely did any journal, excepting *Tribune*, venture the suggestion that the arms embargo be lifted, and never with vehemence or pertinacity; infrequent and exceptional was the call to Britain (and France) to impose a blockade on Iberian shores to render non-intervention effective. This political and moral failure derived from two sources: fear of British involvement in a war with Germany and Italy and, paradoxically, unwillingness to wander from the fold of Government policy and popular consensus. 'Unpopularity' was a bugbear, and the charge of 'war-mongering' was a shaft to the heart of all who came after the Great War.

Without a doubt, the *Spectator* was the leading proponent of appeasement among the Liberal and left-wing weeklies. While always flaunting its liberal and democratic credentials, the journal only reluctantly and, at times, equivocally expressed sympathy for the Republican cause. For the duration of the Civil War, the journal was definitely anti-Franco but only marginally pro-Loyalist. Somewhat belatedly, on 7 August 1936, it branded Franco a 'rebel' and charged him with presenting Europe 'with the choice between a Fascist and a Communist Spain'.[117] (In the liveliness of their anti-Communism, Wilson Harris and Wrench conceded nothing to Sidebotham and Garvin.) A Fascist victory, noted the journal, would enhance Italy's Mediterranean position and imperil Gibraltar and the sea-route to India. Nonetheless, asserted Wilson Harris, 'the only possible policy for [Britain was] to work for the isolation of the conflict'; though entitled to arm the Republic, Britain was under 'no obligation' to do so, and 'it would be folly to do it at the risk of provoking Italy and Germany to counter-measures'.[118]

This fear of 'counter-measures' impelled the *Spectator* to endorse the Government's posture of non-intervention through thick and thin; mounting evidence of growing Italian and German intervention left the journal unmoved. In mid-October Wilson Harris stated:

> The policy of Non-Intervention ... has unquestionably justified itself. The opposite policy would have caused serious trouble even here [i.e., Britain] and would have split France in half. More than that, the Spanish Government would probably have lost on balance, for Germany and Italy would have displayed much more vigour in arming the insurgents ... than Britain and France would have in supplying the Government in the ordinary way of trade.[119]

In the following week with somewhat greater candour the *Spectator* argued that the supreme task of European statesmen was to avert general war. On its own, this consideration afforded 'justification for the policy of Non-Intervention' pursued by 'European' governments. British and French provision of arms to the Republic would 'gravely endanger' peace.[120] Only in December 1936 did the *Spectator* admit that Germany, Italy and Russia were massively involved in the Civil War. But though agreeing that a Fascist victory in Spain would pose 'a grave threat' to vital British interests, Wilson Harris pleaded for the continuance of non-intervention by the democracies. Paradoxically, Russian aid to the Republic soothed the journal's conscience: for it was able to assert that both combatants enjoyed the assistance of 60,000 'foreign volunteers', diminishing the need for a reversal of British policy.[121]

Illustrative of the *Spectator*'s attitude to the Spanish problem, and exemplifying appeasement, were its treatments of the Guernica, Almeria and *Deutschland* incidents. The journal called the bombing of the Basque town an act of 'sickening butchery' and laid the blame squarely at the feet of Franco's airplanes. Allegations that German aircraft and pilots were involved were 'not convincingly substantiated ... We are not, therefore, yet driven to think Herr Hitler capable of condoning a crime so damnable.' (At issue, of course, was not Hitler's 'condonation' but German authorship.) Nor, suggested Wilson Harris, was the act compatible with Hitler's note to Eden calling for the prohibition of aerial attacks upon civilians. A week later the *Spectator* conceded that that 'crime beyond palliation' had been committed by German 'planes and bombs'. The journal registered surprise at the press campaign being waged in Germany against the British press treatment of Guernica, 'for there has been on the whole, a tendency in this country to suspend judgement' as to who was responsible. The journal added that the German press campaign 'did not prove German guilt'. Two weeks later, hidden in a news item reviewing recent Spanish developments, such as Mola's success against the Republicans in the north, appeared the brief sentence that 'the admissions of a German airman shot down last week appear to have proved conclusively that the destruction of Guernica ... was due to German airplanes flown by German pilots'. As if to balance this damaging anti-German admission, the next sentence read: 'On the other hand, the explosion on *HMS Hunter*, off Almeria ... can be attributed only to a floating mine.'[122]

Care not to offend German sensibilities, and remarkable evenhandedness, also characterised the *Spectator*'s handling of the (Republican) bombing of the cruiser *Deutschland* and of the (German) retaliatory shelling of Almeria; agility of language camouflaged a perversion of values. The linked incidents began when the German vessel was bombed by two Republican aircraft (not under orders), while it lay anchored in the rebel-held harbour of Ibiza; it was questionable, given its naval patrol duties under the aegis of the Non-Intervention Committee, whether the vessel should have been there at all; it is possible that the cruiser fired first on the approaching aircraft; and it is by no means difficult to understand Republican pilots who felt that Germany was not a non-combatant in the Spanish arena. The bombing occurred several weeks after Guernica. The shelling of Almeria, Hitler's act of retribution, was simply a deliberate attack on a civilian centre. Wilson Harris had this to say:

> The attack on the *Deutschland* was an act of criminal folly indistinguishable from crime. The bombardment of Almeria was a criminal act made the more criminal by the fact that it was the fruit not of folly but of deliberate policy. [But] the impulse on which Herr Hitler acted is no doubt intelligible enough ... Dictators cannot hesitate in such cases ... The provocation to Herr Hitler, it must be conceded, was intense.[123]

A touch of absurdity was added to this performance some weeks later when Wilson Harris registered bewilderment at Germany's withdrawal from the naval patrol arrangements on the pretext of an alleged torpedo attack on the *Leipzig*. The editor noted that there was no proof to corroborate the German story. He added, however: 'To say that is not to call in question for a moment the Captain of the *Leipzig*'s belief that there was an attack.'[124] The *Spectator* persisted in its support of non-intervention for the duration of the Spanish Civil War.

About a fortnight after the outbreak of the Spanish Civil War, Sir Walter Layton, *The Economist*'s editor, outlined his views on the nature of the conflict in a speech delivered at the Liberal Summer School in Oxford. He said: 'We cannot concur in the attempt to reverse by violence the verdict given by a free electorate'; 'if Spain becomes Fascist, it will be another blow to the Western democracies' – France would be surrounded by Fascist states and Britain's imperial communications would be imperilled. If these were the premises, his conclusion, obliquely stated, was dismissive of logic: 'We must never give the impression of endeavouring to build up a rival block against Germany.'[125] Several months later Graham Hutton, an *Economist* Assistant Editor, wrote in a similar vein: the revolt of the generals pitted reaction against democratic majority government. And of British policy he wrote: 'The British Government displayed an ominous preoccupation with the internal politics of Spain to the exclusion of any profound regard for British long-run interests.' As such, it was 'pitiably misguided'. Like his editor, however, Hutton refrained from suggesting the adoption of a firmer course.[126]

From the first, *The Economist* came out clearly and unequivocally in support of the Republic. The journal noted the German and Italian intervention and defined it as being close to 'an act of war'. It urged Britain and France to invite the European Powers to halt aid to the warring factions and to cordon off Spain against all outside help.[127] Though the journal regarded the conflict as 'a life and death struggle between democracy and the forces of reaction', it concurred with British and French non-intervention for 'the sake of European peace'.[128] *The Economist* gently chided the Government for its arms embargo, commenting that it 'might have been suitable action as part of an agreed neutrality plan'; in the light of external support for Franco, the ban was tinged with a definite 'anti-Government bias'. But while strategic interests and moral 'duty' seemed to point to the need for British support of Madrid, *The Economist* forbore to issue the necessary call.[129]

For the duration of the war, *The Economist* remained deeply unhappy with British and French policy. On 10 October 1936 it declared: 'There can be no justification for continuing the embargo at the Spanish Government's expense.'[130] The journal continued to view the war as but a part of the wider European struggle between aggressive dictatorships and unresisting democracies. It warned that if Britain allowed its potential allies to be demolished piecemeal, its own turn would inevitably come, with disastrous consequences.[131] But a reversal of non-intervention was never consistently, openly or firmly argued before 1938. *The Economist* realised that 'the primary purpose' of non-intervention was 'not to secure Non-Intervention, but to prevent the clash of arms between other Powers anywhere except in the Spanish arena,'[132] and it thought that Britain was pursuing a policy of 'peace at almost any price' which would result in 'a permanent Italo-German occupation ... of the Peninsula'.[133] But, throughout 1937, the journal failed to repeat its earlier call for British arms for Madrid, and never once suggested direct aid to the Republic comparable to that given to the Nationalists by Italy and Germany. Nor was an Anglo-French quarantine of Spanish shores against all foreign comers, come what may, ever mooted. Criticism of non-intervention there was, in profusion; insistence, firmness and a staunch advocacy of an alternative were lacking.

A decisive change of course was intimated in *The Economist* of 11 September 1937. The journal called upon Britain to place herself at the head of 'a defensive but resolute coalition' of peaceful powers before it was too late. But absent from this Churchillian cry was a constructive application to the Spanish problem.[134] Only with the *Anschluss*, in March 1938, did the journal come out openly with what, so to speak, had been on the tip of its tongue for so long. It repeated the call for a 'united front' and added: 'We must inscribe our first "No" on the face of Spain.' But it still refrained from saying exactly how this might or should be done.[135] Despite its protracted hesitations and inability to 'come out with it', *The Economist*, in relation to Spain, was the firmest anti-appeasement advocate among the serious weeklies.

The fear of embroilment in a general European war determined *Time & Tide*'s attitude to the Spanish Civil War. From the start, the journal had only sympathy for the beleaguered Republic, hatred and contempt for its Spanish and foreign assailants. Occasionally, as after Guernica, sympathetic verbiage was translated into calls for real British firmness against the dictator states. But this was rare.

The journal reacted to the revolt of the generals with unequivocal support of the Madrid Government and unreserved condemnation of British neutrality. It urged that Britain rescind the arms embargo.[136] But the growing evidence of German and Italian intervention, and perhaps the realisation that this marked a departure from the national consensus, prompted a sharp about-turn: the journal feared that British involvement would lead to European war. On 8 August Lady Rhondda came out in support of 'Non-Intervention', but urged that the democracies erect a sea and air cordon around Spain to prevent all foreign interference in the conflict.[137] In the following months, however, *Time & Tide* back-pedalled further and dropped its advocacy of the sea and air cordon, despite the growing German and Italian involvement. Non-intervention was approved, for it helped to 'keep up the difference between a European war spread over Europe and a European war confined to Spain.'[138] Britain, argued the journal, could not risk covert or open support for the Republicans because 'British aerial rearmament is too far in arrears.'[139] Hence, 'the strong legal case that the Spanish Government . . . is the only side which has the right under international law to buy arms cannot be allowed to weigh against the imperative need to prevent general war.'[140]

But conscience afflicted Lady Rhondda. The assault on Guernica evoked a plaintive condemnation of non-intervention: 'That is not neutrality. That is deliberately, if indirectly, to throw the whole weight of Britain on the side of the German and Italian bombers.' Assuming a calculated vagueness, the journal called upon the Western democracies to allow the Republic to purchase 'the means to defend its helpless population.'[141] Lady Rhondda, however, soon reneged. British policy, the journal argued on 10 July 1937, was determined, rightly, by two considerations – first, a desire to avoid European war and second, a desire to deny Italy and Germany a permanent foothold in the Peninsula. Concerning the second point, *Time & Tide* assured its readers that Franco, if victorious, would expel his erstwhile foreign colleagues. The journal concluded with a reaffirmation of its commitment to British policy.[142]

As in the case of *The Economist*, the *Anschluss* prompted *Time & Tide* to a somewhat mealy-mouthed reversal. With Barcelona about to fall, it called upon France (!) to 'support' the Republicans in their hour of need, and upon Britain to back France.[143] The call was not repeated thereafter.

'The Spanish war, which had begun in the summer of 1936, had seemed to me the last proud moment of hope. There seemed an off-chance of defeating Fascism in Spain instead of merely waiting until we had to fight for nothing but national survival', wrote Kingsley Martin in 1968. But the British Government reacted only with 'craven indolence', and the Republic was allowed to perish. The Second World War, as a struggle for survival, followed.[144]

If this judgement was harsh, so too, in the light of its oft-avowed principles, must be that delivered against the *New Statesman*. Beatrice Webb's view of the editor at the time tended, if anything, towards magnanimity: 'He vacillates between . . . complete isolationism in foreign affairs and helping the Spanish Government and thus risking war.'[145] The *New Statesman*, during that civil war, tended to steer a middle course between these extremes.

The journal's views on the merits of the conflict were clearly and dogmatically presented in editorial comment and in contributions from Geoffrey Brereton, Cyril Connolly and others: the struggle was one between Democracy and Fascist Reaction; victory in Spain was crucial to stopping, if not actually toppling, the Hitler and Mussolini regimes. The fate of 'collective security' and of Europe was at stake.

In face of the Fascist challenge, on 1 August 1936 the *New Statesman* urged the establishment between Britain, France and Russia of a 'united front', mirroring the Republicans' internal 'popular front'.[146] But fear of European holocaust quickly asserted itself. Though acknowledging Italian intervention on the Franco side, Kingsley Martin on 8 August commended the French and British adoption of non-intervention; the democracies were acting 'wisely, in our view'. British and French 'one-sided neutrality [was] conceived in fear', the *New Statesman* diagnosed on 22 August. But it neither offered nor recommended an alternative course.[147]

By October 1936, for all practical purposes, Kingsley Martin's vacillation was at an end. While constantly sniping at Western non-intervention, he too opted for the line of least resistance. The canker, affecting the journal as well as the governments concerned, was clearly perceived: 'The dread of war demoralises the pacific masses, both British and French'; 'The fear of war accounts, as in the Abyssinian affair, for a complete renunciation of action.'[148] Far from urging even the reversal of the arms embargo, the journal argued that British rearmament was to be opposed as war could be its only upshot, a war so devastating as to render meaningless the concept of victory. Kingsley Martin could console his readers only with the happy reflection that the German and Italian 'volunteers' had failed to swing the tide of Spanish battle. He urged that Britain open negotiations with Germany in order to assuage the Reich's demands for raw materials and colonies.[149]

While eliciting indignation, Guernica served mainly to reinforce the *New Statesman*'s fear of a British adoption of any policy smacking of firmness: 'Guernica is a rehearsal, not only for Bilbao and Madrid, but also for London and Oxford', he argued on 8 May 1937. He flatly abjured rearmament: 'London cannot be guarded by armaments . . . No amount of rearmament will save English towns.'[150]

Nor did Italian submarine attacks on shipping in the Mediterranean in the summer of 1937 shake the *New Statesman*'s endorsement of non-intervention. In the first leading article of 5 June 1937 C.M. Loyd stated: 'There will, of course, be people who will demand a complete reversal of policy on the part of Britain and France, and urge that "Non-Intervention" be abandoned, even at the risk of war. This might sound like doing belated justice to the Spanish Republic.' But this was incorrect. A reversal of British policy leading to unchecked competition in armaments, he argued, would probably favour the insurgents; British and French adherence to non-intervention might yet lead to the withdrawal from Spain of the foreign 'volunteers'; and, in any case, how could the precipitation of a 'general calamity' help the Spaniards?[151]

With despair and tenacity Kingsley Martin, through the summer of 1937, continued to cling to non-intervention. The presumed alternative – European war – was too frightful to contemplate, still less to precipitate. Conscience was sorely tried but its voice, always and ultimately, was stilled. In July, dubious battle was joined between two exponents of appeasement, Kingsley Martin and J.M. Keynes. At the end of June Kingsley Martin had hinted that the continuation of German and Italian intervention might compel a British abandonment of non-intervention and a 'return to the position that ought never to have been abandoned' — that is, allowing the Republic to purchase arms.[152] Somewhat disturbed, Keynes, chairman of the journal's board of directors, wrote to the editor plaintively interpreting the quoted passage as indicating a desire to terminate non-intervention.[153] Kingsley Martin rejoined with some further bluster in the *New Statesman*'s pages on 3 July. Some day, he argued, Britain might steel herself to make a stand; but he did not enjoin her to do so.[154] The 'dispute' reached a climax in the following issue of the *New Statesman*, which printed, side by side, articles by the two disputants. Keynes contended that 'the claims of peace' were paramount. Hence peace must be prolonged, hour by hour and day by day, for as long as possible: 'If we are at peace in the short run, that is something. The best we can do is put off disaster . . . if only in the hope that "something will turn up".' In any case, if war was inescapable, Russia and France needed more time to prepare. (Britain was not mentioned.) In his 'rebuttal', the editor agreed that war was not inevitable and that the claims of peace were paramount. Mere words followed. The policy of delay, espoused by Keynes, was 'not a peace policy': 'The distinction lies not between a peaceful and a war-like policy, but between a definite policy of opposition to aggression and an indefinite one of condoning it where it is not inimical to imperial interests and arming to resist it where it is.' No call followed for Britain to make a stand in Spain or, for that matter, anywhere else.[155] Perhaps Keynes's summation, in a letter to Kingsley Martin, was the most illuminating part of the exchange: 'There is no pleasing a really bellicose pacifist! They have got you both ways.'[156]

The *New Statesman* continued, through its silence, to consent to non-intervention. The *Anschluss* evoked a curious performance. It appeared then that Czechoslovakia was next on the Nazi 'list'. The journal, therefore, called for British and French 'support' of the Spanish Republic; no clarification of what was meant by the term was offered. Spain, asserted the journal, presented 'an incomparably more propitious field to the Western Powers, if ever they mean to make a stand, than Czechoslovakia. Prague, indeed, might be better defended in Barcelona than on the slopes of the Sudeten range.'[157] Kingsley Martin went on to advocate a cession of the Sudetenland to Germany. In other words, since Czechoslovakia was the contemporary flashpoint, that was where Hitler had to be placated. Suggesting a vague firmness in Spain was mere sugar-coating for the bitter pill of appeasement in the Sudetenland. Alexander Werth, the *New Statesman*'s Paris correspondent, later protested against this. Why, he wrote to Kingsley Martin on 2nd September, did the editor appear to believe that Spain was 'more important' than Czechoslovakia? The opposite was the case, asserted Werth.[158] By 1938, for all practical purposes, Spain had already been written off by the British Government; hence, at this late hour, a spurious militancy over Barcelona was a 'safe' salve to conscience. The desirability of commitment to Czechoslovakia was now the issue. So the *New Statesman* called for a Sudeten transfer. Needless to say, such 'firmness' over Spain was not repeated in the journal's pages.

The controversy in the Labour Party over policy on Spain had been *Tribune*'s midwife; the journal had specifically and primarily come into being in January 1937 in order to mobilise public support for the Republic. Through the remainder of the Spanish conflict *Tribune* called for British financial and military aid for the Republic. It did not, however, ever plead for British or French intervention in the conflict on the German, Italian and Russian models; such advocacy would have been politically suicidal to its proponents. Perhaps nothing better demonstrates the sway of appeasement in Britain during the 1930s than the total unwillingness of the Labour Left to contemplate British intervention on the side of the Spanish Republic though, to judge from their words at least, nothing should have enjoyed greater moral and political sanction.

VI

1938 – THE *ANSCHLUSS* AND THE CZECH CRISIS

A brief glance at attitudes in the weeklies to the Austrian and Czech questions before 1938 demonstrates that the views adopted in 1938 had little or nothing to do with perceptions of the rights and wrongs of Versailles. Attitudes to the *Anschluss* and to the Sudeten problem were determined mainly if not solely by attitudes to Nazi Germany and as functions of appeasement. Fear of war with Germany and of air attack upon Britain loomed large in the evolution of postures towards the two problems before 1938.

Between 1933 and 1935 the weeklies, with rare exceptions, supported the independence of Austria and the territorial integrity of Czecho-slovakia, even to the extent of urging British commitments to these ends. During 1936–37 almost all the weeklies came to abjure such commitments. By 1938 most of them accepted, with reluctance, resigna-tion or indifference, both the *Anschluss* and the dismemberment of Czechoslovakia. Especially instructive is the evolution of attitudes towards the Sudeten problem between March and September 1938.

THE *ANSCHLUSS*

Before 1933 all the weeklies, save for the *Saturday Review*, the *British Weekly* and the *Tablet*, favoured Treaty revision. The Sudetenland, quiescent, received practically no attention. Austria was another matter. The proposed customs union between Austria and Germany in 1931 – seen by many as but a preliminary to full political union – elicited little criticism and much support in the serious weeklies. Garvin's pronouncements at the time, while strongly worded, were not atypical: 'The economic union between Germany and Austria is in itself natural and sound'; the Treaty prohibition of *Anschluss*, 'a decree of force', was 'inimical to the future of peace', he wrote in the *Observer* in May 1931.[1]

By 1935, however, and equally typically, Garvin defined Austria as 'the keystone' of European peace and called a commitment to its independence 'the acid test of British Policy'.[2] A similar call was issued by Oldmeadow in the *Tablet*; British adhesion to a French–Italian guarantee of Austria was necessary because 'the bigger the phalanx of Austria's guarantors, the less will be the military liability of each'.[3] For a time after the Rhineland *coup*, even under Woodruff, the *Tablet* persisted in upholding Austrian independence; Austria's Catholicism temporarily overrode the temptations of appeasement. Woodruff lamented: 'the real trouble which faces Baldwin's Government is that nothing has been done to prepare public opinion in this country for any really strong action in central Europe.'[4]

Austrian independence, under sustained attack by Hitler, even evinced the unlikely occasional support of Herbert Sidebotham in the *Sunday Times*. But he always opposed any formal British guarantee. Until Kemsley's take-over in 1937, Hadley, the paper's editor, continued to uphold Austrian independence and to endorse a British commitment to it; it was 'a cardinal necessity for the peace of Europe', he declared.[5] *Truth*, too, occasionally expressed an interest in the maintenance of Austrian independence. In the summer of 1933, seeing Germany grow 'Nazier and nastier', the journal assured Dollfuss that the Western democracies would not allow the Reich to 'swallow Austria'.[6]

Such were the views of the Right. The Liberal and left-wing weeklies were, if anything, more outspoken in support of Austrian independence. *The Economist*, the *New Statesman*, the *Spectator* and *Time & Tide* all acknowledged that for Hitler, aggressive and evil, the incorporation of Austria was both an end in itself and a means to further expansion in eastern Europe. Austria, they believed, as 'a vital strategic position in Europe's cockpit', must not be abandoned.[7]

In the course of 1936–37, however, fear – of Germany, of Italy, of war in general and of air attack in particular – took its toll. The previous nearly unanimous support of Austrian independence vanished; talk of a British guarantee was replaced by a resigned silence in expectation, as it were, of the inevitable. Erosion set in in all weeklies. For instance, in May 1936 Kingsley Martin warned in the *New Statesman* that a German seizure of Austria would gravely imperil Czechoslovak security; he failed, however, to repeat his previous call for a British commitment to the integrity of either. In July 1937 Lady Rhondda, in *Time & Tide*, relegated Austria to a mere parenthesis: 'When the *Anschluss* has been achieved (and there would seem to be nothing that could avert it, save a general European war, which is desired by no one)' then, she warned, Czechoslovakia would be mortally threatened.[8] Even *The Economist* and *Tribune*, which, as we shall see, repeatedly urged British commitment to Czechoslovak integrity, usually forbore to demand a similar guarantee for Austria, despite their oft-repeated assertion that the fall of the latter would render impossible the continued independent existence of the former.

By the end of 1936 the *Observer* had written off Austria. The prospective *Anschluss* was, Garvin wrote, 'about the last question on earth in which British policy should dream of interfering'.[9] Hadley's occasional firm noises notwithstanding, this was also the policy of the *Sunday Times*, particularly after Kemsley's take-over. Complete alignment was then achieved between the views in Hadley's leaders and those in Sidebotham's leader page commentaries. Sidebotham, despite occasional lapses, had long promoted the cause of *Anschluss*; his constant refrain was that nothing in eastern Europe was remotely worth the life of a British grenadier. By 1937 the *Tablet* had come full circle with regard to Austria. In November of that year Woodruff declared: 'Our position is that we don't greatly mind what the frontiers in central Europe are, but we do greatly care that there shall be no frontiers which are indefinite sources of contention';[10] this applied equally to Austria and Czechoslovakia. Though having cast off the eccentricities of Lady Houston's editorship, the *Saturday Review* retained her faith in the weak right arm of appeasement: 'This country', declared the journal, 'can have no objection to a powerful Germany ... on the face of it, we have no immediate interests in Austria and Czechoslovakia. It would be impossible to raise any popular enthusiasm for a war on their behalf.'[11] *Truth*, too, in the course of 1936–37, consigned Austria to extinction, usually by referring vaguely to the need for a 'reconsideration' of central European frontiers.[12]

Perhaps the disaffection from the cause of Austrian independence owed something to a distaste for its clerical, authoritarian regime. Yet certainly Schuschnigg was no more a 'Fascist' than Dollfuss had been; and in the wake of Dollfuss's suppression of the Socialists in February 1934 even the left-wing journals continued to support embattled Austria in her conflict with Germany. Nor was the iniquity of Saint Germain often cited in the Liberal and left-wing weeklies. These weeklies, when considering central Europe, normally focused on democratic, French-aligned Czechoslovakia rather than on Austria. Yet given what was perceived as the interlocking fate of the two countries, it is somewhat difficult to explain the espousal of commitment to Czechoslovakia side by side with the relative indifference displayed towards Austria. Perhaps the knowledge, before 1936, that Italy, in this instance, was on the side of the angels, made the support of a British guarantee seem less risky; so, too, did Germany's relative weakness. The failure, however, to urge such commitment after the creation of the Axis probably owed more to fear than to disaffection or ideological antipathy. Commitment to Czechoslovakia too, as we shall see, fell off markedly during 1936–37 and, with precipitancy, after March 1938.

A sigh of relief was emitted by the right-wing weeklies when the *Anschluss* finally came to pass; an echo of it was to be heard in some Liberal journals as well. It could have been worse, some seemed to be saying – Austria could have offered armed resistance, Czechoslovakia or France might have intervened.

The German invasion, however, found few outright defenders in the weeklies. Garvin, an exception, laid the blame squarely at Schuschnigg's feet: the Nazi invasion had issued from 'a headlong precipitancy of challenge on the part of the Viennese regime'. But he found the *Anschluss* distinctly unsettling. The moral for the British people, Garvin declared, was that 'while utterly refusing to be involved in Europe this time, [Britain] should extend [her] rearmament without delay'. Forecast and justification merged in Garvin's assertion that the separation of the Germans of Germany, Austria and Bohemia ran 'against nature, history, geography and economics', and could not last.[13] Approval of the German *coup* was also implicit in his assurance that the *Anschluss* removed 'an obstacle to European settlement'.[14] That Czech security was now fatally undermined left Garvin unconcerned; Czechoslovakia, too, was in the nature of an 'obstacle to European peace'. Two months passed before Garvin allowed himself an oblique condemnation of the *Anschluss* in the pages of the *Observer*:

> The methods by which the *Anschluss* was achieved, and some of the utterances before it, suggested to the general world a spirit violent and incalculable that might prove on other occasions sudden and lawless in the seizure of opportunity.[15]

The *Tablet*, too, refrained from condemning the *Anschluss*. Rather, it noted that 'the extent of the welcome accorded to Hitler in his first return to the land of his birth has been an impressive spectacle'.[16] Woodruff discovered grounds for dissatisfaction insofar as 'the ruthless German action has played directly into the hands of the Left-wing elements in France and Britain'.[17] Certainly, Hitler's methods were deplored; Germany would have done better to implement the *Anschluss* gradually and imperceptibly.

Initially the *Sunday Times* reacted to the *Anschluss* with surprise and anger; Sidebotham called it 'a black day for Europe', and, for himself, 'a deep and bitter disappointment'. It was, he declared, the first instance, save for Spain, of a German assault on the independence of another State. Unlike Garvin, Sidebotham refused to regard Schuschnigg's threatened plebescite as justification for the invasion. He wrote:

> So long as Germany's policy with her neighbours was determined
> by what was right and just, Germany could count on a great
> deal of sympathy in this country. But when the criterion is ...
> [only] 'what have I the power to do?', the whole atmosphere is
> tainted.[18]

A week later, however, Sidebotham retreated to his customary position.
He condemned the method of the *Anschluss* while approving of its
substance and stressing its inevitability; castigated Churchill as a 'peace
defeatist'; totally rejected all talk of a commitment to Czechoslovakia;
and abjured alliance with France or obligations arising from France's
eastern entanglements. Above all, Sidebotham feared the eruption of
a new world war which, consisting mainly of mutual air raids, would
plunge Britain into 'deepest hell'.[19] Hadley, too, preferred to condemn
the method rather than the substance of the *Anschluss*.[20] Both hoped that
progress towards European appeasement would continue and that Hitler
would display 'humanity' towards his opponents and towards the Jews in
Austria. Like the *Observer*, the *Sunday Times* called for an increase of
Britain's anti-aircraft defences.[21]

The *Saturday Review*, similarly, reacted to the *Anschluss* with a call for
greater efforts of rearmament. It urged also that Britain contract alliances
with France and Italy. If Hitler, who was apparently incorrigible, had
to be fought, it were better that Britain first secure her Mediterranean
flank. The journal persisted, however, in rejecting all commitments
in eastern Europe. Referring to Czechoslovakia, the *Saturday Review*
declared that 'too early a statement of our intentions might well be
dangerous'.[22] *Truth*, too, reiterated the call for rearmament: 'Every
National consideration – and every private consideration, too – must
yield to rearmament', it stated.[23] It condemned the *Anschluss* on more
grounds than those of method but, confusedly, offered justifications for
Hitler's action. Austria, stated *Truth*, had been 'artificially separated from
Germany'; 'the *status quo* is far from satisfactory and peace depends upon
its rectification.'[24]

The left-wing and Liberal weeklies were unanimous in their verdict
on the *Anschluss*: it was an unjustifiable act of naked aggression. *The
Economist*, the *New Statesman*, *Time & Tide* and *Tribune* saw it as but
a prelude to further aggression by Germany in eastern Europe. The
Spectator demurred, venturing that perhaps Hitler would be satisfied
with the incorporation of his native land. In any case, argued Wilson
Harris, Hitler's intentions towards Czechoslovakia were certainly 'of
a different order from his designs on Austria'.[25] As a result of the

Anschluss, the *New Statesman* called for British participation in a 'grand alliance'. *The Economist* and *Tribune* reiterated their previous call to the same effect. *The Economist*, alone of the Liberal and left-wing weeklies, was moved by the *Anschluss* to press for greater British rearmament.

In retrospect the strangest thing about the weeklies' reaction to the *Anschluss* was the speed with which Austria and its population were written off and forgotten. Only *Tribune* made a point of urging British non-recognition of Austria's annexation by Germany. It was as if men, despite their professions, had for years resigned themselves to the elimination of Austria; a similar reaction, if even more muted, was to characterise the Italian conquest of Albania a year later. Following Abyssinia, States, apparently, had become as perishable and disposable as consumer goods.

The weeklies immediately deemed the annexation irreversible; the possibility of achieving a German withdrawal, through diplomatic pressure or military threat, was not even mooted. Political discussion in the wake of the *Anschluss* immediately focused on Czechoslovakia; 'What next?' rather than 'What of Austria?' typified the approach. And much of it was of the order of 'one down and one to go'. Without exception, the journals viewed Czechoslovakia as next on the German 'list'. Many contemporaries, unlike some later historians, perceived that German foreign policy ran to an order if not to an immutable timetable and plan; after the Nazi occupation of Prague, a similar absorption with the fate of Poland was to characterise the weeklies.

CZECHOSLOVAKIA AND 'MUNICH'

The weeklies devoted scant attention to Czechoslovakia and the Sudeten problem before 1937. Neither was, nor was seen to be, a burning issue. Sudeten rights (and Czech 'wrongs', for that matter) were rarely mentioned. Rather, Czechoslovakia was universally regarded in Britain as the only enlightened and meritorious Succession State, her statesmen, Masaryk and Beneš, as paragons of civilised wisdom and democratic virtue. Even *Truth*, Conservative, revisionist and pro-appeasement, saluted Czechoslovakia, on Masaryk's re-election to the Presidency in 1934, as 'the sole successful experiment in liberal democracy that has emerged from the post-War settlement'.[26] Similar sentiments were expressed in the *Observer*, the minorities problem notwithstanding.[27] As late as April 1937 the *Sunday Times* published a major article in support of Beneš' refusal to grant autonomy to the Sudeten Germans.[28]

Liberal and left-wing views of the Czech Republic were still more enthusiastic. In 1937 *Time & Tide* described Czechoslovakia, which had done 'all that is reasonably possible' to placate its Sudeten minority, as 'highly civilised and truly democratic'.[29] *The Economist* mixed enthusiasm with political firmness: 'Once again', it stated in February 1937, 'Czechoslovakia has proved itself to be, as she claims to be, a country with a thoroughly western standard of enlightenment . . . [and] entitled to receive our covenanted support if . . . she were eventually attacked.'[30] The Sudetenland, thought Graham Hutton, had rightly been given to Czechoslovakia in 1919 because of 'economic . . . and military necessity'.[31]

As with Austria, erosion set in with respect to Czechoslovakia during 1936–37. In the *New Statesman*, Kingsley Martin in July 1936 noted the lack of 'real will to check Hitler' in Britain. The National Government, he assured his readers, would never fight for Czechoslovakia. But, then, neither would he. He argued: 'Even if the Covenant were still operative [when Czechoslovakia was attacked], it does not ask us to 'fight' in central Europe, but obliges us not to remain neutral [and] to co-operate, according to the express definition of our obligations, with those who are fighting, by imposing a financial and trade embargo on the aggressor.'[32] *Time & Tide* discovered a similar formula in mid-1937. 'We do not believe', declared Lady Rhondda, 'that Britain would have her people behind her if, in the event of German meddling in Czechoslovakia, she adventured on war on behalf of that unhappy country. Nor do we ourselves believe that she would be justified in doing so', whatever the merits of the Czech case. 'We hold', concluded the journal, 'that Britain would be fully justified in maintaining an attitude of benevolent neutrality towards the Czechs, or any other nation attacked, in offering them diplomatic and possibly material support.'[33]

By the autumn of 1937, the *Spectator* too recognised the imminence of a Czech crisis. Czechoslovakia, declared Wilson Harris, was 'the single effective obstacle' on Germany's path of expansion eastwards; its existence was 'irreconcilable with the achievement of Germany's *Drang nach Osten*'; and the Sudeten minority represented 'the spearhead' of that drive. He agreed that the Sudeten Germans were better treated than any other eastern European minority and that the cantonisation of Czechoslovakia was 'impracticable'. But, Wilson Harris concluded, 'if Berlin is seeking to make capital of the grievances of the *Sudeten-Deutsch*, that is a double reason why Prague should see that all genuine grievances disappear'.[34] Among the weeklies, only *The Economist* and *Tribune* continued, through 1937, to call for a British commitment to Czech territorial integrity.

Having adopted full-fledged appeasement, Garvin, by the end of

1936, wrote off Czechoslovakia as the most artificial State in Europe, 'a diplomatic creation with no sufficient national basis either in geography or race'. And this was compounded by the existence of the Czech-Russian Pact, 'the very plague-carrier of European politics'.[35] Between March 1936 and March 1939 there was, in fact, no more distinguished proponent in Britain of the cause of German racial unification than the *Observer*'s editor. In May 1937, lumping together Austria and Czechoslovakia, he argued: 'For a thousand years both these countries have had a special historic connection with the main body of the German race ... and there is bound to be again some kind of close and lasting association.'[36] The *Saturday Review*, the *Tablet* and the *Sunday Times* all abjured a British commitment or involvement in eastern Europe; the configuration of frontiers and the relative weight of powers east of the Rhine moved them not at all.

Of the Conservative journals, *Truth* alone during 1936–37 remained peculiarly divided over the problem of Czechoslovakia; a sincere admiration for Czech accomplishments vied with a desire to conciliate Germany, at almost any cost. On the one hand the journal declared: 'The question has been asked in certain quarters, not entirely disinterested, whether Czechoslovakia is not an artificial conglomeration of races, unfit to be preserved at all.' Actually, it was 'the most homogeneous' of the Succession States and 'the surest guarantee against German expansion to the South'.[37] On the other hand, *Truth* stated: 'So long as the Czechs continue to hold Eger and Pressburg, the Lithuanians Memel, and the Rumanians Transylvania, there is a distinct possibility not only that there will be German aggression in Europe but that Englishmen will think that aggression justified.'[38]

The *Anschluss* pushed Czechoslovakia to the top of the international agenda and inaugurated the 'Czech crisis'. What was Britain to do? Between March and September 1938 the debate in the weeklies, as in Whitehall, turned upon the desirability of extending a guarantee to Czechoslovakia and, taken further, of participation in the Franco-Russian–Czech alliance system. There was little argument about immediate German intentions; Hitler aimed to 'neutralise' Czechoslovakia and to 'remedy' the plight of the Sudeten minority. Many, not only on the Left, believed that the Nazis desired the dismemberment and dissolution of the Republic: assuaging Sudeten grievances through 'home rule' or cession would effectively emasculate Czechoslovakia. Granting one minority autonomy (or more) would encourage Hungarians and Poles to demand the same. Disintegration was clearly on the cards. Political 'neutralisation' implied the same result; without her

French and Russian alliances, Czechoslovakia, despite her allegedly efficient army, was a nation at the mercy of voracious neighbours.

To those who urged a British guarantee before September 1938, the Sudeten problem, in a profound sense, was an irrelevance: the problem of Europe was Nazi aggressiveness and expansionism, not this or that bit of territory, German-speaking or otherwise. Besides, Czechoslovakia was a mainstay of the French security system; its dismemberment or dissolution would undermine French security and, by extension, Britain's. In a narrower sense, the Sudetenland was relevant. The guarantee was seen by its promoters as the means whereby Britain would enable Czechoslovakia to extract tolerable terms from Germany. With a British guarantee added to French and Russian commitments, the Czechs could successfully oppose cession of or disruptive 'home rule' for the Sudetenland and preserve intact their territorial integrity and defences. Such a guarantee, its proponents hoped and believed, would deter Germany from attack and peace would be secured. A British guarantee would represent *de facto* adherence to the Franco-Russian alliance. The 'united front' or 'grand alliance' thus constituted would also serve to 'contain' Germany elsewhere should Hitler shift his attention to other corners of Europe.

Supporters of appeasement vehemently opposed a guarantee to Czechoslovakia. They repudiated the notion that Britain had any interests east of the Rhine compelling involvement to the point of war. Rather, they argued that the extension of German political influence in eastern Europe was natural and inevitable if not laudable. Some, such as Wilson Harris of the *Spectator*, genuinely admired Czechoslovakia but failed to translate such sympathy into political commitment. Others, with varying degrees of sincerity, denied the merits of Czech democracy or culture. Rather, they pointed repeatedly to the evils of the 'non-nation-State', to Czech discrimination against minorities and to legitimate Sudeten grievances. Underlying all was the assumption that Hitler's intentions were irrevocable and that if Czechoslovakia did not submit, war would ensue. A British guarantee would compel participation in that war. In addition, many supporters of Government policy genuinely detested Communism and refused to contemplate war in alliance with Soviet Russia or to support a state (Czechoslovakia) seen to be in some manner 'infected' by the Soviet malaise.

Many proponents of appeasement in 1938 argued that once Sudeten claims were met, Hitler would cease to pursue a policy of expansion and would allow the newly-constituted Czechoslovakia an independent existence. That they were deluded is now obvious. Some, as will be shown, were also insincere. During and after Munich, all of them opposed a British guarantee to 'rump' Czechoslovakia despite professions of sympathy for that state and despite alleged belief in the sincerity of Hitler's pledges. Before Munich no proponent or opponent of appeasement argued that Czechoslovakia should be sacrificed to gain time for Britain to rearm in order to confront Germany at a later date; this was a post-Munich justification of what came to be seen as a shameful and impolitic settlement. Perhaps Garvin was an exception, but if his support of Munich was so grounded, it was never made explicit in the pages of the *Observer*. On the contrary, before Munich only *The Economist* and *Tribune* bothered to make the necessary calculations of relative strengths. They argued that a world war fought after the 'neutralisation' and dismemberment of Czechoslovakia would be more difficult to win than one fought before. Usually, and especially during September, advocates of a Sudeten cession concluded their defence by asserting that Britain was simply unprepared materially (especially in the air) for war against Germany. The loss of Czech fortifications, armament works, divisions, or the will to resist was rarely considered in terms of the effect on Britain's military position.

The New Statesman

The *New Statesman* between March and September 1938 encapsulated the dilemma posed by Czechoslovakia. The journal, as it were, embodied Britain's conscience, Britain's fears and Britain's ultimate failure. Kingsley Martin was 'deeply emotionally involved in the Czech crisis'. His sympathy and admiration for the Republic and his knowledge of its problems dated from a visit to Prague in 1935. Frontier revision, he learned then and was to acknowledge many years later, 'would not in reality solve anything, since Hitler was interested not in the Sudetens, but in destroying the Republic'.[39] This observation, however, was to find little echo in the *New Statesman* in 1938. Irresolute incoherence, firmly rooted in fear, was to characterise Kingsley Martin's public and private avowals concerning Czechoslovakia up to the signing of the Munich agreement.

The *Anschluss*, Kingsley Martin told Dalton, 'had produced . . . a mass panic. People [in Britain] were terrified by the exhibition of combined brutality and efficiency.'[40] Shock and terror pervaded the *New Statesman*'s pages. In oblique justification, the journal called the German invasion of Austria 'a sequel to the stupid arrangements made by the victors in 1919'. But this was already spilt milk: Czechoslovakia was now the problem. Britain, no doubt, should support France and Russia in defence of the Republic. But could she? The answer proffered was an ambiguous 'no'. The *New Statesman* argued:

130

What is in the way of a prompt and unambiguous declaration of British policy? Fear? Insular egoism? Lack of imagination which cannot picture the consequences of a Nazi-Napoleonic era? All these things play a part, but once more conscience makes cowards of us. The Czech chapter of the war settlement was no more perfect, to use mild words, than the rest. Was it defensible to include 3½ million Germans in this Slav State? It was not necessary.

Britain should make 'a public promise' to support France and Czechoslovakia. But what Czechoslovakia? On this point the journal was relatively clear:

> London, Paris, Moscow and Prague should at once converse to discover the best way of removing [the Sudeten] blot on the character of the Czech Republic. Should it be by cession – a clean but drastic cure; or by cantonal autonomy, a scheme the Czechs have rejected? ... we do not dogmatise over details [!] It is enough to say that the Czechs, well-meaning, tolerant and liberal to minorities though they have generally proved themselves to be, would be wiser at once to rid themselves of the terrible menace of disgruntled and now excited Germans within their frontiers. Till that is done, or until enough has been done to satisfy reasonable neutrals, some element of hesitation will always qualify British support for this threatened democracy.[41]

To underline its preference for a solution involving cession, the *New Statesman* on 26 March 1938 published articles by Keynes and C.E.M. Joad. Keynes called upon Germans and Czechs to reach 'a reasonable solution' to the Sudeten problem, 'even if this involves a rectification of the Bohemian frontier. Racial frontiers are safer and better to-day than geo-physical frontiers.'[42] More candidly, Joad declared: 'We should urge the Czechs to cede the German-speaking part of their territory to Hitler without more ado ... To withstand Hitler now is to increase the risks of war.'[43] The indefensibility of a Czechoslovakia shorn of its Sudeten fringes was casually or deliberately ignored; so too were the prospective fate of such a 'rump' State and the various appetites of Polish and Hungarian irredentists, Slovak separatists and German militarists.

The state of Kingsley Martin's mind and the real motor of his political thinking at the time is revealed in a diary entry of Hugh Dalton's. Kingsley Martin

> said that Chamberlain had at least got a coherent foreign policy, whether right or wrong. He took the view that this country was

so weak in arms, and London so indefensible, and France so weak, that we could not afford to antagonise in any degree a German–Italian combination . . . [Kingsley Martin] said that he . . . felt that things had gone so far that to plan armed resistance to the dictators was now useless. If there was a war, we should lose it. We should therefore seek for the most peaceful means of letting them gradually get what they wanted. But he feared that this would not be the view taken either by the British imperialists, when aroused, or by the Left Book Club and similar groups which were bent on war against Fascism.[44]

Thus the *New Statesman*'s prompt and early abandonment of Czechoslovakia following the *Anschluss* becomes intelligible; the duplicity of arguing Treaty revision as a dictate of conscience rather than of fear while at the same time purporting to uphold the concept of collective security becomes equally apparent.

The Czech crisis gathered intensity through the summer of 1938; the end of August and September witnessed its culmination. The *New Statesman* boldly entered the fray on 27 August with a statement urging cession of the Sudetenland. 'The question of frontier revision', declared Kingsley Martin, 'difficult though it is, should at once be tackled. The strategical value of the Bohemian frontier should not be made the occasion of a world war. We should not guarantee the *status quo*.'[45] The question, however, was not Hitler's interest in the alleged plight of the Sudeten minority but Hitler's intention of destroying Czechoslovakia *in toto*, as Kingsley Martin acknowledged shortly afterwards. Hitler aspires 'not only to free all German peoples, but to regain European paramountcy. We should view the Czech crisis in this perspective', he wrote on 17 September.[46]

Several *New Statesman* staff members disapproved of the editor's line.[47] Both Gedye, the Geneva correspondent, and Alexander Werth, the Paris correspondent, protested. Werth chided Kingsley Martin: 'To let Germany get away with Czechoslovakia is to hand over the whole of Europe to Fascism.'[48] Perhaps to stiffen the editor, Werth assured him that France would fight and, together with Britain, win. But protests availed little. Kingsley Martin, absorbed by fearful imaginings, was unrepentant and immovable. To Gedye he replied:

The comment [of 27 August] in the form made may have been a mistake [but] I have always held . . . that the right solution was for the Czechs to redraw the frontier in certain places . . . I know the great difficulties, psychological, strategical (which, I believe, much exaggerated now [!]), economic and racial that are involved. I still hold . . . that Czechoslovakia should have cut the ground from under Germany's feet by destroying the fortifications in some places and rebuilding them in the less good strategic ground, thus excluding some of the most difficult areas . . . The problem of the world is to defeat Fascism without general war. If we get general war the experts, who are, of course, always wrong, think it would probably be an affair of ten years or so, and that neither the Czechs nor ourselves nor anyone else much would be left. To shrink from this . . . does not seem to me in the circumstances cowardice . . . In view of the alternative any postponement is to be welcomed . . . I am deeply sorry if I have given an impression of cowardice at a critical moment.[49]

Kingsley Martin's weakness over Czechoslovakia was reinforced by a stream of personal letters from Keynes. Keynes argued that Britain should attempt to 'bluff' Hitler; but 'if the bluff is called, back out'.[50] He preferred the 'cleaner and *safer* remedy' of outright cession to plebiscites and cantonisation.[51] Aylmer Vallance, too, confirmed the editor's worst fears.[52] Perhaps it was to him that Kingsley Martin alluded when he wrote to Keynes on 13 September: 'I heard to-day from an excellent source that the strategic and military position is regarded as almost desperate . . . I gather that the Government thinks . . . that the German air fleet can accomplish to a large extent a blockade of England almost at once, and that the French air position is appallingly bad.'[53] This appreciation was given expression in the pages of the *New Statesman* several days later. In an article on air raid precautions, Kingsley Martin argued that the method of 'counter bombing' was no solution to the problem of Britain's vulnerability. The Spanish war experience had demonstrated 'that even where there is reasonable protection, 500 aeroplanes each dropping two tons of bombs would, on average, kill 2,000 people' each day – and Britain was bereft of shelters or trenches.[54]

Such beliefs could have no issue other than capitulation. Yet Kingsley Martin was able to criticise the infirmity of others though it was based on foundations akin to his own. 'I fear', he wrote to Keynes on 19 September, 'that the "sell-out" is going to be complete . . . I am inclined to think that the result now is worse than a world war.'[55] On 17 September he had praised Chamberlain for displaying 'unusual courage' and for the 'departure from ineffectual old-style diplomacy'; apparently he had hoped that the Prime Minister would pull off the miracle of saving Czechoslovakia, British honour and the peace.[56] Yet a week later he turned stridently critical, condemning the Anglo-French proposals – the essence of which the *New Statesman,* in advance of its peers and the Government, had been advocating since March – as 'the murder of a nation' and a 'surrender to Hitler'. Talk of guaranteeing a rump Czechoslovakia he condemned as 'a final mockery', 'as if the viper and the scorpion were to guarantee the well-being of the shorn rabbit'. In a crowning hypocrisy, Kingsley Martin asserted 'that fear of war is no sufficient explanation for the terrible part played by [the British and French] Governments'; Chamberlain had returned to Britain with a peace 'that is without honour or security'. Though nothing was yet sealed, the *New Statesman* declared that it was 'too late to save Czech integrity'; hence it refrained from calling for a reversal of posture and for a belated assertion of firmness towards Hitler.[57]

Yet a few days later, the *New Statesman* welcomed the Munich settlement. On 1 October the journal stated: 'Everyone must share in a feeling of immense relief that war ... has been at least postponed and very possibly averted.' To be sure, the terms of the agreement were lamentable, indeed humiliating; but once signed and sealed, there was no danger in berating them. The only immediate point of hazard was the question of the guarantee to rump Czechoslovakia. The *New Statesman* chose to sidestep the problem by arguing that 'there is no frontier that can be guaranteed'. Otherwise, the journal endorsed the Labour Party call for a new international conference to rectify the remaining wrongs of Versailles, re-distribute colonies and legislate for the protection of minorities.[58] Kingsley Martin persisted in condemning rearmament; he castigated those whose 'only notion of security is to redouble our air force'.[59]

Some three weeks after Munich, Hugh Dalton, Leonard Woolf, Douglas Jay (formerly of *The Economist*), Ivor Thomas, Ivan Black, and Kingsley Martin and R.H.S. Crossman of the *New Statesman* discussed the new international situation. Crossman, recorded Dalton, argued against Anglo-French (and Anglo-Russian) staff talks for fear that these might provoke a German pre-emptive strike. The blow of Munich, and perhaps the proximity of the fear-stricken Kingsley Martin, had undermined his previous anti-appeasing convictions.[60] As before Munich, the *New Statesman*'s editor was plagued by a general fear of Germany and a particular fear of air attack. Dalton recorded that Kingsley Martin 'fears [that] firm stands in future may be to fight a war. [He believes that] many of the facts are very bad, e.g. as to the Air Force. German fighters are 100mph faster than ours ... we cannot stand up to Germany ... Germany now is [militarily] equal to a nation of 140 millions'. Rather than advocating a military alliance, Kingsley Martin advised that Britain link up 'economically' with the U.S. and the Soviet Union in order 'to preserve a democratic Byzantium in the West'.[61]

134

The Spectator

Some six weeks after Munich Wilson Harris, editor of the *Spectator*, declared at Chatham House: 'Given the situation at Munich, Neville Chamberlain could have taken no course except the one he had taken.'[62] Years later he elaborated in his autobiography: 'Having regard to both our own and France's glaring unpreparedness, I held and have not ceased to hold, that even the most desperate attempt to save the peace was worthwhile.'[63]

Wilson Harris's acquiescence in German designs upon Czechoslovakia following the *Anschluss* was less precipitate than Kingsley Martin's. In March 1938 he vaguely supported a British commitment to Czechoslovakia; in April, he rejected Sudeten demands for autonomy in view of what he believed to be Germany's real aim, the outright absorption of the Sudetenland.[64] Nor, at the start of September, did he evade what he believed to be the main issue. He wrote that only 'nominally' was 'the degree of autonomy to be conceded to the Sudeten Germans' the issue; 'actually, it is whether the next step in German expansion is to be taken . . . at Czechoslovakia's expense'. He dismissed Sudeten allegations as well: 'The Sudeten Germans are not downtrodden.'[65]

In fact, the *Spectator* 'held out' until 16 September, a notable achievement (given its well-established support of appeasement); this probably owed much to the editor's admiration for Czechoslovakia. Wilson Harris wrote:

> Let Germany have [the Sudetenland] and she has the whole of the elaborate fortifications . . . ; she has the Skoda munitions works at Pilsen . . . ; in other words, she has what would be left of Czechoslovakia at her mercy. That is why a plebiscite . . . would be suicide for Czechoslovakia.[66]

But, in the same issue, the *Spectator* revealed the seed of its anxiety and eventual reversal. Goronwy Rees, the assistant editor, wrote:

> This country is still utterly unprepared for the greatest danger modern war implies – that of murderous attacks from the air, delivered with such efficacy as to break the morale of the population and destroy the great cities and those who live in them.[67]

Implicit, perhaps, was the writer's desire that Britain should arm. But, in the circumstances, the more obvious and immediate message was that Britain simply could not engage in war for the present.

With the publication of the Anglo-French proposals the *Spectator*'s divergence from and resistance to the course of British policy disappeared.

135

'In the face of the demoralisation the past few days have wrought', wrote Wilson Harris on 23 September, Churchill's suggestion that a stand could yet be made 'may well be questioned'.[68] Wilson Harris was obviously and deeply angry at the Anglo-French collapse following Berchtesgaden. He wrote:

> Britain, France and Russia are not prepared to go to war in resistance to Germany's resolute, unflagging, undiverging eastward march. And so it comes that Dr Beneš received his ultimatum not from Herr Hitler ... but from Mr Chamberlain and M. Daladier – acting under the law of agency.

It all represented 'a terrible victory for Herr Hitler'.[69] But, and this was the crucial point, Wilson Harris suggested no alternative; nor did he broach the practicality of offering resistance to Hitler.

Henceforward, the *Spectator* argued that the avoidance of war was worth the price paid:

> The [Anglo-French] proposals ... have been criticised in these columns ... as consistent neither with reason nor with justice. That criticism stands, but it must be subordinated to the larger considerations which the Prime Minister so impressively laid before the House of Commons.[70]

In effect, Wilson Harris argued that avoidance, and perhaps even postponement, of war constituted the highest reason and the highest justice; at the forefront of his mind was the spectacle of British unpreparedness and the prospect of air attack. As he put it a week later:

> And though war may only be postponed, and that not for long, and will, if it comes, be engaged in by this country in conditions much less favourable than existed ten days ago, yet the fact remains that while there is no war there is always the chance of preserving peace.[71]

(It is worth noting that years later Wilson Harris argued that the year 'gained' at Munich 'was of more value to the defence than to the attack'.[72]) Also on the 'credit' side, the *Spectator* chalked up the 'fact' that the Munich settlement approximated, in its terms, the Anglo-French proposals rather than Hitler's Godesberg 'Diktat'.

In the wake of Munich, the *Spectator* partly 'turned': it urged massive rearmament,[73] the conclusion of an Anglo-French military alliance and 'a definite association' with Russia, the United States, Scandinavia and the Low Countries. But the journal still entertained hopes, however diminished, of achieving a settlement with Hitler by way of

136

appeasement.[74] It completely rejected appeasement only in the wake of the German occupation of Prague.

The Economist

Since the close of 1936 *The Economist* had been urging a British commitment to Czech territorial integrity. On the eve of the *Anschluss* the journal hailed the Republic as 'the bastion of Europe', a State the West could not afford to sacrifice.[75] Through the spring and summer of 1938 *The Economist*, while willing to contemplate Czech concessions to Sudeten Germans, flatly rejected solutions based on autonomy, cantonisation or cession.[76] The journal's position was forthrightly put on 19 March: the western democracies must 'compel Herr Hitler to give Czechoslovakia not intolerable terms ... And, having satisfied ourselves and the world that justice is being done, we ought then to say to Herr Hitler: "Hands off! Resort to force at your peril. We draw the line here!"'[77]

The Economist was bewildered and angered by the succession of Nazi and British pressures which ultimately elicited Beneš's Fourth Plan (offering the Sudeten Germans cantonal autonomy). That plan, in the journal's view, 'came as close to the Sudeten demands as is possible without disrupting the Czechoslovak State'; it represented the Czech 'limit of safety'. It was time, thought *The Economist* on 10 September, that Britain start applying pressure on Germany; 'after all, [Britain was] mediating, not arranging the terms of Czech surrender'. But the journal feared the worst: 'We cannot ask [the Czechs] to believe that their national existence is a reasonable price to pay for a few weeks of British security.' Britain, it urged, 'must bindingly guarantee the new [Fourth Plan] status of Czechoslovakia'.[78]

The Economist greeted the flight to Berchtesgaden with gratitude and apprehension; gratitude for the prolongation of the peace, and apprehension in view of the terms which might emerge. 'Canossa' was mentioned: 'If the peace of Berchtesgaden turns out to be the rewarding of the aggressor in return for his mere promise to be good for a while, then we have merely gone a step further towards our own doom.'[79]

With the publication of the Anglo-French proposals, *The Economist's* disillusionment was swift and complete; expediency, not justice, was their origin. The mooted guarantee to the rump State, declared the journal, was worthless without Russian participation. It advised that if Germany offered no concrete proofs of its intention to desist from aggression, Britain should 'stand firm':

> The alternative to giving way is, of course, to run the grave risk of immediate war. But if the risk of immediate war is one horn of our

terrible dilemma, the virtual certainty of ultimate war is the other. And in war next year, or the year after, we shall be weaker than we are today, however much we rearm ... In a war today, Germany would have to fight on two fronts.[80]

Given Layton's penchant for balanced argument, here indeed was resolute language; nothing as forceful appeared in any journal before March 1939.

Berchtesgaden and the Anglo-French proposals appeared to have saved the peace; however unjust the portion meted out to the Czechs, Armageddon had been averted. Godesberg once again conjured up the spectre of annihilation, even among the most truculent exponents of collective security. Hence, the greatness of the relief felt at the result of the Munich conference. Even *The Economist* uttered 'a prayer of thanksgiving' and accorded Chamberlain 'the lion's share of the credit' for averting world war.[81]

In the weeks that followed, defenders of the Munich settlement attempted to play up the differences between its terms and those presented by Hitler at Godesberg. *The Economist*, on the contrary, emphasized their similarity: 'Broadly speaking the [Godesberg] ultimatum has been conceded in full', it stated on 15 October.[82] Certainly, war had been averted but 'the peace has been purchased at the price of the overwhelming defeat of ... international principles', not to mention Czech territory and independence. Peace, concluded *The Economist* bleakly, might hold up for longer than the six months predicted by Harold Nicolson; but it was not to be 'peace in our time'.[83]

Time & Tide

Soon after the *Anschluss Time & Tide* clarified what it believed to be Hitler's immediate aims – to exploit the Sudeten problem in order to incorporate the Sudetenland in the Reich and to bring about the dissolution of Czechoslovakia.[84] But, despite its conviction that the fall of Czechoslovakia and of the rest of eastern Europe would vastly weaken the position of the western democracies, *Time & Tide* refused to endorse a British commitment: 'Further commitments by this country might precipitate the war they would be meant to avert', declared Lady Rhondda.[85] As pressure on the Republic mounted, the journal shifted a little and supported a 'friendly political and commercial association' between Britain and the states of the Little Entente.[86]

At the start of September *Time & Tide* put the issue clearly: Hitler's onslaught against Czechoslovakia aimed at the extinction of the Republic's independence, putting 'the ultimate independence of Great Britain and

France ... in question'. A Sudeten cession would increase, not lessen, the chance of war, and would certainly give Germany vastly better starting conditions should it erupt.[87] On 17 September *Time & Tide* was still firm:

> The possibility of this country being involved in war [soon] ... is so terrible a thing to contemplate that it is not altogether surprising that there should be some who ... are ready to allow Herr Hitler to play such tricks with the map of Europe ... But the survival of Czechoslovakia is vital ... to England ... and there are risks too grave to be taken even for the sake of securing a few months more of fear-haunted twilight.

The journal was contemptuous and condemnatory towards both *The Times* and the *New Statesman* for suggesting a Sudeten cession.[88]

Chamberlain's acceptance of 'self-determination' at Berchtesgaden left *Time & Tide* mortified; history might well judge it 'a disaster for England'.[89] The journal roundly condemned the Anglo-French capitulation:

> The French and British Governments have had to choose between the possibility of a terrible war and the certainty of a shameful peace. They have chosen the latter. Even if they were right, even if by preserving the peace they were not inviting an even more terrible war, they might have shown a little more sense of dignity, and some consideration for the friendly Power they have now condemned to extinction.[90]

It was, above all, the humiliation and indignity of it all which affected Viscountess Rhondda; this was not the behaviour of the World Power she had known in her childhood. The journal went on to argue, perhaps with more than a touch of self-condemnation, that the western democracies might have avoided both war and ignominy by showing 'a more menacing attitude' before the climax of the crisis in September. It predicted: 'For a time there will be peace in Europe – a terrible and shameful peace'; then Hitler would turn upon Britain and France.[91] The question, therefore, was between 'war now and war not yet', for Hitler was bent on world domination.[92]

Like everyone else, *Time & Tide* rejoiced at 'the immeasurable blessing' afforded by the Munich settlement's deferment of war. Lady Rhondda later recalled that while writing her leader of 1 October on Munich, 'nine-tenths' of her 'mind and heart were stricken with not only shame but the certainty of ultimate disaster'; but 'one tenth was filled with a blessed feeling of relief: There will be no bombs tonight ...'.[93] The settlement, concluded *Time & Tide*, was 'terrible ... by whatever yardstick we measure it – by honour, by security, by prestige'; that Britain would come to 'wholly regret' it was more than implied if less than definitively stated. Nor, asserted the journal, were the terms of Munich any better than those presented by Hitler at Godesberg. It called for massive rearmament and economic mobilisation as well as for the replacement of the country's political leadership.[94] Throughout the Czech crisis, however, *Time & Tide*'s moral outrage and idealistic outpourings far outdistanced its willingness to espouse firm, concrete commitments and policy.

Tribune

Tribune's treatment of the Czech crisis was persistently marred – in terms of its professed political aims – by a refusal to countenance British rearmament or conscription; marred, as well, by constant declarations that 'British labour' would never fight under Chamberlain in an 'imperialist war'. Through 1937 and until August 1938 the journal urged the Government to guarantee Czechoslovakia. Such a guarantee, it argued, would deter Hitler from aggression and avert world war.[95] Similarly, it continued to press for a 'united front' with France and Russia.

By the start of September 1938, however, *Tribune* began to sound a hesitant, ambiguous note; the crunch had been reached. While castigating Chamberlain's policy, the journal abruptly ceased to call for a commitment to Czechoslovakia. Instead, it declared:

> British Labour in this crisis must keep its head. There must be no talk of national unity under Chamberlain's banner ... Moreover, the fight in which Labour is interested is not the immediate diplomatic clash between Berlin and Whitehall [!] It is concerned rather with the building of a genuine peace front against the Fascist international ... British Labour should refuse to co-operate in the arms speed-up, should oppose any future war plans of the Government so long as it refuses to give arms ... to the Spanish Government.[96]

Under the circumstances, such a declaration – like a similar one made in the *New Statesman* in March – meant the abandonment of Czechoslovakia; the two journals differed only in that *Tribune* had consistently advocated arms for Spain while the *New Statesman* had not.

Nonetheless, *Tribune* continued through September and October to criticise Chamberlain's 'sell-out' at Berchtesgaden and Munich, arguing that war postponed was not war averted, and that national dishonour and still greater weakness were the outcome. But, positively, the journal propounded nothing save empty slogans about the need to 'fight fascism'.

On 30 September *Tribune* clarified its position on the ultimate issue when it declared: '*Tribune*, like every other newspaper in the world, greets the postponement of war with heartfelt relief.'[97] Unlike *The Economist* and, to a degree, *Time & Tide*, *Tribune* never advanced the calculation that war now was preferable to war later, nor urged that a stand be made. With most others, abhorrence of war and fear of devastation led to effective acquiescence in Czechoslovakia's dismemberment.

For Liberals and the Left, the Czech crisis and Munich presented no moral dilemma; their courage rather than their convictions were put to the test. Despite Sudeten grievances – and especially after successive Czech concessions – the issue was generally regarded as clear-cut: the Nazi regime was inherently evil and bent upon territorial aggrandisement; the democratic Czech Republic was the imminent victim; and cession of the Sudetenland to Germany would seal the Republic's fate and greatly enhance the Reich's power for further evil. The test, for Liberals and the Left, involved the lengths to which they were ready to go in seeing their convictions upheld and implemented. As it turned out, the crisis vividly outlined the hiatus between the convictions and the willingness to act upon them.

For the Right the Czech crisis posed a different and fundamental dilemma. Ultimately, it involved first principles, honour and pride. Proponents of appeasement had long discounted the notion that Nazi Germany posed a threat to Britain and the West. For years, they had preached the virtues of non-involvement in eastern Europe and had virtually invited Hitler to do as he wished with the Succession States (so long as violence was not inordinately and embarrassingly employed). German predominance east of the Rhine was viewed as natural and inevitable, rectification of the wrongs of Versailles as just; Britain must not involve itself in world war in order to preserve a *status quo* which denied self-determination to over 3 million Sudeten Germans. Munich should have been the crowning achievement of appeasement, the fullest realisation of expediency and morality.

But it was not, and this was realised during September and October by those who had for years supported that policy. Paradoxically, Munich dealt appeasement a mortal blow. The manner in which that Agreement was reached, rather than its terms, proved decisive in the evolution of British policy and thinking; the revulsion from appeasement in March 1939 owed as much to memories of Munich as to the German occupation of Prague. To most observers it appeared that Hitler had obtained the Sudetenland at Munich by employing subversion and the threat of war and that the statesmen of appeasement, Chamberlain and Daladier, had visibly submitted to fear rather than to the dictates of conscience or long-term expediency. It came to be sensed that the real aims of German foreign policy were clearly reflected in the means by which they were pursued, and that professions of Treaty revision were but a cloak for wider designs which would inevitably impinge on British security. The balance of power was visibly being subverted.

Long-standing proponents of appeasement such as Garvin discovered that the morality of righting Treaty wrongs was as nothing compared to the immorality of the murder of a friendly state. Hitler (and Chamberlain) had successfully manoeuvred Britain and France into a position whereby they, in fact, engineered the dismemberment, indeed suicide, of a democratic Republic. The shame of it, coupled with the palpable humiliation of bowing to fear, issued in a novel 'Never Again' – never again to submit to Nazi *Diktats* of force. With Munich, the heart went out of appeasement. Henceforth, it was understood by right-wing as well as Liberal and left-wing journals that Nazi expansionism, not the need for treaty revision, was the compelling contemporary issue. Britons were no longer able to view appeasement as moral, though there were still many, until 'Prague', who remained attached to it on grounds of expediency. Ironically, Munich marked the end of indifference to the fate of the states of eastern Europe. And through the Runciman Mission, the settlement itself and the mooted guarantee to 'rump' Czechoslovakia, Britain had become inextricably involved.

The Sunday Times

For years, the *Sunday Times* had been preaching the virtues of British indifference to the fate of eastern Europe. It was, argued Sidebotham, the price which must be paid for peace in western Europe and for an Anglo-German accommodation. Until the summer of 1938 the price seemed not exorbitant. However, the Czech crisis increasingly brought home to him the moral, political and strategic consequences of his professions; and Hadley, during the spring and summer, tortuously struggled to cast off the chains of appeasement *vis-à-vis* the Czech problem.

Neither, however, discarded appeasement. In 1944 Hadley published his apologia, *Munich: Before and After*.[98] In it he justified British policy and the Munich settlement on the grounds that 'the claims of peace were paramount',[99] and that Britain and France had been militarily unprepared. Somewhat inconsistently, he also laid the blame for the capitulation at France's feet and argued that had France fulfilled her obligations towards Czechoslovakia, Britain would have unreservedly supported France in the ensuing conflict, whatever the exact order or nature of events.[100] These views are worth recalling in the light of the

Sunday Times's actual avowals during the crisis.

Hadley made his basic position clear in May 1938. Britain, he argued, had a right to pressure Czechoslovakia to grant the Sudeten Germans 'everything not inconsistent with . . . integrity and independence'; they already enjoyed 'more favourable conditions than any other racial minority in central Europe'. Hadley ruled out Sudeten autonomy as it would eventually lead to cession: and 'if the democratic Powers allowed such a change to go through unchallenged, the balance of Europe would be destroyed, perhaps beyond recovery and almost certainly beyond recovery without ultimate war'.[101]

Through the spring and summer Hadley published strongly pro-Czech articles. In one, the French ex-minister P. Etienne Flandin argued that hegemony on the Continent was the issue and not Sudeten grievances.[102] In June, in a full-length, leader-page contribution (in place of Scrutator's), the American journalist Virginia Cowles flatly opposed cession of the border areas to Germany.[103] At the end of July even Sidebotham displayed unwonted understanding for Beneš's reluctance to cede the Sudetenland.[104] However he advised Czechoslovakia to discard her alliances and adopt a Swiss-style neutrality.

In September Sidebotham showed first signs of discontent with his refrain – that Britain had no interest in eastern Europe compelling commitment or war. He now intimated that German domination of eastern Europe might well increase British (and French) insecurity. On 11 September he acknowledged his 'sins' when writing that one *could* argue that nothing between the Rhine and the Dardanelles was of any concern to Britain: 'But these arguments, sound or unsound, are not such as *should* be pressed now, for they are much the same arguments by which the Germans have been persuading themselves that, when it comes to the pinch, we shall do nothing.' He condemned the *Times*'s leader of 7 September – which advocated Sudeten cession – as encouraging Germany 'in extreme courses'. He went so far as to say that the link between peace on the Rhine and peace beside the Danube was 'inexorable'.[105] On the same date Hadley declared that Czechoslovakia, in the Fourth Plan, had reached the limit of concessions 'if the limiting factor be the continuance of their country as a free State'.[106]

But on 18 September, with capitulation in the air after Berchtesgaden, Hadley and Sidebotham swung adroitly behind Chamberlain. Hadley, for his part, ominously noted Britain's anti-aircraft deficiencies; Sidebotham paved the way for an acceptance of the Sudeten cession. Sidebotham contended that if Britain and France were to sacrifice their young on behalf of Beneš's Republic, the two had a right to lay down their conditions, and Czechoslovakia a duty to respect those conditions. The cause of Czechoslovakia's independence commands our greatest respect; but, after all, no nation is truly independent that makes immeasurable calls on its friends for protection against its enemies.[107]

A week later Hadley and Sidebotham came out openly in favour of a Sudeten cession; both, however, admitted that the Nazis' 'whole policy, at home and abroad, is indissolubly wedded to the idea of force as the only law' and that Germany appeared bent upon the total dismemberment of Czechoslovakia.[108]

With the conference over, the *Sunday Times* accorded Chamberlain the highest praise. Mussolini and Hitler, who had had the 'courage that dared go back on an ultimatum', were also lauded. Daladier and Franklin D. Roosevelt received citations; only Beneš remained unmentioned.[109] The *Sunday Times* greeted the settlement itself with a 'boundless' sense of relief; 'a paean of joy echoed all around the world from Munich'.[110] War had been avoided. Hadley, wisely, restricted his defence of Munich mainly to arguing that 'neither Great Britain nor France were sufficiently prepared in armaments or in ARP for a great war'. Air fear was a sufficient explanation: 'It was not our naval weakness that handicapped us in the crisis. The instant peril, which war would have precipitated, was in the air.'[111] Sidebotham assumed, or was delegated, the task of offering a more comprehensive justification. 'Emotional joy over the deliverance of humanity', he wrote, 'is not the only or necessarily conclusive argument for the settlement.' At bottom, he argued, 'no settlement would have been lasting that had not ceded to Germany the provinces which are predominantly German.' Germany was not, as Hadley had previously implied, bent on the destruction of the Czech Republic: 'the terms of Munich . . . have proved that that interpretation was wrong.' But what, then, of Hitler's stance at Godesberg? 'The moral of Godesberg would seem to be that, in international as in personal relations, where two explanations are possible of what is said or done, the more creditable of the two is usually the right one.' Such novel theories aside, Sidebotham made clear his disapprobation of a British guarantee to 'rump' Czechoslovakia, and concluded matters with the soothing reflection that 'Czechoslovakia has suffered grievously, but more in present pride than in future happiness'.[112]

The Observer

In the *Observer* Garvin through 1938 was guided by one major consideration: 'The [Great] War had been the horror of all history; and we all know that another war, if there were to be another, would be worse.'[113] Garvin was certain that after the *Anschluss* contemporary Czechoslovakia could not, and in view of the danger, should not be preserved; the peril to Europe was of Czech, not German, origin. The Sudeten Germans must be granted 'equality' and the Republic must adopt a Swiss-like political neutrality, he argued in May.[114] He was stung, apparently, by accusations that appeasement was 'a policy of fear'; he repudiated such charges as 'baseless and unworthy'. Chamberlain, he thought, on the contrary, had displayed 'decisive courage' when issuing his warning in March that a war erupting in central Europe might ultimately draw in Britain as well as those attacked or bound by formal obligations. But 'any more challenging and adventurous foreign policy', he argued, 'would be not so much spirited as criminal.'[115]

Through the summer of 1938 Garvin urged the Czechs to grant the Sudetens cantonal autonomy: British policy must aim at 'meeting the German claim ... to racial self-government ... while maintaining the integrity of Czechoslovakia'.[116] Privately, however, in a letter to Waldorf Astor, he acknowledged that 'Hitler ... has never swerved since 1920 in his demand for German "self-determination" in Bohemia and Moravia-Silesia'. If Britain went to war to prevent a plebiscite 'what would history say ... ?'; it 'would be one of the stupendous crimes and follies of all time', he argued. The Czechs were dragging their feet, he complained on 30 August, and Britain was 'not yet holding the balance fair'.[117]

Astor responded by endorsing Garvin's preference for a cantonal arrangement but feared 'that the Himmlers and Goebbels [would] persuade Hitler to reject every Czech proposal' and would precipitate war. Yet an unlikely source of hope remained: 'It seems to me', wrote Viscount Astor, 'that the *Observer*, because of its past line, might turn the scale with Hitler against war and keep the moderates [dominant?] in Germany.' Garvin had voiced deep fears concerning Britain's aerial unpreparedness. 'As to preparedness, in some ways we are better off than in 1914', Astor assured his editor.[118]

A week later Garvin reacted to the publication of Beneš's Fourth Plan. The Czechs, he wrote to Astor,

> at the last minute have produced the really big plan of autonomy that ought without doubt to mean a settlement. Thank God for that. If Hitler did not accept it substantially ... he would not have a real supporter in the world among the nations. It looks as if they [i.e. the Czechs] could scarcely have gone further now.[119]

In print, however, while guardedly approving the Czech Plan and flatly rejecting cession, Garvin warned: 'It is no use for the Czechs to speak of their limit of concession, in their own estimate, when Britain and the British Empire and others are expected to stake their all without any limit.'[120]

The coordinates of Garvin's perplexity were thus clearly defined. Justice and morality were now embodied in the Czech solution to the Sudeten crisis. But Hitler, he sensed, would demand cession. Without capitulation to Hitler's demands, world war would follow. And world war must be avoided; British military weakness and Germany's vast power forbade it. 'I'm quite certain', he wrote to Astor, 'the relative power of Germany is just now greatly under-estimated.'[121] Hence it remained an over-riding necessity for Britain to 'work harder than ever for common sense settlements and the world's peace, even if sentimentalism [i.e., anti-Nazi or pro-Czech feelings] can play no part'.[122]

A week later, on 18 September, Garvin publicly fell into line with Chamberlain's capitulation and supported a Sudeten cession: 'Britain and the Empire', he wrote, 'will not go to war against the doctrine of self-determination.' He acknowledged that cession would render Czechoslovakia's position 'hopeless', but 'a peace of surrender'– which he professed to be 'a peace of honour'– was preferable to world war.[123] Such was the argument he advanced in the *Observer*. To Astor, with greater candour, he wrote that a Sudeten cession would 'mean the disappearance of Czechoslovakia from the map'. Were Britain to contemplate war, it would be against a coalition comprising 'Germany, Poland, Hungary, Italy [and] Japan ... while Russian aid is unreliable in every way'. Moreover, Garvin hinted at still darker circumstances: 'It is a hideous dilemma (far worse than is yet suspected outside a few ... But I speak this to no one but you.).' Apparently he had heard further disheartening news about Britain's military, and especially aerial, unpreparedness.[124] Thus, while staunchly justifying appeasement and the dismemberment of Czechoslovakia in the *Observer*, in private, to Astor, Garvin's thoughts at last led him elsewhere; justice and political considerations, he seemed to imply, called for war; but Britain's unpreparedness forbade it.

Munich left Garvin humiliated and shattered. He attempted to justify the settlement on grounds other than fear, but his heart was not in it. Munich had saved Czechoslovakia from 'total destruction'; Munich, in contrast with the Godesberg terms, had assured that 'many humanities, decencies and conveniences [were] preserved instead of savage conquest and panic flight'; Hitler and Chamberlain had 'become friends for good'.[125] But when Garvin wrote that Chamberlain had been 'a thousand times right' in accepting the settlement, it was as if he were counting the number of Hitler's bombers. As he put it, 'while Britain was being bombed, Czecho-Slovakia would have been irrevocably crushed'; the superiority of the Luftwaffe, he wrote, had been 'a dominant factor behind the ultimatums and the "squeeze"'.[126] On 2 October the *Observer* declared:

> A great city has become a great peril ... It is a commonplace that London is the most vulnerable area upon the whole earth ... London has had its glimpse of reality ... It has been shown something of what war means now that the air has become its chief theatre.[127]

A month later Garvin wrote to Astor complaining of Chamberlain's lack of drive in promoting rearmament. For lack of air power and anti-aircraft defences Britain had been 'disgracefully reduced' to the 'position, in effect, of a second-class power by comparison with Germany'. He was 'all for peace with strength ... But this peace with humiliating weakness ... is something worse than I ever saw in my time', Garvin declared. Munich had driven him to insomnia and melancholy, and to the 'very bottom of the pit'.[128] As before Munich, but with still greater insistence and vigour after it, the *Observer* pressed for British rearmament, especially in the air.

The Tablet

From the start of the Czech crisis, the *Tablet's* attitude to the Sudeten problem was frankly stated. 'There can be no prevention of German growth, nor should it be attempted, provided always that the Germans have the good sense to proceed step by imperceptible step', declared Woodruff in May 1938.[129] Woodruff recalled that in the 1920s he had considered Czechoslovakia a 'model democracy'; in the late thirties Sir Robert Hodson had succeeded in convincing him that Czechoslovakia was an artificial, patchwork state dominated by a repressive Czech core.[130] Whatever the merits of such recollection, the *Tablet* by September 1938 was easily persuaded of the virtues of the principle of self-determination. Accepting German arguments or *Diktat* 'at the pistol's point' was, admitted Woodruff, unpleasant; but, he argued, 'a war to-day could not conceivably be fought to force a German minority to continue under the Czechs. There would have, in any event, to be a new form of constitution and new frontiers, and it is much better to have them before [a war] than after it.'[131] The journal praised Chamberlain's flights as an 'endeavour to get beyond angry feelings, the resentment, even the detestation which is felt for the crueller features of the German movement'.[132]

Woodruff was ruffled, at Munich-time, by suggestions that British policy was determined by fear rather than considerations of justice: 'Insufficient weight', he contended, 'was allowed in judging the British action to British recognition of the merits of the [Sudeten] case and too much was attributed to the desire for peace at any price.'[133] But after the agreement was concluded, he admitted: 'It is true that the vivid forecasts of aerial war, as well as the treatment of the last war in literature, have built up a powerful sense of indiscriminate death and destruction, and that war has been brought home to the ordinary populations as never before in modern times.' Peace had been saved; no further justification of British policy was needed.[134]

Woodruff used the opportunity of Munich to offer a blanket justification of German and Italian foreign policies since 1933; Germany and Italy had 'practically entirely' acted in repudiation of 'different onerous clauses ... It has been a kind of aggression which consists of throwing off handcuffs and chains, of disregarding arbitrary prohibitions.'[135] In the following months, while also calling for massive British rearmament, Woodruff, unlike Garvin, failed to display unease or remorse over the dubious achievements of Munich.

Truth

Before the *Anschluss* Henry Newnham, editor of *Truth*, had displayed genuine sympathy for the Czech Republic. By May 1938 *Truth* effectively echoed the Nazi line: the Czechs were urged to abandon their alliances and assuage Sudeten grievances.[136] Newnham was also forthright as to what Britain's attitude should be:

> The exotic combination of consonants in 'Czechoslovakia' has always seemed to me a factor on the side of peace. There is a healthy prejudice in this country against going to war over what looks like printer's pie.[137]

The ostentatious German military preparations of July–August 1938 riled *Truth*. Once again the Germans were proving themselves to be 'bad Europeans', Newnham stated.[138] But though 'Hitler's methods' failed to inspire sympathy, he had 'a case', thought the journal.[139] In early September it pressed for Sudeten 'home rule'. By 14 September, *The Times* and the *New Statesman* having broken the taboo, *Truth* felt able to urge a Czech cession of the 'Egerland'; but it firmly rejected a cession of the whole Sudetenland as it 'would leave the Czech State at Germany's mercy and existing only on sufferance. That is not to be thought of.'[140] With Chamberlain's capitulation at and after Berchtesgaden, the unthinkable became the acceptable, if not desirable. In not objecting to the British acceptance of a Sudeten cession, *Truth* succinctly declared: 'All the world over the average man recoils from the thought of war.'[141] But, evidently, Newnham found the reversal difficult to stomach: 'Individually', he wrote, 'the whole nation wanted to see Britain stand firm as a rock, and let Hitler turn aside or break himself. Better informed than the public, the Cabinet evidently thought otherwise; its reasons, in the circumstances, must be very cogent.'[142] The implication – of British military weakness – could not have been lost on the journal's readers. Indeed, on 28 September *Truth* ascribed German military confidence, and, implicitly, British infirmity, to a German 'ray' capable of destroying aircraft in flight.[143]

Truth justified Munich with the usual arguments that it had averted world war and that the Sudeten issue was no cause for one. Idiosyncratically, the journal singled out Runciman as responsible for the terms of the settlement: 'Exceptional authority attach[ed] to [his] views ... His conclusion ... provided the only possible foundation for the determination of [British] policy.'[144] Newnham apparently believed that Runciman's Report had constituted the basis of Government policy rather than that Government policy had determined the content of the Report. Perhaps even more eccentric were the conclusions of Nigel Tangye's survey of the post-Munich strategic situation. Tangye argued that 'the "betrayal" of Czechoslovakia by the British Prime Minister is one of the most astute and personally courageous diplomatic moves in history'. This was so because Chamberlain had succeeded in 'depriving' Hitler of most of Czechoslovakia, leaving Czech air-fields and air-power intact.[145]

The offering of such questionable arguments was indicative of the depth of Newnham's dissatisfaction with the Agreement. So, too, was *Truth's* subsequent attack upon those who bemoaned the 'shame' of Munich:

> Not one soul has a right to criticise the Government for lack of firmness unless he put himself in the forefront of the advocacy of rearmament in those early and (as we now see) supremely important days when it was an unpopular cause.[146]

CONCLUSION

The *Anschluss*, by its suddenness and completeness, allowed of two possible responses: advocacy of resistance to Germany; or an acceptance, however riddled with misgivings, of the *fait accompli*. No weekly thought the German invasion merited an immediate recourse to arms and only a few, in its wake, called for British preparation to resist. Yet only a minority of the weeklies had, before the event, deemed an *Anschluss* inevitable or just. The majority of the weeklies had, occasionally or consistently, called for British commitment to Austrian independence;

149

such calls decreased in frequency and insistency as Germany's power and aggressiveness increased over 1935–37. The *Anschluss* moved most to anger or resignation but not to a demand for action. Yet all agreed that the event, besides inflicting an injustice, had greatly strengthened Germany and undermined the security of the West's allies in eastern Europe.

The next item on the Nazi agenda, as all the weeklies immediately recognised, was Czechoslovakia. The Czech crisis unfolded between March and September 1938. It culminated at Munich.

Few journals argued that the Munich settlement had been engineered by Britain and France with morality in mind or that it had achieved anything approximating justice. Perhaps, in the eyes of some cosmic deity, Munich 'was a triumph for all that was best and most enlightened in British life; a triumph for those who had preached equal justice between peoples; a triumph for those who had courageously denounced the harshness and short-sightedness of Versailles'.[147] This was not how any of the weeklies saw things at the time. Both the substance of the settlement and the manner of its accomplishment were recognised by appeasers and exponents of collective security alike as humiliating and immoral.

That the Munich solution to the Czech problem was not conceived at the time as a dictate of justice was attested to by people as diverse in outlook as the (then) appeaser Garvin and the ostensible proponents of collective security, H. Wilson Harris and Kingsley Martin. Still more formidable is the proof afforded by the evolution of attitudes on the problem in the weeklies before September 1938. Except, perhaps, for the *Tablet*, no journal regarded a cession of the Sudetenland to Germany as a just solution; few pro- or anti-appeasement weeklies recommended anything like it. As late as mid-September, Wilson Harris of the *Spectator* and Garvin of the *Observer* strenuously argued that some degree of Sudeten autonomy was the maximum Beneš must be compelled or allowed to concede. All were genuinely and deeply shocked by the Anglo-French capitulation in the wake of Berchtesgaden.

The real argument, during and in the wake of the crisis, focused on the question of whether the settlement was impolitic as well as immoral. Views on the wisdom of the settlement turned upon three questions: were German 'acts of aggression' limited to the rectification of Versailles-based grievances and were they now, as promised, at an end? Should the Sudeten or other disputes in eastern Europe be the occasion of British involvement in a new world war? And was Britain, in September 1938, militarily sufficiently prepared for war, or was war against Hitler, if necessary and inevitable, preferable at some later point in time?

In September 1938 it was in answering these questions and on this plane that proponents of collective security joined hands with outright appeasers such as Sidebotham in the *Sunday Times*. Before then, appeasers argued that nothing in eastern Europe was worth British commitment to the point of war; ostensible anti-appeasers, that Hitler's designs ultimately threatened the security of western as well as eastern Europe and that it was better to stop Hitler before German power further increased and before the West was denuded of further allies. But in September, with war just around the corner, almost everyone took cover. Appeasers and anti-appeasers alike shunned the thought of a new world war; both succumbed to air fear. The imminence of war and air attack only impelled pro-appeasement papers like *Truth* and the *Sunday Times* to re-emphasize their indifference to the fate of eastern Europe. When faced with the crunch, 'anti-appeasement' weeklies such as the *New Statesman* pointed to the sky, soon to be infested with bombers, and pleaded for a postponement. Save for *The Economist* and *Time & Tide*, the advocates of 'resistance to Fascism' refrained from voicing assessments as to whether war was preferable in September or at a later date in relation to the shifting balance of power. War, simply, was too horrible a prospect to contemplate; and such calculations might well have prompted the conclusion that war was preferable before the sacrifice of Czechoslovakia rather than after it.

Hadley, then, was right when he wrote in 1944 that the British press was 'all but unanimous' in the acceptance of Munich and its terms, and in praising Chamberlain's efforts and sacrifice on behalf of the peace.[148] But Hadley erred when he stated:

> Many knew of our unpreparedness, of the serious shortages of military equipment and especially of the inadequacy of the defences against air attack. Yet there was no remotest sign of panic. Whatever the handicap, war would be faced with grim resolution.[149]

It was true that the public did not scurry underground at every belligerent noise from Berlin. But in the weeklies a virtual stampede took place between March and October 1938. In March all the weeklies, save the *New Statesman*, refused even to contemplate a solution to the Sudeten problem based on cession to Germany; most, as well, abjured even a solution based on cantonisation. As the months passed, the clamour grew for British pressure on Prague to extract progressively greater concessions to Henlein and Hitler. By mid-September all the weeklies agreed to Sudeten autonomy; by its end, all, save perhaps *The Economist* and *Time & Tide*, conceded the Sudeten cession, and all loudly praised Chamberlain for saving Britain and Europe from the affliction of war. If this reversal was not a product and symptom of 'panic', then the word has no meaning. The justice of Sudeten claims had not measurably increased between March and September; British fears had. The praise accorded Chamberlain upon his return to Britain with 'peace in our time' was of an hysterical variety like that of one accorded a last minute stay of execution. Later, indeed, many felt shame. And it was largely this sense of shame that in March 1939 compelled the extension of the guarantee to Poland, an impolitic gesture (in view of the lack of a Russian alliance) to a nation unsympathetically regarded (in view of its participation in the plunder of Czechoslovakia).

VII

1939

The pogrom of 'Crystal Night' (11–12 November 1938) followed sharp on the heels of Munich. In most of the weeklies, it was dismissed as irrelevant to the international situation, reflecting upon and touching only the Reich's internal affairs. Almost alone among supporters of Chamberlain, Wilson Harris of the *Spectator* was moved to argue that 'the events of the past week have obliterated the word appeasement, for the present, at any rate, from the political vocabulary'.[1] Like the *Observer*, most of the weeklies buried their comments on the pogrom in insignificant news round-up items.[2]

Though most of the weeklies continued to endorse rearmament, many, between Munich and Prague, entertained the belief that appeasement was on the verge of success. Official sponsorship of this idea was not lacking. On 10 March 1939 Sir Samuel Hoare announced the imminence of a new golden age in international affairs. Some weeks before, rumours of a Nazi onslaught in the West had proved groundless.

But the respite afforded by Munich was short-lived. The German regime was bent upon the elimination of Czechoslovakia, as the opponents of appeasement (and, indeed, some of its supporters) had opined during the crisis. Nazi-sponsored Slovak secessionists engineered a new crisis which, on 15 March, culminated in the occupation of Prague by German troops. Events had moved swiftly and, for most, unexpectedly; practically no time had been allowed the British Government or press to examine options.

But this *fait accompli* was different. Hitler had departed from what many Britons still regarded as his (acceptable) aim – the political unification of all Germans and the revision, albeit unilateral, of Versailles' 'injustices'. A non-German state had been crushed and occupied. And, in doing so, Hitler had violated solemn pledges and assurances given at Munich. For Englishmen, deception had been added to humiliation. That humiliation, it now appeared, had been undergone in vain; the agreement's political inexpediency and moral dubiety were now clearly seen.

Chamberlain was apparently willing to allow the German *coup* to pass without serious issue. In the Commons, on 15 March, he and Simon temporised. But the nation, including many of Chamberlain's own colleagues, revolted. The firm Birmingham speech of 17 March was the initial result; the Prime Minister in effect announced the bankruptcy of appeasement. Guarantees to Poland, and then to Rumania, Greece and Turkey, followed; negotiations were started with Russia in order to conclude a military alliance. At the end of April Germany denounced the Anglo-German Naval Agreement, a fit conclusion to the era of appeasement which had begun shortly before that pact was signed.

During the spring and summer of 1939, as the Anglo-Russian talks dragged on, German pressures mounted on Poland; Hitler demanded a swift solution to the 'problems' of Danzig and the Corridor. Smigly-Ridz and Beck remained obdurately unwilling to offer concessions under threat; Britain and France, reluctantly, stood by the guarantee. Russia remained the great enigma. Without her, the guarantees to Poland and the rest of eastern Europe remained without teeth; Britain and France could declare war, in the event of fresh German aggression, but they could not directly assist the Poles or anyone else in eastern Europe.

Munich had been a severe blow to Russia. She had lost an ally and buffer state, and any faith she may have had in France and Britain. Stalin had been humiliated by Russia's exclusion from the conference table. The obvious reluctance of the British to meet Russian demands at the Moscow talks convinced Stalin of the desirability of changing course. The Molotov–Ribbentrop Pact, concluded on 22–23 August 1939, startled the West – though an augury had been afforded by the prior replacement of the western-oriented Litvinoff. Britain, some said quixotically, stuck by its guarantee to Poland. On 1 September Hitler invaded the Corridor and, two days later, Britain and France declared war on Germany.

In March 1939 the weeklies were unanimous in their insistence that the invasion of Czechoslovakia was no grounds for British involvement in world war; in September, they all supported war. This change in the climate of opinion from appeasement to support of resistance between Prague and the invasion of Poland was accurately reflected in the weeklies. It was not however as immediate, stark or complete as some later commentators made out. Attitudes to five major issues serve as indices of this change: (a) Treaty revision in general and the revision of the status of Danzig and the Corridor in particular; (b) the Polish guarantee and alliance; (c) a Russian alliance; (d) rearmament and conscription; and (e) the inclusion of Churchill, Eden and Labour representatives in the Cabinet. The shift from appeasement to resistance in the weeklies, it will be seen, revealed itself in relation to these issues.

154

Reactions to the German invasion of Bohemia and Moravia were unanimously hostile; they varied, from weekly to weekly, only in the degree of indignation displayed and in the assessment of conclusions to be drawn about Britain's foreign policy. The *New Statesman*'s attitude was predictable. 'Hitler is in Prague', stated the journal, 'as those who understood the Nazis predicted last September. At last the Führer has discarded the pretence that German policy was bound by "the morals of nationalism" and aimed solely at the overthrow of Versailles's "injustices".'[3] Kingsley Martin expressed guarded approval of Chamberlain's Birmingham speech. He confessed that appeasement had had much 'to commend it': 'We were all conscious of the evils of Versailles and of the post-War policy of France ... Appeasement in such a situation carried with it the appeal to pacifism and co-operation as opposed to military preparation and economic rivalry.' But that policy, he concluded, had not been feasible due to 'the nature of the Nazi regime'; it was not understandable economic compulsions (as he himself had usually argued) but 'the will to power' that had provided Hitler's motivation.[4]

However, Kingsley Martin's support of resistance to Hitlerism was wavering and ambiguous, even in the wake of Prague. On 1 April he warned that in the absence of an Anglo-French–Russian guarantee to Poland, that country would soon fall prey to German designs.[5] Yet, a bare week later, Britain having extended the required guarantee, the *New Statesman* castigated the Chamberlain Government for entering into 'this dangerous commitment'. The only possible defence of Britain's action, thought Kingsley Martin, rested on the belief that Germany 'was not yet ready for world war'. He had no sympathy for the Poles or for their Government, a right-wing dictatorship which had only just participated in the plunder of Czechoslovakia. Moreover, and here lay his main line of argument, the guarantee was ineffectual as Britain could afford no help to an invaded Poland; Russia alone could do so. Britain, he argued, should have withheld the guarantee until a Russian alliance had been concluded and until Poland had accepted Soviet assistance in the event of war. As it stood, the guarantee would not avert war but simply assure Britain's participation in it should it erupt. 'It is a strange proceeding', declared the *New Statesman*, 'to sacrifice Spain and Czechoslovakia and then, with only France as an ally, to embark on the more dangerous task of defending the vital interests of Poland.'[6]

As before Prague, Kingsley Martin's advocacy of resistance to Nazism was ambivalent. From the first, his conception of the Russian alliance was of an instrument designed to avert war rather than fight and win one. He refused, even after Prague, to regard war with Germany as inevitable. Perhaps some genuine anti-appeasers shared this view. But none would have written, in May 1939, that 'a collective peace system is poor sense if it means no more than a military alliance'. Apart from alliances, believed Kingsley Martin, 'a world peace conference' was needed to revise the Versailles settlement. In effect, the *New Statesman* was advocating negotiated concessions over Danzig and the Corridor. The conclusion of a Russian alliance, for Kingsley Martin, only facilitated the offering of these concessions. The journal continued to press this position until the outbreak of the world war.[7]

On rearmament, conscription and the inclusion of Churchill in the Cabinet, the *New Statesman* followed the Labour Party's negative line. Churchill had long been a bugbear of the Left; conscription was decried as a 'Fascist' method; and rearmament, as always, portended war (though the *New Stateman*'s opposition to it, in the final months before the invasion of Poland, was muted).

The invasion of Czechoslovakia hardly affected *Tribune*'s posture. It continued to place all its eggs in a single basket – a Russian alliance. All else it dismissed as insincere or dangerous. It continued, until the outbreak of war, to oppose rearmament and conscription under a Conservative Government; and it dismissed the Polish guarantee as 'eyewash' preparatory to another Chamberlainite sell-out. The journal believed that Chamberlain would 'never stand up to Fascism'; only the conclusion of a Russian Pact would mark and consolidate a real reversal of policy. Like the *New Statesman*, *Tribune* also regarded such a pact as a means of averting war rather than as an aid in fighting one. But it never suggested pacifying Hitler by offering him slices of Poland.[8]

A few days after the occupation of Prague, *Time & Tide* put its finger on Kingsley Martin's perennial dilemma: was peace with Hitler possible? To reply 'no', thought *Time & Tide*, was 'so infinitely depressing that a large number, perhaps the majority of the people of this island, are inclined to force themselves to believe that the answer may after all be "yes" . . . '. But if the answer were a definite 'no', as the journal believed, then the policy of appeasement 'had to go', for 'each new act of appeasement is merely feeding the tiger'.[9] The journal happily noted the reversal of Britain's posture in the wake of Prague: Britain was at last leading the effort to establish an anti-German containing front. Indeed, this is what the journal had been preaching since the spring of 1938. It now called for the speedy conclusion of alliances with Russia, Poland and

Rumania. However, *Time & Tide* cast grave doubts on Chamberlain's suitability for the tasks ahead. Hence it called for his resignation and for the formation of a 'government of national concentration'.[10] *Time & Tide* suspected that Chamberlain really desired an alliance system exclusive of Russia: 'To the ordinary mind this plan seems mad, so mad as to be almost incredible.' Moreover, the Prime Minister still seemed bent on appeasing Italy in the hope of dividing the Axis; *Time & Tide* regarded such hopes as delusive.[11]

A week later the journal relented; the guarantee to Poland had been extended. *Time & Tide* still questioned the finality of Chamberlain's change of heart but forbore from reiterating its call for his replacement. Instead, it demanded the inclusion of Churchill and Eden in the Cabinet.[12] It was to repeat this call (adding Duff Cooper to its list of prospective ministers) through the summer of 1939. It continued, also, to demand a swift and positive conclusion to the Moscow talks.

For years, *Time & Tide* had grudgingly concurred with the Government's limited rearmament programmes. In 1938 it demanded ever greater efforts of rearmament. Through 1939 it continued to press in this direction. In April, it 'welcomed wholeheartedly' the Government's announcement of conscription and chided the Opposition for its policy: 'There is nothing Fascist about conscription', declared the journal.[13]

Through the spring and summer of 1939 *Time & Tide* feared that the Government would revert to appeasement. In May, in this connection, it criticised Chamberlain for returning Ambassador Henderson to Berlin.[14] The journal never demanded or suggested any assuaging of German grievances over Danzig and the Corridor. It appreciated, given German mobilisation and threats, that this amounted to appeasement. It was with a certain sense of relief that the journal greeted the outbreak of war: the long wait was at last at an end.

The Economist used the occupation of Prague as an opportunity to berate those 'well-meaning, truth-fearing folk' who believed that by a few concessions, Hitler could be bought off or converted to pacifism. 'Nazi Germany', asserted the journal, 'is a robber-state . . . It will be restrained . . . only by force as naked and brutal as its own.' The invasion of Czechoslovakia had revealed, as *The Economist* had long contended, that British policy since Munich was 'naive, amateurish and ill-informed'. The journal concluded its leader of 18 March by quoting Eden to the effect that Britain had better align herself with like-minded states to achieve the containment of Germany.[15] *The Economist* had intermittently called for an alliance with Russia since the autumn of 1937. It now wrote:

The fatal weakness of the western democracies' policy in the face of Herr Hitler's successive *coups* has been the reluctance of their leaders, on class and ideological grounds, to consult and co-operate with the Soviet Union.

The Economist hinted darkly that should an Anglo-Russian alliance fail to materialise, a Russo-German pact was not improbable.[16] During the following months, the journal repeated its call for the conclusion of an alliance with Russia, deeming it 'the sheet-anchor' of any defensive coalition.

On 25 March *The Economist* pleaded for the extension by Britain of 'full and formidable' guarantees to Poland, Greece and Turkey;[17] it also demanded the incorporation of Churchill, Eden and Labour Party representatives in the Cabinet.[18] Commenting on its sister journals, *The Economist* acutely observed:

> Most of the supporters of appeasement in fact have been desperately unhappy. They have rejoiced at the permission [afforded by the occupation of Czechoslovakia and Chamberlain's *volte face*] to speak their minds out.[19]

The journal rejoiced at the extension of the guarantee to Poland, viewing it as a genuine token of Chamberlain's conversion. But it insisted that an alliance with Russia must be concluded swiftly; without it, the anti-German coalition would be feeble. In support of this view the journal argued:

> an Anglo-Russian agreement presents the best chance of avoiding a war and the virtual certainty of winning it if it cannot be avoided.[20]

As in previous years, *The Economist* clamoured for rearmament; it now came out unhesitatingly in favour of conscription. It reprimanded those like Kingsley Martin who desired a peace conference to effect yet more Treaty revisions in favour of Germany: 'The opinion is frequently heard', it declared, 'even on the Left, that the conclusion of the Russian alliance will be the moment to make a fair offer to Germany. But this is most dangerous doctrine.'[21] Rather, *The Economist* demanded that Germany de-mobilise and stressed that the limit of concession had already been reached.

Despite its prevision, the journal was appalled by the Molotov–Ribbentrop Pact, which it called 'the single biggest piece of perfidy in history'. It was fully cognisant of the damage done to the West's strategic position. But it remained unhesitatingly committed to the Polish guarantee and the principle of resistance to Nazism.[22] It turned its gaze westwards, looking to America to take Russia's place in the scheme of containment.

Munich had converted the *Spectator* from full support for appeasement to a hesitant advocacy of a Russian alliance. On 27 January 1939 Wilson Harris wrote:

> After the rude shock the balance of power in Europe has suffered since Munich, every conceivable effort should be exerted to maintain and consolidate relations with Russia. The regime existing in Russia is utterly alien to our political ideas, but that is Russia's concern, not ours.

The journal criticised Whitehall's shunning of Russia as 'a dangerously expensive luxury'. While studiously avoiding the word, 'alliance' was what the *Spectator* had in mind.[23]

With Prague, the *Spectator* finally abandoned appeasement. It concluded that Hitler's driving motive was 'a lust for power'; to achieve Continental hegemony, it declared, he would 'lie, deceive, threaten and rape'.[24] Even the Germanophile Wrench, the *Spectator*'s proprietor, found Prague too much. A year later he referred to the event as 'the turning point' in his agonised assessment of relations with Germany.[25]

What Britain should now do was indicated by Wilson Harris on 24 March. He called for the admission of Churchill and Eden to the Cabinet; though a Quaker and a pacifist, he pleaded for the institution of some form of conscription and he supported a binding pact of mutual defence between Great Britain, France, Russia, Poland and the lesser states in eastern Europe. 'Nothing', he argued, 'could do more to give pause to Herr Hitler and confidence to the world.'[26]

The *Spectator* maintained this posture until the outbreak of the world war. On 7 April it asserted that Chamberlain's extension of the guarantee to Poland had earned the country's unanimous approval.[27] In July it chided Sir Arnold Wilson (formerly, a regular contributor to the journal) for urging concessions over Danzig. 'The incorporation of Danzig in the Reich ... is palpably impossible', declared Wilson Harris.[28] Wrench, during that critical summer, visited Berlin and found it 'a shattering experience for a life-long lover of Germany'. He was bewildered by the extent of the hatred for Britain which he found there.[29]

In the wake of the occupation of Prague there was unanimity among the Left and Liberal journals on only one major point – the need to conclude an alliance with Russia. The Polish guarantee, supported heartily by the Liberal weeklies, was dismissed by *Tribune* and the *New Statesman* as insincere or impolitic or both. For the Left, conscription remained a bugbear; rearmament was abjured on grounds of principle; and Churchill at or near the helm remained an alarming prospect. Yet for all that, the Left too had perceptibly moved from reluctant support of appeasement (or empty asseverations of 'collective security') to a reluctant endorsement of the need for resistance. Even in the *New Statesman*, Kingsley Martin's occasional pleas for further Treaty revision were the exception rather than the rule. For the Liberal anti-appeasement journals, namely *The Economist* and *Time & Tide*, Prague had acted as a confirmation rather than as a catalyst: appeasement had been and was wrong, and Hitler's latest *coup* had providentially revealed as much to the hitherto weak, blind and uncaring.

Munich had driven Garvin reluctantly into the anti-appeasement camp. He harboured few illusions about that settlement, either privately or in the *Observer*: 'The sequel of Munich has been a bitter tale', he asserted at the start of 1939. Hardly had the ink dried on the agreement 'before the Utopian hopes of the moment began to fade and vanish . . . The general situation was rather worsened than improved.'[30]

The invasion of Czechoslovakia evoked Garvin's full fury: 'A stark tyranny . . . darker than Napoleon's trod down and trampled out with giant iniquity the political life and freedom of another nation and another race. The last rag of human decency was discarded this time.' Hitlerian foreign policy, he declared, was governed by 'colossal megalomania'; it aimed 'at the absolute domination of all eastern Europe between the Baltic and the Black Sea' and, ultimately, 'supremacy in the world'.[31] Like all who had pursued the mirage of appeasement, Garvin felt personally deceived. As he complained to Astor on 16 March: 'Most odious and intolerable is the systematic deception they employ in order to make dupes of those of us who have honestly wished to be friends.'[32]

What was Britain to do? The *Observer* reacted favourably to Chamberlain's Birmingham speech but thought it insufficient. Britain, it declared, 'waits for something more'. In explication, the paper went on to call for a British and French 'understanding with Soviet Russia . . . without regard . . . for prejudices and doubts'.[33] Privately, Garvin was yet more critical of the Government. He wrote to Astor: 'I doubt whether the Cabinet yet comprehends the breadth and urgency of the business . . . or the size of the game that Hitler is attempting.' He expressed the hope that Chamberlain would yet effect 'the dramatic stroke' of an immediate alliance with Russia.[34] He advocated conscription and full mobilisation of Britain's economy in the rearmament effort.

Like Kingsley Martin, Garvin was dissatisfied with the Polish guarantee. His heart was set on a Russian alliance; anything less he deemed insufficient and perhaps counter-productive. In the *Observer* of 9 April he argued that Britain should either not have gone so far (i.e., the Polish guarantee) or gone farther (i.e., the Russian alliance).[35] In June he wrote to Astor: 'The Polish guarantee may have been inevitable but it raises what is the most dangerous of all points in our relations with Germany, and why we gave it without first making absolutely sure of Russia as well as Turkey I shall never be able to understand.'[36] Through the spring and summer of 1939 Garvin pressed ceaselessly for the conclusion of the Russian alliance. In June, he was among the most vocal supporters in the British press of the Russian position that the Baltic states must also receive British and French guarantees.[37]

Occasionally, in those months of crisis, Garvin suggested colonial concessions to Germany.[38] But usually he stuck firmly to his re-born adherence to containment. 'If we flinch', he wrote to Astor in late June, 'we are finished, for we shall be isolated, and pushed rapidly from European surrender to surrender of Empire.'[39] Danzig, he declared in July, was 'the acid-test' of British resolve, 'the touch-stone of all our pledges'[40] – it must not be conceded. He repeatedly called for Churchill's inclusion in the Cabinet.[41]

Garvin promptly and accurately interpreted the significance of the Molotov–Ribbentrop Pact. It meant, he wrote on 27 August, that 'all the restraints on Nazi aggression against Poland' had been removed; Germany, he forecast, intended to dismember Poland, perhaps with Russian assistance.[42]

At the start of 1939 Sidebotham, in the *Sunday Times*, reflected that 1938, after all, had not been such a bad year: 'We not only avoided a war with Germany', he declared, 'but laid down in the exchange of notes at Munich the foundation on which a permanent peace might be built.' He found 'no inconsistency between the Nazi philosophy of politics and the hope of European appeasement'.[43]

The occupation of Prague inaugurated a revolution in the *Sunday Times*'s foreign policy. Echoing the thinking of most Conservative appeasers, on 19 March Sidebotham declared: 'Hitler has deceived us.' Until then, he believed, Germany had 'had a case'; for the latest *coup*, all pretexts were hollow. Both Hadley and Sidebotham offered reluctant acclamation of the Birmingham speech. But neither suggested anything concrete which went beyond it.[44]

Given the gravity of events, Kemsley himself went into print. Concerning the paper's past policies he was unrepentant. 'I have come to two conclusions', he stated; '(1) that in the so-called policy of appeasement there is nothing to regret and much of which we may be proud; and (2) that though, through no fault of ours, it has not achieved its purpose in the case of Germany, yet it has given to this country a moral strength . . . of value incalculable.' He admitted that the *Sunday Times* had often laid itself open to the charge of carrying tolerance towards Nazi deeds to inordinate lengths. But, he maintained, it had been done in 'the cause of peace'. Munich had been sensible and just: how, he asked, could Chamberlain have known that Hitler would prove faithless?[45]

Disillusion with appeasement did not rapidly convert the *Sunday Times* to advocacy of its alternative. Certainly it exhibited no desire to outdo its new-born mentor in resistance, Chamberlain. On 26 March Sidebotham, apart from pressing for more rearmament, weighed up Britain's options – alliance with Russia and/or with other states in eastern Europe. He concluded by rejecting any extension of Britain's commitments.[46] Nonetheless, the *Sunday Times* fell smartly into step in the wake of the extension of the Polish guarantee. As Hadley put it: 'At this stage, it has become evident that if we leave Europe to its fate, it will fall under the sway of a single aggressive military despotism . . . If Poland and Rumania go, Holland, Denmark and Switzerland will go also.' But Hadley carefully stressed what he believed to be the transient nature of the Polish commitment: 'It is not a guarantee for all time but during the period before the present diplomatic consultations are concluded.'[47] He called the guarantee an 'assurance'; and he voiced the hope that a negotiated peace, by way of Treaty revision, would swiftly be concluded. Less wishful thinking was displayed by Sidebotham, who admitted that a revolution in British foreign policy was indeed and permanently under way: 'a united front of resistance to German aggression' was being established under British tutelage.[48]

By mid-summer 1939 the *Sunday Times*, while still holding out hopes for a negotiated solution to the Danzig dispute, had come almost full circle in its attitude to British commitments in eastern Europe. It persisted in regarding a Russian alliance with grave misgivings; but it allowed that 'a new Locarno of the East might well scatter the clouds of war overnight.'[49] Despite a last-minute personal effort by Kemsley to discover conciliatory trends in Berlin,[50] the *Sunday Times* stuck by Chamberlain over the Polish guarantee. On 3 September the paper declared: 'The pledge is sacred.' Danzig, it asserted, was not the issue: 'We are dealing with a threat to the peace and liberties of the world.'[51]

Through the summer of 1939 the *Sunday Times* pressed for ever more rearmament and supported the institution of conscription; but, presumably for party political reasons, it failed to endorse the growing clamour for the expansion of the Cabinet, and would have nothing to do with the incorporation in it of Labour representatives.

Woodruff emerged from Munich with his pro-appeasement convictions intact. The occupation of Prague and Chamberlain's Birmingham speech only marginally affected his thinking. Only on 25 March 1939 did the *Tablet* allow itself even a hesitant criticism of Hitler's *coup*. It stated: 'The action of the Führer . . . places him in the category of the great adventurers and out of the category of the great statesmen.'[52] Criminality, as distinct from 'adventurism', was nowhere mentioned. Woodruff, however, clearly understood that Germany's latest transgression had destroyed 'the bases of Chamberlain's policy'.[53] But beyond endorsing conscription and rearmament Woodruff would not go.

The *Tablet* was horrified by the turn events had taken, particularly because they seemed to point towards a Russian alliance. The Polish guarantee, in the *Tablet*'s view, was bad enough; the journal forbore from openly condemning it. But courting Russia – to Catholics an incarnation of Anti-Christ – was something else:

> That the British Government has found itself driven to make its present overtures to the avowed enemies of our civilisation and religion is in part due to the pressure of uninformed public opinion, which now finds it convenient to forget that the things it most detests in Germany are to be found on a larger and more dreadful scale in the territory under Moscow.

If the choice lay between a concessionary peace with the right-wing dictators and an alliance with the Soviet Union, Woodruff's preference was clear. 'The worst enemies of peace today', he declared, 'are those who limit their analysis to a denunciation of the harsher features of German and Italian policy . . . '[54] The journal called repeatedly for negotiations over Danzig and the Corridor.

Through the spring and summer of 1939 the *Tablet* persisted in its opposition to alliance with Russia. It greeted the Molotov–Ribbentrop Pact with ill-concealed relief and an air of 'I told you so'. In September, Woodruff resigned himself to war with Germany; but war with Italy – the residence of the Pope – to his mind remained unthinkable.

Munich had done little to curb *Truth*'s appetite for appeasement; neither had 'Crystal Night' nor the rumours of January 1939 concerning a prospective German invasion of the Low Countries. In February the journal rejoiced at the visit to Berlin of a British delegation of industrialists.[55]

Truth bided its time before pronouncing on the German assault on Czechoslovakia. Initially, it merely expressed the hope that 'a fatal blow

163

has not been struck at the future peace of Europe'; as usual, it found 'the method' rather than the substance of the German *coup* 'disturbing'.[56] But in the following week, Conservative anti-appeasement having been legitimised by Chamberlain in Birmingham, *Truth* spoke out more firmly. The Nazis had 'torn off the mask' and were palpably seeking 'world hegemony by ruthless force', it declared. The hopes of Munich had been dashed. The journal resigned itself to 'the radical re-orientation of the British Government's foreign policy'. *Truth*, however, quickly denied remorse over appeasement; Munich had been necessary and just. Now, it declared, the British public was united in support of a defensive posture of resistance. But the journal continued to reject a grand alliance as provocative and condemned any thought of 'preventive war'.[57]

Truth was unhappy with the extension of the Polish guarantee. In comment, it all but rejected it. 'There is an obvious danger', it stated, 'in simply cheering the announcement of "a firm front" against the totalitarian countries.' Like the *Sunday Times*, it preferred to view the commitment to Poland as an interim device. On the wider issue, *Truth* was forthright and hopeful: 'It may be assumed that Poland would not consider a reasoned request for the re-inclusion of Danzig in East Prussia to be a threat to her independence.' The journal urged the Polish Government not to 'exploit' the British commitment by persisting in intransigence.[58] Unfortunately, the journal noted in May, the guarantee had had 'the not wholly welcome' effect 'of stiffening Poland's attitude towards German claims in relation to Danzig and the Corridor'. It cautioned that 'if Poland's valour outruns discretion, Herr Hitler may be presented with an excuse for annexation capable of logical defence'.[59] Nor were the strategic drawbacks of the Polish guarantee lost on *Truth*. It firmly abjured a Russian alliance. But it stressed:

> Without the 100 per cent military co-operation of the USSR, a British guarantee extended to every State northeast and south of Germany is an appalling commitment ... Yet the participation of Russia in mutual assistance pacts is not merely a doubtful factor; it would be highly unwelcome to most of the countries most closely exposed to German attack.[60]

Unlike the anti-appeasement journals and the recently converted *Observer*, *Truth*, through the spring and summer of 1939, opposed Churchill's inclusion in the Cabinet, perhaps seeing in him an assurance of a war they still deemed avoidable.[61] But it continued to press for greater measures of rearmament and economic mobilisation, and supported the Government's institution of conscription.

Truth maintained this posture through the summer of 1939. The

British people, it declared, refused 'to fight for Danzig'. It argued:

> If we set aside the ideological passions of Mr Victor Gollancz and his tribe in the tents of Bloomsbury, the truth is that no appreciable section of British opinion desires to reconquer Berlin for the Jews or to see the Vistula . . . run red with British blood for the greater glory of Marshal Smigly-Ridz and Polish political romanticism.[62]

Such arguments were confined to *Truth* alone. Perhaps though, by their uniqueness, they may serve as an index of the weeklies' almost unanimous rejection of fear-engendered hysteria and confusion as war drew near in the summer of 1939. If nothing else, appeasement, by its eventual repudiation, had succeeded in unifying the country and in concentrating its mind wonderfully for the trial ahead.

CONCLUSION

As indicated, the alleged consensus brought about in British public opinion by the German occupation of Czechoslovakia was not as solid as many later commentators recalled.[63] Die-hard Conservative and Catholic appeasers, such as Woodruff (the *Tablet*), Kemsley (the *Sunday Times*) and Newnham (*Truth*), remained eager and hopeful of reaching a compromise with Germany based on concessions by Poland. They were uneasy with the Polish guarantee on strategic and political grounds; they appreciated that the determination of British participation in war had passed into Polish hands and was dependent upon what they regarded as Polish obduracy. Even greater disquiet was fostered by the Russian negotiations. Life-long anti-Bolsheviks and Conservative and Catholic appeasers found it well-nigh impossible to stomach the prospect of an Anglo-Soviet alliance, even if that were the sole avenue of escape from war; and if it furnished no escape, the prospect of fighting in alliance with 'murderous Reds' remained abhorrent and forbidding.

Nor was the Left completely happy with the Polish guarantee. Its strategic shortcoming (i.e., the absence of a Russian alliance) was obvious and its dangers appeared legion. For more than a year the Left, represented by the *New Statesman* and *Tribune*, had been preaching a Russian alliance. But, public professions aside, Kingsley Martin was filled with pessimism as the prospect of its conclusion grew more likely. Perhaps it would provoke rather than prevent a German onslaught and world war? The real drift of Kingsley Martin's thinking was revealed in his continuous espousal of a world peace conference; by this route, he joined the ranks of the die-hard appeasers who, despite Prague, were still bent on propitiating Germany.

Near-consensus was achieved in the weeklies, after Prague, over rearmament and conscription. Liberal support for rearmament and mobilisation now matched the clamour from the Right. While *Tribune*, unmoved, continued to oppose both, the *New Statesman* muted its criticisms. The Liberal, Leftist and some Conservative journals also joined hands in calling for the expansion of the Cabinet to include prominent anti-appeasers.

Altogether, to judge from the weeklies, the occupation of Prague and the ensuing Polish crisis brought the British nation substantially closer to reconciling itself to a new war against Germany. What had been unthinkable to the vast majority of the nation in September 1938 was now accepted, with varying degrees of resignation and despair. No journal spoke out against honouring the Polish guarantee or against the British declaration of war, though the pro-appeasement journals such as the *Tablet* and *Truth* (and Kingsley Martin in the *New Statesman*) continued to hope until the last moment that a compromise solution could be worked out at the expense of Poland.

VIII

CONCLUSION

In looking at the weeklies, this study has attempted to investigate a fresh body of evidence concerning British attitudes to Germany in the 1930s. The aim has been to discover what those attitudes were, what underlay them and what policies they issued in. It is hoped that some new light is thus shed on the era and on the mechanism of appeasement. The popular dailies furnish a good guide to British public opinion in the thirties; private and Cabinet papers are useful in determining the concerns and thinking of the country's political elite. The value of the evidence of the weeklies lies somewhere in between. They accurately reflected, across the Left-Right spectrum, the assumptions, concerns and politics of the educated classes. With amplification, they also echoed the drift of popular public opinion; and, to a degree, they reflected and perhaps influenced the assumptions and policies of the nation's political elite.

The policies of the weeklies during the successive crises of 1935–9 have been examined in detail; some light, in this respect, has been shed on the early thirties as well. Despite manifold differences between the journals, a common pattern of advocacy (and lack of it) emerges in the realm of foreign policy. Put simply, before March 1939 no weekly, with the inconsistent exceptions of *The Economist* and *Time & Tide*, was genuinely willing to contemplate war against Germany, Japan or Italy. With respect to Germany, Hitler's actions before March 1935 did not necessitate such contemplation (though perhaps the doctrinal thrust of Nazi ideology and *Mein Kampf* should have); German foreign policy was generally restrained if only, as many in fact remarked, because Hitler was too busy consolidating his rule and rearming. From March 1935 until March 1939, despite numerous displays of German aggressiveness in practice and in intention, the weekly press was almost unanimous in its rejection of 'confrontation politics'. Nor did similar displays by Italy and Japan elicit any greater firmness.

Broadly speaking, the posture adopted by the weekly press was one of appeasement. Middlemas's distinction between 'passive' and 'active' (or 'positive') appeasement[1] is useful in surveying the policies of the weeklies. But whereas he employed the distinction as between the

167

National Government's policies before May 1937 and after it, when applied to the weeklies the distinction must be between left-wing and Liberal weeklies on the one hand and Conservative weeklies on the other. The former normally confined themselves to 'passive' appeasement, the latter to a combination of the 'passive' and 'active' varieties. From 1933 until October 1938 the bulk of the left-wing and Liberal weeklies adhered to appeasement in the sense of refusing to advocate its alternative or any measures which might have made concrete their ostensible commitment to resistance to Fascism and collective security. For example, before 1937 they evinced almost no support for military alliances with France and Russia and none at all for a British commitment anywhere to the point of war. All supported the Government's refusal to contemplate military sanctions against Italy in 1935–6 and, through a silence of consent, upheld the refusal to arm the Spanish Republic. All supported the Government's inaction following the German rearmament proclamations of March 1935, the Rhineland *coup* of March 1936 and the *Anschluss* of March 1938. 'Passive' appeasement meant condoning or advocating inaction. In addition, left-wing and Liberal journals occasionally pursued 'positive' appeasement; the *New Statesman*'s policy in March and August 1938 concerning the Sudetenland and the occasional advocacy in the *New Statesman, Time & Tide* and the *Spectator* of colonial concessions are cases in point. Normally, however, left-wing and Liberal appeasement was characterised by acquiescence in the Government's willingness to offer concessions without reciprocity and acquiescence in German *coups* without a suggestion of firm and concrete reaction.

Conservative journals by and large supported the successive lines of the National Government – 'passive' appeasement under Baldwin and 'positive' appeasement under Chamberlain. Usually they were more forward than the Government in the espousal of each. The *Sunday Times* and the *Tablet* (under Woodruff) were normally willing to endorse more concessions than a Government constrained by sensitive public opinion and by even more sensitive, menaced friends on the Continent. Thus Sidebotham positively preached *Anschluss* for years while the Government merely refused to commit itself in advance to the defence of Austrian independence; thus the various Conservative weeklies between March and September 1938 demanded increasingly greater concessions from Czechoslovakia while the Government, similarly inclined, was unable to broach its desires in public.

So, while the left-wing and Liberal journals continued through the thirties to offer lip service to collective security and vehemently to condemn Nazi acts at home and abroad, the difference between them and the frankly pro-appeasement weeklies was little manifested in all that concerned advocacy of British policy. In effect, all supported British infirmity before 1938 and most did so until March 1939.

In his study of the British press, Gannon accepted Hadley's judgement that until March 1939 appeasement enjoyed the tacit or explicit approval of almost all Britons.[2] However, Gannon's explanation of the roots and motives underlying the adoption and promotion of that policy is not supported by the evidence of the weeklies. Gannon argued that appeasement was a product of 'confluence' or coincidence: appeasement, he contended, was not the consequence of attitudes to Nazi Germany or fears of war with Germany so much as the by-product of a variety of related and unrelated attitudes and policies adopted before Hitler's rise to power towards different issues – Versailles, rearmament, Bolshevism, Czechoslovakia, Poland, Britain's vital interests, and so on. Gannon wrote:

> Thus it was that when Hitler came to power in January 1933, he and his new regime were simply slotted in amongst the already important and divisive issues *which in fact determined* the reactions of the different British newspapers to the new leader and Government itself... [H]e appeared to each British newspaper in a well-defined context *which had little or nothing to do with himself* ... Hitler and his demands were like a funnel into which British attitudes on every question from armaments to xenophobia were poured: what emerged from the funnel was the single policy of appeasement. [My italics – B.M.][3]

To judge by the weeklies, such an interpretation is erroneous. In the thirties, Hitler was seen as the central phenomenon of European politics; no subject received more attention in the weeklies. Attitudes to all issues in the realm of foreign affairs turned upon, were amplified by and changed in accordance with reactions to Hitler and to the nature and aims of his regime. Attitudes to Versailles and treaty revision swiftly changed with the onset of Nazism and changed again with the revelations of German military might; long-held attitudes to rearmament and alliances underwent similar changes, as a result. Thus Gannon's funnel metaphor needs emendation. Given that the funnel represented the changing European situation along the time-bar, one might say that attitudes to all issues were poured into its mouth, passed through a filter – representing Hitlerism – at its centre and emerged almost invariably changed beyond recognition from its spout. At the centre of the European drama stood Nazism; perceptions of everything else were conditioned by the changing reactions to that central and brutal reality.

169

Britain's vital interests were variously perceived by the Conservative, Liberal and left-wing weeklies at the start of the 1930s. In the course of that decade, to judge from the weeklies, perceptions changed. In the case of the bulk of the left-wing and Liberal weeklies the change was radical. Among the Conservative journals, the degree of change differed from weekly to weekly; radical changes occurred only in the *Observer*, the *Tablet* and the *Saturday Review*.

On one issue there was almost total agreement among the weeklies throughout the thirties, regardless of political persuasion; the security of the lands lying West of the Rhine was seen as a vital British interest. 'Locarno' more or less defined the commitment entailed. All agreed that a foreign – by which was meant German – invasion of the Low Countries and France would constitute a vital threat to British security. The seriousness with which this traditional menace was viewed was enhanced by the contemporary belief in the efficacy of air power. It was understood by all that German control of air bases in the Low Countries and in Northern France would add immensely to the Luftwaffe's potency *vis-à-vis* England. Nor was the ultimate threat of seaborne invasion ever lost sight of when considering the safety of the Channel ports.

However, perceptions of French inviolability as a vital British interest posed a grave and ultimately insoluble problem for most Conservatives. Conservatives – with exceptions, as shall be shown – repudiated the notion that Britain had any vital interests in eastern Europe; they were wont, in this connection, to distinguish between 'vital interests' and mere 'interests'. But since the end of the Great War France had based her security in large measure on eastern alliances. Seen inversely, France was committed to the preservation of the territorial integrity of the Succession States. For Conservatives, France's eastern 'entanglements' meant that she might be drawn into war with Germany on behalf of some Polish or Czech tract of land of little concern to Britain. In the course of such a conflict France might well be assailed by Germany. And this would impinge on a vital British interest. Conservatives wished France to abandon her eastern bonds, but she showed no inclination to do so. Though this irked Conservatives like Sidebotham, they remained unable to repudiate the commitment to France as it would increase her insecurity and, in turn, that of Britain. Hence the French connection remained a necessary fact of life even for the staunchest advocates of appeasement.

Conservatives and Liberals agreed that Imperial possessions and the sea-routes which linked them were vital interests, to be preserved and secured to the point of war. They were particularly adamant about the safety of the 'Middle Seas' (that is, the North Sea and the Mediterranean). Journalists like Sidebotham, Garvin and F.A. Voigt (of the *Manchester Guardian*)[4] averred that these seas were literally Britain's 'life-lines' and that the security of British passage through them was vital to the safety of the mother country. This explains both the pertinacity of Garvin's and Sidebotham's espousal of Anglo-Italian agreement (to secure the Mediterranean), and also Garvin's and Lady Houston's disquiet over the Anglo-German Naval Agreement (which seemed to connote a renewed naval challenge in the North Sea and in the Atlantic). Japanese expansion in Asia and in the Pacific also appeared to threaten Imperial interests.

Left-wingers, averse to the concept of the Empire, were of a different persuasion. Though unsympathetic to Japanese and Italian imperial designs, they did not believe that Britain's safety or interests compelled war on account of far-flung domains or trade-routes. Their attitude to the 'Middle Seas', however, was ambivalent insofar as they acknowledged that a threat to passage through them might well imperil Britain itself.

In the years of appeasement, Conservative, Liberal and left-wing perceptions of vital interests conflicted most dramatically over eastern Europe. Between 1936 and March 1939 the Conservative weeklies consistently and vehemently argued that nothing in eastern Europe was of vital interest to Britain; the revision of frontiers, the dismemberment of states and the subversion of regimes in eastern Europe were no cause for involvement in war. Liberals and left-wingers rarely concurred explicitly though perhaps Kingsley Martin's opinions, that neither the Sudetenland nor Danzig were sufficient causes for world war, were more commonly held than voiced. Yet Conservatives, Liberals and Leftists were almost at one between 1933 and 1935 and again in 1939 in regarding eastern European developments and issues as vital British concerns. Among Conservatives, Garvin, Oldmeadow and Lady Houston before 1936 often warned that Germany must not be allowed to expand at the expense of her eastern neighbours. A greater, expanded Reich, they argued, would inevitably undermine the security of the West. Dissimilar and similar reasoning brought most Liberal and left-wing journals to the same conclusion. And in 1939 all adopted the common position that indeed vital British interests were at stake in Germany's eastward drive and that Danzig was 'worth' a world war.

Theoretically, the German subversion of the eastern European *status quo* should have been repugnant to the Right as well as to the Left from the beginning of the thirties, and should have compelled advocacy of British involvement to the point of war. Conservatives (and Liberals) were heirs to the doctrine of 'the balance of power'. For centuries, Britain had intervened on the Continent to prevent the supremacy of a single, militant Power. Such supremacy was seen as always and ultimately detrimental to British security. This, in fact, lay behind Britain's entry into the Great War. Hitler's rise and the Third Reich's expansionist pursuits signified a new bid for European hegemony to minds as diverse as those of Garvin, Sir Walter Layton, Lady Houston and Lady Rhondda. As such, Britain's vital interests as interpreted by balance of power theory compelled involvement.

Left-wing and Liberal beliefs were taxed by the emergence and intentions of Hitlerism on another plane. In foreign affairs the Liberals and the Left subscribed to the concept of 'collective security'. The theory enjoined all states to band together to prevent aggression or chastise the aggressor. In a sense, this was a mutation of 'balance of power' doctrine with a moral cloak super-imposed. It was a product of the Great War and was formulated against the backdrop of the failure of the Kaiser's bid for Continental supremacy. What were seen as the expansionist aims of Hitlerism in eastern Europe (and Italian and Japanese ambitions elsewhere) set fair to challenge and threaten the vital interests of Britain as well as 'morality'. Should collective security fail, went the theory, aggressor States would be tempted to pursue expansionism indefinitely. Ultimately, as *The Economist* and *Time & Tide* often stressed, such policies could only end in a frontal assault upon Britain and its Empire.

For the Left and the Liberals, German and Italian expansionism were perilous in another sense. Fascism and Nazism were regarded as above all a mortal threat to democracy and the liberal tradition. Besides subverting potential allies, German and Italian ambitions imperilled democratic norms and structures in France, Czechoslovakia and Spain. The European crisis was thus seen as an ideological struggle between the forces of democracy and of 'Fascism'; 'Fascism' was on the offensive, and Hitler's crusade against democracy, it was seen, could not but result in challenge to Britain.

Thus, both from the Conservative 'balance of power' perspective and from that of supporters of 'collective security' and democracy, the preservation of eastern Europe from aggression constituted a vital British interest. It is a measure of appeasement's dominance in Britain during the 1930s that neither balance of power nor collective security theories were pressed with ardour or firmness by their proponents before 1938. Conservatives, Liberals and left-wingers, all in some measure, denied their principles and their conceptions of vital interests in the pursuit of or acquiescence in the conciliation of Germany. The left-wing weeklies

172

almost invariably pointed out the threat to collective security posed by German attacks and ambitions in eastern Europe and Spain. But almost as invariably they forbore from urging a British commitment to block these designs. Conservative journals, between 1935 and 1939, starkly denied that vital British interests were anywhere involved or at risk in Hitler's eastern ambitions despite their concurrent appreciation that the European balance of power was gravely imperilled. Fear of Germany (and of Italy and Japan) had significantly eroded conceptions of vital national interests.

Some recent interpreters of appeasement have argued that Hitler did not aim at European hegemony and that appeasers in the thirties, in promoting their policy, acted in consonance with this belief. They have contended that appeasement was pursued on the basis of two inter-connected assumptions: first, that the peace treaties of 1919 were unjust and were in need of revision; and second, that the principal object of German foreign policy under Hitler (as before him) was indeed the rectification of the wrongs of Versailles. This view is not borne out by the evidence of the weeklies and must be dismissed before a correct assessment of the roots of appeasement may be reached.

The problem of the relationship between perceptions of Hitlerism and the espousal of appeasement should also be viewed from another angle. Previously it has been argued that appeasement, in the sense of a policy designed to right injustices and as pursued haphazardly in the 1920s, was a child of liberalism. This is not true of appeasement as pursued between 1935 and 1939. Liberal beliefs in the immorality of war and general premises about human nature and political affairs precluded a swift and accurate understanding of Nazi ideology and undoubtedly set the psychological and 'philosophical' scene for appeasement. But they were not its motor force or 'cause' in the thirties.

From the early thirties most British observers, to judge from the weeklies, sensed, if without full understanding, that Hitlerism spelt European war. Nor did a 'guilty conscience' over Versailles and a moral impulse to revise the peace settlement have much to do with appeasement. At stake was a new bid for European hegemony. Revisionism was a convenient inheritance from the twenties for those who felt, in the post-1933 situation, that the advocacy of appeasement demanded a moral dressing to make it palatable. The 'guilty conscience' and revisionism between 1933 and 1939 served as camouflage for the support of policies prompted by totally different considerations.

The weeklies afford a surfeit of evidence for this conclusion. However hazily, during 1933–4 most of the weeklies perceived that Hitler's advent had revolutionised the European situation. Despite a variety of misconceptions and an understandable reluctance to admit that affairs had taken a great turn for the worse, most felt that Hitlerism posed a grave threat to all of Europe, including Britain, and that it was politically hazardous (as well as immoral) to implement treaty revision in favour of a Nazi Germany. Most acknowledged that the violence displayed by Nazism towards its internal enemies was but a prelude to the violence it would, when ready, employ against its opponents abroad. Garvin, for example, an ardent appeaser between 1936 and 1938, wrote to Astor in mid-1933:

> This new barbarism in the centre of Europe must end by putting Western civilisation in dire peril . . . The one thing to keep hold of and never let go unless we mean to be undone is this: that a systematic creed of violence can only lead to violent deeds, that the absolute suppression in Germany of all advocacy of peace and the organised glorification of war *must* lead to war itself.[5]

Nor at this time was Garvin taken in by Hitler's occasional pacific sops: 'Hitler's terms . . . are plausible enough to deceive the birds . . . well-contrived groundwork for supremacy.'[6] Hence Garvin was clear about treaty revision: 'While these conditions remain, Treaty revision in every effective shape or form is rendered impossible.'[7]

From the other end of the political spectrum Kingsley Martin, despite his inability to fathom the hold of 'race' doctrine in Germany, was clear about the threat posed by Hitler's Reich to European peace. Nazi foreign policy, he wrote in May 1933, 'is not merely an assertion of the legitimate rights of Germany . . . They are deliberately challenging the peace of Europe'.[8] War, he declared, was 'the God of the Fascists'[9] and 'Hitler's Germany . . . promises – blatantly and openly – another great war'.[10] As he put it in February 1934:

> We do not see why we should join in the general game of self-deception about Hitler's foreign policy . . . [Hitlerite moderation] is one of the things people believe because they very much want to believe them. The evidence points in the opposite direction. Hitler's foreign policy has been clear from the very beginning. The map of the Greater Germany, which is to be won for the Teutonic race, is plastered all over Germany and impressed on the minds of every German school-child . . .[11]

Even the most consistent advocates of appeasement among the weeklies, *Truth* and the *Sunday Times*, soon after Hitler's assumption of power sensed the danger. As *Truth* put it in May 1933:

> The Hitlerite danger is not likely to be confined to Germany ...
> Germany is making ready to fall on her neighbours, and there is
> no shadow of doubt that nothing but her unreadiness is ever likely
> to deter her from that objective.

The journal declared that 'every word' of the peace treaties must
stand until Hitlerism was replaced by something less bellicose.[12] Even
Sidebotham of the *Sunday Times* cautiously indicated his fears:

> The idea that there is in this country any desire to interfere in
> German internal politics on behalf of the persecuted Jews or
> Marxists or trade unionists may be dismissed at once ... But
> in international politics, what a nation does at home creates a
> certain presumption about what it is likely to do in relation to its
> neighbours.[13]

He did not, however, come out against treaty revision. *Time & Tide*,
long a proponent of revisionism, did. Britain and the West, declared
Lady Rhondda in 1933, must remain 'committed by honour and by
common sense alike ... to stand by the Treaties'.[14] Yet despite these
early perceptions of the danger of Hitlerism and the concomitant rejection
of treaty revision favourable to the Third Reich, from 1935 until the end
of 1938 there was almost total unanimity in the weekly press about the
virtues of appeasement and argumentation in its support based ostensibly
on rediscovered revisionist impulses.

Indirect proof that revisionism was camouflage for the pursuit of
appeasement rather than its motivation is afforded by contemporary
attitudes to Mussolini's attack on Abyssinia and to the foreign interventions in the Spanish Civil War. Versailles's rights and wrongs were
relevant to neither. Yet during 1935–8 a virtual consensus existed
in the weeklies in support of the Government's 'non-interventionist'
policies: all effectively abjured political and arms support for the Spanish
Republic and Ethiopia and all rejected military sanctions against Italy. For
Conservatives such as Garvin there were, certainly, additional motives.
They were willing to contemplate, indeed desired, an Anglo-Italian *entente*
and detested Spanish Republicanism as an offshoot of Bolshevism. No
such considerations impelled the Liberal and left-wing weeklies. They
simply toed the Government line almost consistently during both conflicts,
their determination to avoid war overcoming scruples and convictions.

Thus A.J.P. Taylor's argument that appeasement represented an
apotheosis or consummation of liberalism, 'a triumph for all that was
best and most enlightened in British life ... a triumph for those
who courageously denounced the harshness and short-sightedness of

Versailles',[15] has no basis in the evidence of the weeklies. Perhaps magnanimity and courage came into it in the 1920s; appeasement in the 1930s was unmarked by these virtues. Certainly a degree of ignorance prevailed concerning Nazi ideology and its ultimate aims; but it was not so total as to preclude an appreciation that Hitler threatened the peace of Europe and, ultimately, British security. Many, if not most, acknowledged early in the day that Hitler's ambitions transcended treaty revision. Once the gospel of the British intelligentsia, revisionism was not the motor force of appeasement between 1935 and 1939.

Attitudes to rearmament and alliances doubtless affected thinking about policy towards Germany. The reluctance of liberals to contemplate rearmament and the forging of alliances, and the popular unwillingness to see money spent on rearmament rather than on social betterment certainly tied the hands of those in Whitehall who advocated firmness towards Hitler. But the inverse connection was even more pronounced and decisive. Perceptions of Hitlerism and of the growing militancy of Germany between 1935 and 1939 radically altered British attitudes on the questions of rearmament and alliances.

The Liberal antagonism to armaments was most consistently expressed, through the thirties, in the left-wing journals. The *New Statesman* persisted in opposing defence estimates and increases until 1939; *Tribune* always stressed its objection to arms for a Conservative Government while impracticably and in theory supporting arms for a Labour Government (though remaining cautious in its phraseology as to how such arms should then be used). Conservatives and Liberals often retorted that resistance to Fascism and collective security could not be implemented if the Government was denied arms. *Tribune* and the *New Statesman* replied that a Conservative Government would in any event never confront, defy or fight Fascism. *Tribune*, indeed, carried this further by arguing that arming the Government would only strengthen it for an eventual confrontation with the working class. However, criticism of rearmament vanished from the pages of the *New Statesman*, at least, by the start of 1939.

The rise and revelation of the character of Hitlerism brought about a complete reversal of the Liberal journals' attitude to rearmament. Gradually from the spring of 1935 all the Liberal journals came to accept the need for British rearmament; after Munich, they all clamoured for 'massive' rearmament, especially in the air. Even the Quaker-edited *Spectator* tardily joined the rearmament lobby.

The rise of Hitlerism also affected the attitudes of the Conservative weeklies to rearmament. They had never, in principle, opposed rearmament, though before 1933 they often questioned the need for a massive rearming. From 1933 all came out in support of rearmament. Some journals, such as the *Saturday Review* and the *Observer*, demanded far greater expenditure on defence, especially in the air, than the Government was proposing or enacting. Others, such as *Truth* and the *Sunday Times*, were willing to make do with the Government's lead and self-imposed limits. Munich led to a virtual rebellion among the Conservative journals on the matter of armaments: all demanded that the Government scrap its 'business as usual' ruling and arm as fast and as massively as resources would allow.

Even more decisive was the effect of Hitlerism on British attitudes to alliances. At the start of the thirties most of the weeklies exhibited a strong prejudice against political and military alliances as harbingers of war. Most, especially the Conservative weeklies, even felt uneasy about the Locarno commitments. The *Sunday Times*, the *New Statesman* and *The Economist* repeatedly declared that military alliances had been a major cause of the Great War.

After the advent of Hitler, pro-appeasement journals of the Right abjured an alliance with France or with its eastern partners on the grounds that these would involve Britain in world war over non-vital interests. Especially loathsome to Conservatives and Catholics appeared the possibility of an alliance with Soviet Russia; ideological grounds were added to the normal geo-political ones. A similar ideological revulsion informed the Liberal and left-wing rejection of alliance with Italy in a common anti-German front.

The one alliance all Conservatives and Liberals coveted throughout the twenties and thirties was with the United States. This desire overrode their anti-alliance prejudice because an American alliance was seen, if fulfilled, as measurably increasing British security without adding to her obligations. Immediately, it promised the containment of menacingly expansionist Japan. The *New Statesman* and *Tribune*, on the other hand, showed little interest in an American alliance, perhaps because the United States remained the redoubt of capitalism.

The rise of Hitlerism, radically – albeit briefly – altered views on alliances. Previously, both Garvin and Sidebotham had been Franco-phobes and ardent revisionists. In 1934 the *Observer* and the *Sunday Times* clamoured for an open military alliance with France. Sidebotham called for a binding 'air alliance', by which he hoped that Britain could enjoy the benefits of French air power without incurring the land obligations stemming from France's eastern commitments. Garvin realised that such a limited alliance was impracticable and therefore urged full military alliance. By 1935 both had dropped this proposal because they had come to believe that German military power, especially in the air, was

177

already stronger than the combined might of Britain and France; hence the proposed alliance was seen as an entangling liability rather than as an asset. Nonetheless, this marked an abrupt reversal of long-held prejudices against continental commitment and alliances. It prefigured the subsequent reversal of 1939. With the abandonment of the hope of appeasement's success, all the Conservative journals, save for the *Tablet*, came out in favour of alliances with anyone on the Continent willing to enter into them. The reversal was particularly stark with respect to Russia. The fear of Nazi power and intentions was so acute as to overshadow deeply-held ideological prejudices. Anti-Bolshevism, apparently, was not as powerful a compulsion as strategic expediency once the chips were down. Principle, as it were, once again gave way to politic self-interest.

Despite their views of Hitlerism, the Liberal and left-wing journals before 1937 refused anything more binding than the Covenant or less inclusive than the League. But against the backdrop of the League's failure over Abyssinia and the ongoing civil war in Spain, these journals slowly changed their outlook. In 1937 the *New Statesman* hesitantly urged British participation in the 'united front' against Fascism. More convincingly and consistently, *The Economist* from the autumn of that year explicitly called for military alliances with France and Russia. *Tribune*, from its inception in 1937, called for a Russian alliance; *Time & Tide* joined it in the wake of the *Anschluss*. By January 1939 the *Spectator* had been converted to support of an alliance with France and the Soviet Union. Such then was the reversal in thinking about alliances initiated and consummated by perceptions of the Nazi peril.

The problem posed by appeasement, as by most historical controversies, is one of motive and cause. What prompted most Englishmen to subscribe to appeasement toward Germany between 1933 and 1939? The evidence of the weeklies provides both negative and positive evidence on the question. As has been argued, prior attitudes to Versailles and a belief in the justice of German claims had little to do with the espousal of appeasement between 1935 and 1939. Nor, ultimately, had ignorance of the nature and intentions of the Nazi regime. By the time 'positive' appeasement was in full swing under Chamberlain, most intelligent observers recognised the danger it posed to Europe and Britain. Nor did wonted perceptions of Britain's vital interests clearly favour the adoption of appeasement; adherence to 'collective security' or 'balance of power' thinking antedated, and finally triumphed over, the view that the fate of eastern Europe was no concern of Britain's. From early in the day, many observers recognised that Hitler's Germany aimed at European hegemony. Appeasers ignored the indications and attempted to reject this proposition until late in the

178

day. But the question remains: why did they react in this way? Moral abhorrence of war is an insufficient explanation. (Liberals, though detesting war, plunged Britain into the first holocaust in 1914; and, with greater knowledge of costs, did so again, with unanimity, in September 1939.) To judge from the weeklies, appeasement above all stemmed from fear of war. Memories of the Great War, the horror of the trenches and the bungles of generals and politicians, played a part. Of still greater importance was the contemporary awareness of technological innovations in armaments and of Britain's geo-political and military weakness.

During the thirties, all the weeklies showed acute awareness of Britain's unique vulnerability. In terms of commitments and possessions, she was still *the* world power. Her interests encompassed Europe, Africa and Asia and the world's oceans and seas. She was committed to the protection of territories in six continents and to the maintenance of safe sea-routes between them and between them and herself. As in the First World War, a naval blockade of Britain was seen as a mortal peril, given her dependence on imported foodstuffs and raw materials. To this was added the new threat of aerial blockade. The Great War and the world economic depression which followed seemed to have vastly depleted Britain's resources. By the 1930s, her army had all but vanished; her stockpiles of military equipment had become obsolescent or obsolete; and the state of her economy and public opinion forbade any large-scale rearmament. Hence British resources were deemed insufficient to meet her commitments. Put another way, Britain could not meet warlike contingencies on her own in more than one continent or theatre at a time.

Haltingly from 1933, and acutely from 1935, most of the weeklies exhibited a profound fear of British embroilment in conflict in more than one area of the globe. Germany, Italy and Japan emerged as bellicose states determined on a path of expansion. *The Economist* and *Time & Tide* repeatedly warned that a hostile coalition was forming and that its ultimate prey must be the vast, vulnerable and wealthy British Empire. This fear underscored their espousal of collective security. But how could Britain effectively contain Japan in the Far East without American aid? And how could Italy be thwarted in the Mediterranean without at least French collaboration, withheld through her greater fear of Germany? Lastly, how could Hitlerite expansion be checked without an effective and willing coalition of like-minded European partners?

Journals with an imperial or Commonwealth orientation, such as the *Observer*, the *Sunday Times* and the *Spectator*, preferred, given Britain's limited resources, to first secure far-flung possessions and sea-routes. The danger from Hitler could be neutralised by appeasement. But appeasing zeal was curbed by uncertainty as to Germany's ultimate intentions: an expanded and over-potent Reich would over-shadow Europe and imperil British security.

Yet a confrontation with Germany would invite Italy and Japan to do their worst elsewhere. This fear of a war on many fronts dominated all evaluations of British policy towards Germany, Italy and Japan. It cogently indicated the need for appeasement. Potential enemies had to be bought off, even at stiff prices, so that their number might be reduced. As a memorandum produced in November 1937 for the Cabinet by the Joint Intelligence Committee succinctly argued:

> Without overlooking the assistance which we should hope to obtain from France, and possibly other allies, we cannot foresee the time when our defence forces will be strong enough to safe-guard our territory, trade and vital interests against Germany, Italy and Japan simultaneously.[16]

Hence the need for 'any political or international action which could be taken to reduce the number of our potential enemies'.[17]

The problem of the Dominions reinforced the advocacy of appeasement, especially in the Commonwealth-minded weeklies. During the Great War the Dominions had contributed substantially to the Allied war effort. In the thirties they constituted a multiple liability. On the one hand, they enjoyed a British commitment to their defence which, given the Japanese threat in the Pacific, was likely to become operative. On the other hand, through most of the decade the Dominions refused to be drawn into a new Continental war. Imperial and Commonwealth-oriented editors, like Garvin, Wrench and Wilson Harris feared that should Britain embark on war in defence of the Covenant on the Continent, the Dominions would keep out and perhaps sever their ties with the Crown.

Above all, for Britons in the thirties war against Germany connoted the prospect of air attack and devastation. People then regarded the threat of aerial bombing as a later generation regarded the prospect of nuclear holocaust. Through the thirties, the Cabinet and Air Staff envisaged British casualties as running into hundreds of thousands in the first weeks of war against Germany, principally as a result of air attacks upon civilian centres. Indeed, there was a responsible school of opinion that thought that Germany would initiate a new world war by a massive aerial first strike or knock-out blow and that this would incapacitate the country attacked within days or weeks.

These beliefs were clearly echoed in the pages of all the serious weeklies. The Luftwaffe, until the end of 1938, was seen as capable of demolishing London and all of Britain's other major cities. Gas and thermite bombs were particularly feared. Ships, too, were regarded by many as highly vulnerable to aerial assault; and with Britain's traditional shield thus neutralised, what hope was there of a British victory in a new world war?

The belief in the Luftwaffe's potency, which usually outran its actual strength at any given moment, was probably the single most important determinant of appeasement in the thirties. If aerial annihilation was on the cards, and if war would prompt it, then war with Germany must be avoided at any, or almost any, cost. To avoid it, no price paid in eastern European currency was too high for the *Sunday Times* and the *Tablet*. Others, perhaps, were less generous but they too tended that way. It was the Luftwaffe's pre-eminence which made the appeasement of Germany, among the hostile states, the main goal.

Finally, a factor which made for appeasement, at least in those journals in which that policy sat ill (such as *The Economist, Time & Tide*, the *Spectator* and the *New Statesman*), was a fear of 'what the neighbours would say'. Probably few worried that greater militancy would lead to a drop in sales or readership; but all displayed great sensitivity to the judgement of their peers. Given the memory of the Great War, no liberal in the thirties wished to appear to be advocating a course which would lead to a new holocaust. Few were willing to open themselves to the charge of war-mongering, even if principles demanded firmness to the point of war. Thus Layton and Lady Rhondda during the Abyssinian crisis quickly retreated from their initial support of a blockade of the Suez Canal to Italian shipping. They were willing to contemplate war against the Covenant-breaker; but they were less willing to incur the charge of war-mongering. Thus the consensus supporting appeasement was to some degree compounded of unwilling subscribers. As in all situations, majority views tended to exercise a centripetal force; a desire to conform was added to genuinely shared views in the formation of that consensus.

To judge from the weeklies, appeasement died of shame. The humiliation suffered at Munich and the apparent immorality of that settlement were the major cause of the *volte face* which occurred in the wake of the German occupation of Prague. In this sense, it may be said that a nation which had relentlessly pursued a line of expediency for six years abruptly replaced the determinants of its foreign policy by considerations of morality. The extension of the guarantee to Poland was more a moral gesture of defiance than a calculated political expedient; and certainly the implementation of that guarantee on 3 September 1939 ran counter to most strategic or geo-political sense.

Of course, the extension of the guarantee to Poland and the subsequent British moves which led up to the declaration of war reflected the return to prominence of balance of power thinking. Munich and Prague had forced the appeasers to open their eyes to the Third Reich's bid for Continental hegemony. The destruction of Czechoslovakia had palpably increased Germany's preponderance. Munich and Prague precluded any prolongation of illusions about Hitler's intentions. To avert further deterioration of her position, Britain opted for resistance.

Perhaps, too, fear of war had somewhat diminished by 1939. The fear of multi-front war had not vanished; but air fear, to some degree, had. 1938–9 witnessed the first stage of the overthrow of the fear-instilling dogma that 'the bomber will always get through'. To judge from the weeklies, by 1939 many Britons had come to believe that effective defence against air attack was possible. Some too, were aware of the progress made in the production of the tools with which that defence could be accomplished. Perhaps, therefore, it was no accident that the beginning of the disappearance of that fear which had figured so largely in the adoption of appeasement coincided with the gradual rejection of that policy between September 1938 and September 1939.

APPENDIX

CIRCULATIONS

The following figures, culled from various sources, are, I believe, reliable approximations.

	1933	1935–37	1939
The *Spectator*	19,000	22,000	25,000
The Economist	8,000	–	12,000
The *New Statesman and Nation*	15,000	–	30,000
Time & Tide	–	–	20,000
Tribune	–	–	25,000
The *Week-End Review*	6,000	–	–
The *Tablet*	12,000	12,000	13,000
Truth	–	6,000	–
The *Listener*	42,000	50,000	50,000
The *Observer*	–	210,000	–
The *Sunday Times*	187,000 (1932)	270,000	–

Note: In the thirties, the weeklies enjoyed a heyday in influence and readership. Circulations rose, in some cases steeply, in the course of the decade.

Readership and circulation, especially in relation to weeklies, are distinct terms. A daily newspaper's readership is usually computed as being 2–3½ times its circulation. Issues of serious weeklies are usually read by seven or more people, in homes, in libraries and in common rooms. It is possible that special interest weeklies enjoy a still higher readership-to-circulation ratio.

NOTES

CHAPTER I: INTRODUCTION

1. For example, Taylor, *Origins*, devotes only two paragraphs to British fears of air attack in the 1930s.
2. Gannon, *British Press*, pp. 4–5.
3. Goronwy Rees, former assistant editor of the *Spectator*, makes this point when recalling his first impressions of the extreme nationalist *Weltanschauung* in late Weimar Germany. He wrote (*A Bundle of Sensations*, p. 46): 'It seemed to me that no one could seriously believe such a farrago of nonsense ... so brutal and barbarous ... I was firmly convinced that the irrational was the unreal.'
4. See Gilbert, *Appeasement*, passim. Gilbert stresses the changing meaning of 'appeasement' in the course of the thirties but dates the change from 1937; 1935, to judge from the weeklies, seems to me a more accurate dating.
5. Gilbert, *Appeasement*, passim.
6. *Spectator*, 1 Nov. 1935, 'A Spectator's Notebook' by Janus (i.e. H. Wilson Harris).
7. *Spectator*, 18 Sept. 1936, 'A Spectator's Notebook' by Janus.
8. *Time & Tide*, 1 July 1933, 2nd l.a., 'The Nazi Fantasy'.
9. Astor Papers, J.L. Garvin to Waldorf Astor, 31 Aug. 1933.
10. *Time & Tide*, 6 July 1935, 1st l.a., 'Perfidious Albion' by Odette Keun.
11. *Listener*, 19 April 1933, 'What Germany Was Thinking Last Week' by Sir J. Evelyn Wrench.
12. *Sunday Times*, 11 Feb. 1934, book review by W. Horsefall Carter of Wickham Steed, *Hitler, Whence And Whither?*
13. *Spectator*, 16 March 1934, 'Germany To-day: The Nazis and the Churches' by H. Powys Greenwood.
14. *Week-End Review*, 8 July 1933, 1st l.a., 'Where Is Germany Going?'.
15. *New Statesman*, 25 March 1933, 1st l.a., 'The End of a Taboo'.
16. *The Economist*, 24 Feb. 1934, 6th l.a., 'The Young Nazi Mind' by 'A Correspondent'.
17. *Week-End Review*, 18 Nov. 1933, 'Can Nazi Policy Be Reasonable?' by G.E.G. Catlin; Bartlett, *Nazi Germany Explained*, passim.

CHAPTER II: THE WEEKLIES IN THE 1930s

1. Watson, *My Life*, pp. 271–2.
2. Hudson, *Writing Between the Lines*, p. 186.
3. Kingsley Martin Papers, Keynes to Martin and Lord Cecil.
4. Harris, *Life So Far*, p. 247.
5. Ibid., p. 256.
6. Ibid., p. 248. For Harris see also *D.N.B. 1951–60*, 'H. Wilson Harris'.
7. Watson, *Building a Christian State*, p. 10.
8. Harris, *Peace in the Making*, p. 214.
9. Interview with Rees, 15 Jan. 1977.
10. Wrench, *Dawson and Our Times*, p. 266. See also Thomas, *Story of the Spectator*, pp. 6–7.
11. Harris, *Life So Far*, p. 247.
12. Watt, *Personalities and Policies*, p. 125.
13. Watson, *On Building a Christian State*, p. 11.
14. Wrench, *I Loved Germany*, pp. 13, 48.
15. Ibid., p. 20.
16. Ibid., p. 26.
17. Watson, *On Building a Christian State*, pp. 11, 10.
18. Watson, *My Life*, p. 273.

19. Interview with Rees, 15 Jan. 1977.
20. Interview with Rees, 15 Jan. 1977. The *Spectator*'s 'Log-Book' recorded the authorship of unsigned leaders.
21. Harris, *Life So Far*, p. 237.
22. *The Economist, 1843–1943*, p. 26.
23. Tyerman letter to author, 31 May 1977.
24. Tyerman letter to author, 25 Feb. 1977. Interviews with Jay (25 Feb. 1977) and Hutton (5 March 1977).
25. Letter from Tyerman to author, 25 Feb. 1977.
26. Interviews with Hutton, 5 and 14 Feb. 1977, and Jay, 25 Feb. 1977, and letters by Tyerman to author, 16 Jan. 1977, 15 Feb. 1977, 25 Feb. 1977 and 8 March 1977.
27. Letters to author from Hutton, 8 March 1977, and Jay, 8 March 1977, and interview with Hutton 5 Feb. 1977.
28. Tyerman letter to author, 25 Feb. 1977.
29. *The Economist, 1843–1943*, p. 90.
30. Ibid., p. 93.
31. Toynbee, 'Peaceful Change or War?' in *International Affairs*, Jan.–Feb. 1936, p. 31.
32. Hutton, *Is It Peace?*, p. 201.
33. *The Economist, 1843–1943*, p. 93.
34. Layton, 'Whither Europe?' in *Challenge to Europe*, p. 14.
35. Ibid., p. 18.
36. Ibid., p. 13. Also Hutton, *Is It Peace?*, p. 291.
37. Hutton, *Is It Peace?*, pp. 352–3.
38. Tyerman letter to author, 31 May 1977.
39. Toynbee, 'Peaceful Change or War?', p. 27.
40. Interview with Jay, 25 Feb. 1977.
41. Toynbee, *International Affairs*, passim, and Liddell Hart Papers (I/698), Toynbee to Lord Allen of Hurtwood, 11 May 1938. Toynbee's thinking remains problematic mainly because he was convinced both of the necessity of supporting the League and collective security and of the certain doom another world war would bring upon the British Empire and, perhaps, western civilisation. Despite some apparently conflicting evidence, I believe my outline of the evolution of his thinking *vis-à-vis* Germany is correct: until the summer of 1938 he was opposed to concessions to Nazi Germany, excepting colonies; from the summer of 1938 he became convinced that placating Germany must override all other considerations, in view of the prospective destruction another war would bring.
42. Watt, *Personalities & Policies*, p. 125 and Layton, 'Whither Europe?' in *Challenge to Europe*, p. 14.
43. Hutton, *Is It Peace?*, pp. 98, 29.
44. See, for example, Jones, *Diary With Letters*, p. 181. Jones recorded Layton's reaction to the Rhineland coup as focusing on the event itself; by contrast the others gathered at Blickling Hall for the weekend, including Toynbee, preferred to focus on Hitler's peace proposals.
45. *DNB, 1951–1960*, 'Viscountess Rhondda'.
46. *Report of the Royal Commission on the Press*, p. 23.
47. *Time & Tide*, 13 March 1933, 1st l.a., 'Alarums and Excursions'.
48. *Time & Tide*, 21 Oct. 1933, 1st l.a., 'Stand by the Treaties!'
49. *Time & Tide*, 1 April 1933, 'Foreign Affairs' by Norman Angell.
50. *Time & Tide*, 4 May 1935, Review of the Week, 'The Need for Plain Words'.
51. *Time & Tide*, 22 June 1935, Review of the Week, 'A Welcome Agreement'.
52. *Time & Tide*, 21 Nov. 1936, Review of the Week, 'What Next?'
53. *Time & Tide*, 26 Dec. 1936, 1st l.a., 'Dogs in the Manger'; 6 Feb. 1937, Review of the Week, 'Colonies'.
54. *Time & Tide*, 25 Sept. 1937, Review of the Week, 'Germany's Legitimate Grievances'.
55. *Time & Tide*, 9 March 1935, Review of the Week.
56. *Time & Tide*, 12 Oct. 1935, Review of the Week, 'Rearmament Issues'.
57. *Time & Tide*, 14 March 1936, 1st l.a., 'The Crisis'.
58. *Time & Tide*, 21 Sept. 1935, 1st l.a., 'What is Britain's Business? – The League and the

Dictators'.
59. *Time & Tide*, 5 Sept. 1936, 1st l.a., 'Fantastic Quadrille'.
60. *Time & Tide*, 13 Nov. 1937, 1st l.a., 'The Anti-Comintern Pact'.
61. Passfield Papers, B. Webb Diaries, entry for 5 July 1938.
62. Woodruff interview with author 26 March 1977 and letter to author 7 April 1977.
63. Kingsley Martin Papers, memorandum entitled 'British Foreign Policy in the Thirties' by Martin.
64. Dalton Papers, diaries, entry for 8 April 1938.
65. Passfield Papers, Beatrice Webb Diaries, 22 Feb. 1935.
66. Muggeridge, *The Green Stick*, p. 172.
67. Kingsley Martin Papers, Keynes to Martin, 23 April 1933.
68. Muggeridge, *The Green Stick*, pp. 174, 172.
69. *New Statesman*, 26 March 1938.
70. Wiskemann, *The Europe I Saw*, p. 191.
71. For Keynes on appeasement, see Rolph, *Kingsley*, pp. 191–200, and Martin, *Editor*, pp. 255–63.
72. For the acknowledgement of the influence of Brailsford and Joad on Martin, see Martin, *Editor*, pp. 144–9 and 148–52.
73. Interview with Hutton, 14 Feb. 1977.
74. Martin, *Editor*, pp. 80, 184, 255, and Rolph, *Kingsley*, pp. 189–90.
75. Kingsley Martin Papers, Martin to Gedye, 1 Sept. 1938.
76. Martin, *Editor*, p. 35.
77. Ibid., p. 256.
78. Ibid., p. 38.
79. Kingsley Martin Papers, Martin to Zilliacus (undated).
80. Martin, *Editor*, p. 35.
81. Ibid., p. 204.
82. Vallance and Postgate, *Those Foreigners*, p. 261.
83. Martin, *Editor*, pp. 52–3.
84. Dalton Papers, memorandum of talk, 19 Oct. 1938.
85. Interview with Lord Brooke of Cumnor, 12 May 1977.
86. *Truth*, 17 Sept. 1930, 'Entre Nous' and 24 Sept. 1930, 1st l.a., 'German Flappers' by a Truthful Tory.
87. *Truth*, 11 Feb. 1931, 2nd l.a., 'The Suicide of Poland' by A Correspondent.
88. *Truth*, 18 Feb. 1931, 2nd l.a., 'A Circe Among Cities'.
89. *Truth*, 29 July 1931, 1st l.a., 'A Bungled Conference' by a Truthful Tory.
90. *Truth*, 2 Nov. 1932, 1st l.a., 'The Danzig Danger' by a Truthful Tory.
91. *Truth*, 10 May 1933, 1st l.a., 'Hitler Comes to Stay', by Plain Dealer.
92. *Truth*, 12 July 1933, 1st l.a., 'Hitler Against the World' by Plain Dealer.
93. *Truth*, 10 Jan. 1934, 1st l.a., 'Distracted Europe' by Plain Dealer.
94. *Truth*, 6 June 1934, Entre Nous.
95. *Truth*, 18 July 1934, 1st l.a., 'British Foreign Policy' by Plain Dealer.
96. *Truth*, 16 March 1938, 1st l.a., 'Hitler's Coup'.
97. *Truth*, 30 May 1934, Entre Nous.
98. *Truth*, 18 May 1938, Entre Nous, 'Sudeten Volcano'.
99. Gannon, *British Press*. p. 51.
100. Woodruff, interview, 26 March 1977.
101. *DNB 1941–50*, 'J.L. Garvin'.
102. Katharine Garvin, *J.L. Garvin*, p. 82.
103. Ursula Slaghek, letter to author, 24 March 1977.
104. Katharine Garvin, *J.L. Garvin*, p. 51.
105. *Observer*, 17 May 1931, 'Peace & Drifting Backwards' by J.L. Garvin.
106. *Observer*, 6 March 1932, 'Dr Masaryk' by the Diplomatic Correspondent (George Glasgow).
107. Gannon, *British Press*, p. 50.
108. *Observer*, 30 March 1930, 'Britain's "No"' by J.L. Garvin.

109. Astor Papers, Garvin to Astor, Cablegram, 5 Dec. 1932.
110. For example, see *Observer*, 3 March 1935, 'Peace and the Great Plan' by J.L. Garvin.
111. *Observer*, 5 Feb. 1933, 'Whither Germany?' by J.L. Garvin.
112. *Observer*, 20 April 1933, 1st l.a., 'Germany & Britain'. See also *Observer*, 7 May 1933, 'Whither Germany?' by J.L. Garvin, in which he argued against piecemeal concessions to Germany as they would only prompt further demands.
113. Astor Papers, Garvin to Waldorf Astor, 21 Aug. 1933.
114. *Observer*, 17 Sept. 1933, 'Hitler & Arms' by J.L. Garvin.
115. *Observer*, 30 June 1935, 'Peace is One' by J.L. Garvin.
116. *Observer*, 20 March 1938, 'No War and Why' by J.L. Garvin.
117. *Observer*, 22 March 1936, 'Not Now – But . . .' by J.L. Garvin.
118. Gannon, *British Press*, pp. 51–2.
119. *DNB 1951–60*, 'William Berry'.
120. Gannon, *British Press*, p. 54; Gilbert, *Churchill*, Vol. V, p. 1094.
121. *DNB 1951–60*, 'W.W. Hadley'.
122. Ibid.
123. *Sunday Times*, 10 May 1936, 'Abyssinia's Sad Fate' by Scrutator.
124. For example, see *Sunday Times*, 16 April 1933, 'Facing Facts in Europe' by Scrutator.
125. *Sunday Times*, 14 May 1933, 'New Challenge to Europe' by Scrutator.
126. *Sunday Times*, 27 May 1934, 'Russia Wants a Pact' by Scrutator.
127. *Sunday Times*, 11 Nov. 1934, 'Day of Remembrance' by Scrutator.
128. *Sunday Times*, 31 Oct. 1937, 'A Political Look-Round' by Scrutator.
129. Woodruff interview, 26 March 1977.
130. Ibid.
131. *Tablet*, 4 Oct. 1930, News and Notes.
132. *Tablet*, 21 Oct. 1933, News and Notes.
133. *Tablet*, 4 Nov. 1933, 1st l.a., 'Germany's Worst Friends' and 21 April 1934, News and Notes.
134. *Tablet*, 20 Jan. 1934, 2nd l.a., '"Born in The Trenches"'.
135. *Tablet*, 8 Dec. 1934, News and Notes.
136. *Tablet*, 10 April 1937, 2nd l.a.
137. Ibid.
138. *Tablet*, 8 Jan. 1938, 1st l.a., 'Democracies & Dictatorships'.
139. See Attenborough, *A Living Memory*, passim.
140. Ibid., p.151.
141. *British Weekly*, 14 July 1932, 1st l.a., 'Peace & Amnesty of Lausanne'.
142. *British Weekly*, 2 June 1938, Notes of the Week, 'Our Reticence'.
143. *British Weekly*, 19 April 1934, 1st l.a., 'League of Nations and the Church'.
144. *British Weekly*, 12 Sept. 1935, 1st l.a., 'The Inevitable League'.
145. *British Weekly*, 30 May 1935, 1st l.a., 'Christian Scholarship and World Peace'.
146. *British Weekly*, 3 Oct. 1935, Notes of the Week, 'We can No Other'.
147. *Listener*, 8 Feb. 1933, 'Crises in 3 Countries' by Vernon Bartlett.
148. *Listener*, 22 Feb. 1933, 'Hitler and the Junkers' by Vernon Bartlett.
149. *Listener*, 19 April 1933, 'What Germany was Thinking' by Sir J. Evelyn Wrench; see also *Listener*, 22 March 1933, 'Nazi Revolution' by Sir Arthur Salter.
150. *Week-End Review*, 25 March 1933, 1st l.a., 'Rome and Revision'.
151. *Week-End Review*, 10 June 1933, 'Europe from the Train' by Gerald Barry.
152. *Week-End Review*, 14 Oct. 1933, 1st l.a., 'Back to your Kennel' and 21 Oct. 1933, 1st l.a., 'Turning the Crisis to Account'.
153. See Mairet, *Orage, A Memoir*, passim; *New English Weekly*, 18 April 1935, for special note on journal's policy.
154. *New English Weekly*, 12 May 1932, 'Germany's Brave New World' by W. Horsfall Carter.
155. *New English Weekly*, 6 April 1933, Notes of the Week.
156. *New English Weekly*, 14 Sept. 1933, Notes of the Week.
157. *New English Weekly*, 25 May 1935, Notes of the Week.
158. *New English Weekly*, 9 May 1935, Notes of the Week.

159. *New English Weekly*, 4 May 1933, 'A Continental Diary – January–March 1933' by C.E. Bechhofer Roberts.
160. *New English Weekly*, 25 April 1935, Notes of the Week.
161. *Saturday Review*, 8 July 1932, Notes of the Week.
162. *Saturday Review*, 10 Sept. 1932, Notes of the Week.
163. *Saturday Review*, 14 March 1936, 'What A Man!' by 'Kim'.
164. *Saturday Review*, 14 March 1936, 'The Accursed League of Nations' by Lady Houston.
165. *Saturday Review*, 7 March 1936, front page.
166. *Saturday Review*, 14 March 1936, 'Hitler, the Man of Destiny' by Muriel Buchanan.
167. *Saturday Review*, 16 Jan. 1937, News Review item.
168. *Saturday Review*, 6 Feb. 1937, 1st l.a., 'Hitler and the Colonies'.
169. *Saturday Review*, 20 March 1937, 'Books of the Day' and 1 May 1937, 1st l.a., 'Common Sense in Foreign Politics'.
170. *Tribune*, 1 Jan. 1937, 1st l.a., 'What We Stand For in the Struggle for Socialism' and 18 March 1938, 1st l.a., 'Zero Hour Now; Save Peace and Sack Chamberlain'. For general background I have relied on interview with Strauss, 12 Jan. 1977 and Mowat, *Britain Between the Wars*, pp. 580–2.
171. Interview with George Strauss MP, 12 Jan. 1977.
172. *Tribune*, 18 March 1938, 1st l.a., 'Zero Hour Now: Save Peace and Sack Chamberlain'.
173. *Tribune*, 1 Jan. 1937, 1st l.a., 'What we Stand For in the Struggle for Socialism'.
174. Interview with Strauss, 12 Jan. 1977.

CHAPTER III: THE AIR FEAR

1. Air Marshal Sir John Slessor later recalled: 'It was our shocking weakness in the air relative to Germany that mainly occupied the minds of all in Whitehall concerned with defence matters . . .' (*The Central Blue*, p. 182).
2. Howard, *Continental Commitment*, p. 81.
3. Slessor, *The Central Blue*, pp. 151–2.
4. Wrench Papers, ad.ms. 59544(BM), Rothermere to Wrench, 23 Jan. 1936.
5. The phrase 'the destruction of civilisation' cropped up continuously during the thirties in the weeklies, in diaries and in memoirs in reference to the 'coming world war'. It was largely based upon forecasts of the consequences of air attack. The *Observer*, for example, in its first leader of 16 June 1935, acknowledged that many feared that a new world war 'might well mean the end of civilisation'. Sir Robert Bruce Lockhart admitted to his diary during the Munich crisis that he felt 'a craven reluctance to see the end of the world' (Lockhart, *Diaries*, vol. I, p. 397, entry for 25 Sept. 1938). Sir Angus Watson, co-owner of the *Spectator*, in his political tract *On Building A Christian State*, p. 10, wrote that 'humanity must . . . perish' if world war came again.
6. For example, Woodruff, former editor of the *Tablet*, to author, 10 May 1977: 'The [Nineteen] Seventies are very much like the Thirties with the unknown horror of nuclear war taking the place of the unknown horror of aerial war . . .'; Rees, former assistant editor of the *Spectator*, interview with author 15 Jan. 1977.
7. *Sunday Times*, 4 Jan. 1930, 'Disarmament in the Sky' by Eduard Herriot.
8. *Sunday Times*, 20 June 1932, 'Hoover the Disarmer' by Scrutator.
9. *Observer*, 5 July 1931, 'Arms and the Nation', by J.L. Garvin.
10. *New Statesman*, 2 Jan. 1932.
11. *New Statesman*, 30 Jan. 1932, 'The Next Great War' by V. Lefebvre.
12. Taylor, *English History*, p. 450.
13. *Truth*, 25 Jan. 1933, Entre Nous. (*Truth*'s Entre Nous columns reviewed the week's events in much the same way as the *New Statesman*'s Comments. Sometimes items had a heading, sometimes not.)
14. For example, *Saturday Review*, 27 Jan. 1934, 'Britain Must Build More Planes' by Captain H.S. Broad and 7 April 1934, 'An Air Attack on London' by Boyd Cable.
15. *Saturday Review*, 18 March 1933, Notes of the Week.

16. *Saturday Review*, 10 Feb. 1934, 'The Crime Against the State' by 'Kim'.
17. *Saturday Review*, 2 June 1934, 'The Danger of the Saar' by 'Kim'.
18. *Sunday Times*, 28 Jan. 1934, review of Groves's *Behind the Smoke-Screen* by 'the Air Correspondent'.
19. *Sunday Times*, 11 Nov. 1934, 'Day of Remembrance' by Scrutator.
20. *Observer*, 3 Dec. 1933, 'Air and Sea' by J.L. Garvin.
21. *Observer*, 28 Jan. 1934, 'Air and Life' by J.L. Garvin.
22. Astor Papers, Astor to Garvin, 23 April 1934.
23. Astor Papers, Garvin to Astor, 24 April 1934.
24. *Weekend Review*, 11 Feb. 1933, 1st l.a., 'War in the Air – or Disarmament'.
25. Barry, 'The Mirage of Isolation' in *Challenge to Death*, pp. 284–5.
26. *The Economist*, 18 March 1933, 1st l.a., 'War or Peace?'.
27. *The Economist*, 10 March 1934, 1st l.a., 'The Next War', commenting on publication of Brig.-General P.R.C. Groves, *Behind the Smoke-Screen* and Capt. Bernard Acworth, *The Navy and the Next War*.
28. *Spectator*, 27 July 1934, 1st l.a., 'Great Britain and the Air'.
29. *Spectator*, 3 Aug. 1934, 'The Air Attacks on London' by Squadron-Commander P.R. Burchall.
30. *Spectator*, 17 Aug. 1934, News of the Week and 24 Aug. 1934, 'A Spectator's Notebook' by 'Janus' (i.e. H. Wilson Harris, the editor).
31. *Time & Tide*, 3 Feb. 1934, 1st l.a., 'Smoke-Screens'.
32. *Time & Tide*, 24 March 1934, 1st l.a., 'A New Deal for Europe'.
33. *Time & Tide*, 8 Dec. 1934, 1st l.a., 'After the Saar'.
34. *Time & Tide*, 23 June 1934, 'Pacifism and the Air Menace' by Norman Angell.
35. Webster and Frankland, *The Strategic Air Offensive Against Germany*, Vol. I, p. 70.
36. Ibid. p. 89. See also Collier, *The Defence of the United Kingdom*, p. 1.
37. Taylor, *Origin of Second World War*, pp. 16–18.
38. This assertion runs contrary to the sense of such works as Gilbert, *Roots of Appeasement* and Middlemas, *Diplomacy of Illusion*. Both these point to 1937–38 as the years in which British policy came to be determined by fear and a feeling of inferiority, especially in the air, *vis-à-vis* Germany. I hope that the following pages will, in some measure, go towards substantiating my belief that fear in public and Government circles already dictated policy from the spring of 1935. In this connection, the defence White Paper of 4 March 1935 marked a watershed, ending rather than initiating a policy based on strength; such forthright condemnations of Nazi Germany were not to be repeated until after Prague in March 1939. (Of this, more will be said in a later chapter.)
39. *New Statesman*, 23 Feb. 1935, 1st l.a., 'The Air Pact'. See also *New Statesman*, 9 March 1935, 'Comments'.
40. *Sunday Times*, 18 Nov. 1934, 'Have We a Rhine Frontier?' by Scrutator.
41. *Sunday Times*, 28 April 1935, 1st l.a., 'Germany and the Air'.
42. *Sunday Times*, 19 May 1935, 'The Nazi Mentality', by Scrutator.
43. *Sunday Times*, 14 April 1935, 'The Ghost of 1914', by Scrutator.
44. *Observer*, 9 Sept. 1934, 'Defence Against Air Raids' by Nigel Tangye.
45. *Observer*, 17 March 1935, 'Civilians and Air Attack' by Nigel Tangye.
46. *Observer*, 24 March 1935, 'Germany's Yea or Nay' by J.L. Garvin.
47. *Observer*, 28 April 1935, The World: Week by Week – 'The Facts'.
48. Astor Papers, Garvin to Astor, 28 August 1936.
49. *Tablet*, 23 June 1935, News and Notes.
50. *New English Weekly*, 25 April 1935, 'Correspondence'.
51. *The Economist*, 1 June 1935, Notes of the Week.
52. *The Economist*, 28 Sept. 1935, 2nd l.a., 'A Defence Loan?'.
53. *Spectator*, 31 May 1935, 1st l.a., 'Air Peril and Air Pact'.
54. *Spectator*, 31 May 1935, 'Should London Migrate?' by Capt. W.A. Powell.
55. *Spectator*, 28 June 1935, 'The Monster of the Air' by Air Commodore P.F.M. Fellowes.
56. *New Statesman*, 6 July 1935, 2nd l.a., 'Death From the Air'.
57. *New Statesman*, 20 July 1935, 'Comments'.

58. *New Statesman*, 17 Aug. 1935, 1st l.a., 'Air Raid Precautions'; 19 Oct. 1935, 2nd l.a., 'Alternative to Rearmament' by Jonathan Griffin.
59. *Observer*, 15 March 1936, 'Settle or Fight' by J.L. Garvin.
60. *Sunday Times*, 15 March 1936, 'The Crisis and Its Cure' by Scrutator.
61. *Time & Tide*, 14 Nov. 1936, Review of the Week.
62. *Time & Tide*, 5 Dec. 1936, 1st l.a., 'Forced By Its Own Supporters . . .' and Review of the Week.
63. *Time & Tide*, 20 Nov. 1937, 1st l.a., 'Lord Halifax, Gentleman'.
64. *Spectator*, 6 March 1936, 1st l.a., 'Guns and Geneva'.
65. *Spectator*, 18 Sept. 1936, 1st l.a., 'The Shadow of Destruction'.
66. *Spectator*, 12, 19 and 26 Feb. 1937, 'Air War and the Civilian'.
67. Martin, *Editor*, pp. 227–8.
68. *New Statesman*, 22 Aug. 1936, 1st l.a., 'One-Sided Neutrality' and 24 Oct. 1936, 1st l.a., 'The Drift in Europe'.
69. *New Statesman*, 26 Sept. 1936, 1st l.a., 'Labour and Rearmament'.
70. *New Statesman*, 8 May 1937, 1st l.a., 'Guernica and Ourselves'. Slessor, *The Central Blue*, p. 150, later recalled that 'Guernica seemed to provide some confirmation of the fears of those who saw in air power a terrible menace'.
71. *New Statesman*, 27 Nov. 1937, 1st l.a., 'A Talk With Hitler'. *Truth* (5 May 1937, 1st l.a., 'Frightfulness – Swastika Style' by 'Plain Dealer') was prompted by Guernica to write that it had made 'the civilised world shudder' and had been only a 'dress-rehearsal of a new technique of warfare'. Guernica, however, did not elicit from *Truth* any change of policy *vis-à-vis* Spain or any words of sympathy for the Basques or the Spanish Republic. On the contrary.
72. *The Economist*, 27 Feb. 1937, 6th l.a., 'War in the Air'.
73. *Sunday Times*, 27 Jan. 1937, main news page article 'Germany's Plans for Air Defence' by the Air Correspondent.
74. *Sunday Times*, 28 Feb. 1937, 'Britain an Island' by Scrutator.
75. *Sunday Times*, 21 Nov. 1937, 'Air Raids' Wicked Logic' by Scrutator.
76. *Observer*, 21 Feb. 1937, leader page article 'Defence Against Aircraft' by Brig. General P.R.C. Groves.
77. *Observer*, 5 Sept. 1937, book review by Nigel Tangye of *Air Defence and the Civil Population*.
78. *Spectator*, 19 Nov. 1937, 1st l.a., 'War-conditioned Life'.
79. Middlemas, in *Diplomacy of Illusion*, argues that a major shift in British foreign policy occurred with Chamberlain's assumption of office in May 1937, and that this was aligned with a basic change in strategic thinking; Baldwin's dependence upon counter-offensive deterrence was replaced, until March 1939, by an insular defensive, non-Continental strategy. He implies that this was reflected in Chamberlain's abandonment, or at least diminution, of Britain's counter-offensive, bombing capability and a shift in emphasis to fighter production.
    With regard to air thinking, this view seems to me incorrect. The Baldwinian (Scheme F) ratio of 2:1 in bomber:fighter production was in essence perpetuated by the Chamberlain Cabinet even after the *Anschluss* (i.e. Scheme L – envisaging the production of 1,352 bombers and 608 fighters (plus reserves) for the spring of 1940 for the metropolitan air force). A real shift in air policy became apparent only in the wake of Munich, with the adoption of Scheme M which envisaged the production of 1,360 bombers and 800 fighters and the allocation of priority to fighter production (see Collier, *The Defence of the United Kingdom*, chapters II and IV). Even then, however, the bomber:fighter ratio indicates that a belief in deterrence and the necessity for counter-bombing capability was, in great measure, retained. In reality, the shift attested to the growing belief in Government and Services circles that effective fighter- and radar-based air defence was possible.
    While the belief in the omnipotence of the bomber (and the Luftwaffe) reigned (1935–37) and while Britain's material inadequacies in the realm of air defence were legion and obvious (1938–March 1939), appeasement characterised British foreign policy. As Middlemas, *Diplomacy of Illusion*. p. 14, put it: 'To men in the 1930s [war]

was as terrible a prospect as thermo-nuclear war is today. It was the age of the bomber . . . Expert calculations made by the Air Ministry in 1936 suggested that London might suffer half a million casualties in the first three months of war.' See also Howard, *The Continental Commitment*, p. 112 for the official 1936 estimate of 150,000 casualties in the first week of the war. See also Slessor, *The Central Blue*, p. 166.

80. *Spectator*, 14 Jan. 1938, 2nd l.a., 'Air Raids and the Citizen'.
81. *Sunday Times*, 5 June 1938, 'The Meaning of ARP' by Scrutator. See also *New Statesman*, 17 Sept. 1938, 'ARP' by Kingsley Martin: 'In comparison with this problem [i.e., of high explosives] defence against incendiary bombs and gas . . . is comparatively unimportant'. See also *The Economist*, 14 Jan. 1939, 2nd l.a., 'Civilian Defence'.
82. *Sunday Times*, 15 May 1938, 'Government and Air Defence' by Scrutator.
83. *Observer*, 25 Sept. 1938, 'Air Attack and Defence' by the Air Correspondent.
84. *The Economist*, 14 Jan. 1939, 2nd l.a., 'Civilian Defence'.
85. *Time & Tide*, 14 May 1938, 1st l.a., 'The Air Defence Muddle' by Lt. Commander R. Fletcher, MP.; 5 Nov. 1938, 'The Defenceless Citizen'; 18 Feb. 1939, 'Air Defence Chaos'.
86. *Observer*, 7 Aug. 1938, main news page article, 'Our Army in the Air' by the Air Correspondent and 25 Sept. 1938, 'Air Attack and Defence' by the Air Correspondent.
87. Dalton Papers, diary entry for 8 April 1938.
88. *New Statesman*, 17 Sept. 1938, 2nd l.a., 'A.R.P.' by Kingsley Martin.
89. Ibid.
90. *Observer*, 20 March 1938, 'No War and Why' by J.L. Garvin.
91. *Observer*, 3 April 1938, 'The Price of Safety' by J.L. Garvin.
92. *Observer*, 9 Oct. 1938, 'Make Sure' by J.L. Garvin.
93. *Sunday Times*, 2 Oct. 1938, 'The Morrow of Peace' by Scrutator.
94. *Saturday Review*, 26 March 1938, 1st l.a., 'British Foreign Policy'.
95. *Spectator*, 3 June 1938, 2nd l.a., 'Murder From the Air'.
96. *Spectator*, 10 June 1938, 1st l.a., 'The Right to Bomb'.
97. *Spectator*, 24 June 1938, 2nd l.a., 'The Defence of Britain'.
98. *Spectator*, 16 Sept. 1938, 2nd l.a., 'Air Raid Protection'.
99. H. Wilson Harris, *Life So Far*, pp. 251–2.
100. *Spectator*, 7 Oct. 1938, 2nd l.a., 'Defence To-Day'. The *Spectator* also devoted leading articles to the problem of air defence in its issues of 9 and 16 Sept. 1938.
101. *The Economist*, 12 Feb. 1938, 1st l.a., 'Home Defence'.
102. Quoted from Tyerman to author, 8 March 1977. Tyerman himself admits to having suffered acute fear of aerial attack but stresses (letter to author 31 May 1977) that his fear and that of his colleagues was 'quite irrelevant' to *The Economist*'s policies. Graham Hutton (interview with author 14 Feb. 1977) rejected suggestions that he or others suffered from 'air fear' during the thirties; he conceded, only, that there was a shared general 'horror of war'.
103. Martin, *Editor*, p. 266.
104. *New Statesman*, 17 Sept. 1938, 2nd l.a., 'A.R.P.' by Kingsley Martin. Significantly, in May 1938 Kingsley Martin wrote to a Czech friend, Professor Otakar Vocaldo, that should war erupt, 'it would be merely a bombing match in the West as in the East, and I doubt if even God knows what will be the result of that'. In May 1938, as in September, he feared that Czechoslovakia would be completely demolished, were Hitler resisted; apparently he feared the same fate would befall Britain (see Rolph, *Kingsley*, p. 249).
105. Woolf, *A Writer's Diary*, p. 300.
106. Lockhart, *Diaries of Lockhart*, p. 397.
107. Cockburn, *Crossing the Line*, p. 12.

CHAPTER IV: FEBRUARY–JUNE 1935

1. *The Economist*, 2 Feb. 1935, 2nd l.a., 'Franco-British Talks'.
2. *The Economist*, 9 Feb. 1935, 1st l.a., 'A New Start in Europe'.

3. *The Economist*, 16 Feb. 1935, News of the Week.
4. *The Economist*, 23 Feb. 1935, 1st l.a., 'The German Answer'.
5. *Spectator*, 8 Feb. 1935, 1st l.a., 'Buttressing Peace'.
6. *Spectator*, 22nd Feb. 1935, News of the Week.
7. *New Statesman*, 9 Feb. 1935, Comments.
8. *New Statesman*, 23 Feb. 1935, 1st l.a., 'The Air Pact'.
9. *Time & Tide*, 9 Feb. 1935, Review of the Week.
10. *Observer*, 3 Feb. 1935, 'Germany Next' by J.L. Garvin.
11. *Observer*, 29 Feb. 1935, 'Face to Face' by J.L. Garvin.
12. *Observer*, 3 March 1935, 'Peace and the Great Plan' by J.L. Garvin.
13. *Sunday Times*, 3 Feb. 1935, 'For European Peace' by Scrutator and 24 Feb. 1935, 'One Europe or Two?' by Scrutator.
14. *Sunday Times*, 24 Feb. 1935, 'One Europe or Two?' by Scrutator.
15. *Truth*, 6 Feb. 1935, 1st l.a., 'The Very Latest Pact' by Plain Dealer; *Saturday Review*, 9 Feb. 1935, Notes of the Week.
16. *Truth*, 13 Feb. 1935, Entre Nous – 'The Bloom of the Air Pact'.
17. *Saturday Review*, 23 Feb. 1935, Notes of the Week.
18. *Truth*, 6 March 1935, Entre Nous – 'Another Little Pact'.
19. *The Economist*, 9 March 1935, 1st l.a, 'A Black Paper'.
20. *The Economist*, 16 March 1935, 1st l.a., 'The Heart of the Matter'.
21. *Spectator*, 8 March 1935, News of the Week, and 1st l.a., 'The Government and Germany'.
22. *Spectator*, 15 March 1935, News of the Week.
23. *Time & Tide*, 9 March, 1935, Review of the Week and 1st l.a., 'The Rearmament Memorandum' by Norman Angell.
24. *New Statesman*, 9 March 1935, Comments and 1st l.a., 'Hitler's Sneeze'.
25. *New Statesman*, 16 March 1935, Comments.
26. *New English Weekly*, 14 March 1935, Notes of the Week.
27. *Truth*, 13 March 1935, 1st l.a., 'Arms and Security', by Plain Dealer.
28. *Sunday Times*, 10 March 1935, 'Arms, Security and Peace' by Scrutator.
29. *Observer*, 10 March 1935, 'Sanity or Suicide?' by J.L. Garvin, and 1st l.a., 'Necessities of Defence'.
30. *Spectator*, 15 March 1935, News of the Week. *The Economist* was exceptional in that it devoted a News of the Week item to Goering's message. It did not however consider the news of sufficient moment for leader comment; possibly, Goering's was not considered 'the horse's mouth'.
31. *The Economist*, 23 March 1935, 1st l.a., 'Parting of the Ways'.
32. *The Economist*, 30 March 1935, 1st l.a., 'Drawing a Blank'.
33. *Spectator*, 22 March 1935, 1st l.a., 'What Does Germany Mean?' See also the less reserved remarks in the same issue's News of the Week column: France's intention to take up German rearmament in the League of Nations, thought the journal, 'will . . . serve no good purpose'; those who wished the Simon–Eden visit cancelled the journalist called 'emotionalists blind to realities'. Perhaps by 'realities' the journal meant the assumed potency of German arms; for in the 1st l.a., 'What Does Germany Mean?' the journal stated; 'Much of this is not merely intention but accomplished fact.'
34. *Spectator*, 29 March 1935, News of the Week and 5 April 1935, News of the Week.
35. *Spectator*, 29 March 1935, 1st l.a, 'Can Britain Save Europe?'
36. *Spectator*, 5 April 1935, 1st l.a., '1914 and 1935'.
37. *Time & Tide*, 23 March 1935, Review of the Week and 1st l.a., 'What Now?' by Norman Angell.
38. *Time & Tide*, 23 March 1935, 'Notes on the Way' by Wyndham Lewis. Notes on the Way were normally columns contributed by diverse personalities not always reflective of editorial thinking – and certainly not so in this instance.
39. *Time & Tide*, 6 April 1935, 1st l.a., 'Show Down'.
40. *Time & Tide*, 6 April 1935, 'No End of Illusions?' by Robert Dell.
41. *New Statesman*, 23 March 1935, 1st l.a., 'Hitler's Challenge'.
42. *New Statesman*, 30 March 1935, Comments.

43. *New Statesman*, 6 April 1935, Comments.
44. *New Statesman*, 6 April 1935, 1st l.a., 'What Does Collective Security Mean?'.
45. *Sunday Times*, 24 March 1935, 1st l.a., 'The Berlin Visit'.
46. *Sunday Times*, 24 March 1935, 'The Mission to Berlin' by Scrutator and 31 March 1935, 'Danger in Europe' by Scrutator.
47. *Observer*, 24 March 1935, 'Germany's Yea or Nay' by J.L. Garvin.
48. *Observer*, 31 March 1935, 'Steady!' by J.L. Garvin.
49. *Observer*, 7 April 1935, 'Think It Out' by J.L. Garvin and 14 April 1935, 'What To Do' by J.L. Garvin.
50. *Saturday Review*, 23 March 1935, News of the Week.
51. *Truth*, 20 March 1935, Entre Nous.
52. *Truth*, 20 March 1935, 1st l.a., 'Tearing Up The Treaty' by Plain Dealer.
53. *Saturday Review*, 23 March 1935, News of the Week.
54. *Truth*, 27 March 1935, 1st l.a., 'Germany Arrogant and Armed' by Plain Dealer.
55. *Truth*, 3 April 1935, 1st l.a., 'Eden Plays with Fire' by Plain Dealer.
56. *The Economist*, 6 April 1935, 1st l.a., 'The Alternatives Before Britain'.
57. *The Economist*, 13 April 1935, 2nd l.a., 'Rebuilding Peace'.
58. *The Economist*, 20 April 1935, 3rd l.a., 'From Stresa to Geneva'.
59. *The Economist*, 11 May 1935, News of the Week.
60. *Spectator*, 12 April 1935, 1st l.a., 'Stresa and After'.
61. *Spectator*, 19 April 1935, 1st l.a., 'Great Britain's Commitments'.
62. *Spectator*, 26 April 1935, News of the Week.
63. *Spectator*, 17 May 1935, 1st l.a., 'Herr Hitler and Versailles'.
64. *New Statesman*, 13 April 1935, 1st l.a., 'Questions for Stresa'.
65. *New Statesman*, 20 April 1935, Comments – 'Stresa and Geneva'.
66. *Time & Tide*, 20 April 1935, Review of the Week.
67. *Time & Tide*, 20 April 1935, 1st l.a., 'Post Stresa'.
68. *New English Weekly*, 9 May 1935, Notes of the Week. On 23 May 1935 in Notes of the Week, the journal even-handedly condemned all rearmament.
69. *Truth*, 17 April 1935, 1st l.a., 'Much Ado About Stresa' by Plain Dealer. Interestingly, the leader concurred with the 'French' view that Germany contemplated eastward expansion only as a prelude to attack in the West. See also 8 May 1935, Entre Nous – 'The Franco-Russian Pact'.
70. *Observer*, 14 April 1935, 'What To Do' by J.L. Garvin.
71. *Sunday Times*, 14 April 1935, 'The Ghost of 1914', by Scrutator.
72. *Spectator*, 3 May 1935, News of the Week.
73. *Truth*, 1 May 1935, Entre Nous, 'German Sea Power'.
74. *Saturday Review*, 11 May 1935, 'Wilfully Blind' by Kim.
75. *The Economist*, 4 May 1935, 2nd l.a., 'Britain and Germany'.
76. *Time & Tide*, 4 May 1935, Review of the Week and 1st l.a., 'Trumpet of Mars'.
77. *Sunday Times*, 28 April 1935, 1st l.a., 'Germany and the Air' and 5 May 1935, 'After Twenty-Five Years' by Scrutator.
78. *Spectator*, 24 May 1935, 1st l.a., 'The German Proposals'.
79. *Spectator*, 24 May 1935, 1st l.a., 'The German Proposals'.
80. *The Economist*, 25 May 1935, 1st l.a., 'Herr Hitler's offer'.
81. *The Economist*, 25 May 1935, 2nd l.a., 'The Air Debate'.
82. *New Statesman*, 25 May 1935, Comments.
83. *Time & Tide*, 25 May 1935, Review of the Week.
84. *Sunday Times*, 26 May 1935, 'Hitler and Air War' by Scrutator.
85. *Truth*, 29 May 1935, 1st l.a., 'Olive Branch from Hitler' by Plain Dealer.
86. *New English Weekly*, 30 May 1935, Notes of the Week.
87. *Spectator*, 21 June 1935, News of the Week.
88. *Spectator*, 28 June 1935, News of the Week.
89. *The Economist*, 22 June 1935, 1st l.a., 'Naval Agreement'. *The Economist*, incidentally, did not remain happy about the agreement for long. It did not completely reverse its position. But it came pretty close to doing so on 13 July 1935 (1st l.a., 'A Tight Corner'): 'Whatever

may be said for the Naval Agreement with Germany – and, as we indicated at the time, the arguments are in our opinion conclusive in its favour – European countries were disturbed by what they regarded as the indecent haste with which we concluded it and by the implied condonation of Germany's treaty-breaking. And as though to lend colour to these criticisms, Germany has this week revealed that she has one submarine ready' – and others, and battleships, under construction.

90. *Time & Tide*, 22 June 1935, Review of the Week – 'A Welcome Agreement'.
91. *New Statesman*, 8 June 1935, Comments.
92. *New Statesman*, 22nd June 1935, Comments.
93. *Truth*, 1 May 1935, Entre Nous.
94. *Truth*, 26 June 1935, 1st l.a., 'Hands Across the Sea' by Plain Dealer.
95. *Sunday Times*, 23 June 1935, 'The Agreement With Germany' by Scrutator.
96. *Observer*, 23 June 1935, 'Sea Pact and Security' by J.L. Garvin.
97. *Observer*, 30 June 1935, 'Peace Is Close' by J.L. Garvin.
98. *Saturday Review*, 29 June 1935, 'What A Government!' by Robert Machray.

CHAPTER V: ABYSSINIA, THE RHINELAND AND SPAIN

1. *Sunday Times*, 30 June 1935, 'Italy and Abyssinia' by Scrutator; *New Statesman*, 6 July 1935, 1st l.a., 'Mussolini and the League'.
2. *The Economist*, 31 Aug. 1935, 1st l.a., 'British Interests'.
3. *New Statesman*, 6 July 1935, 1st l.a., 'Mussolini and the League' and 24 Aug. 1935, 1st l.a., 'The League, Duce and Empire'; *Time & Tide*, 21 Sept. 1935, 1st l.a., 'What is Britain's Business? – The League and the Dictators' and 5 Oct. 1935, Review of the Week.
4. *Spectator*, 23 Aug. 1935, News of the Week and 1st l.a., 'The Crisis'.
5. *Truth*, 17 July 1935, 1st l.a., 'The Peace of Europe' by Plain Dealer and 18 Sept. 1935, 1st l.a., 'Sanctions' by Plain Dealer.
6. *Sunday Times*, 28 July 1935, 'Italy and Abyssinia' by Scrutator.
7. *Saturday Review*, 25 April 1936, 'Bravo Mussolini!' by Kim.
8. Baldwin Papers, 170 f. 104, Lady Houston to Baldwin, 13 Dec. 1935.
9. Templewood Papers, x;3, Garvin to Hoare, 26 April 1938.
10. *Observer*, 7 July 1935, 'Italy in Arms' by J.L. Garvin.
11. *Observer*, 4 Aug. 1935, 'Fools' Paradise' by J.L. Garvin.
12. *Tablet*, 27 July 1935, News and Notes.
13. *Tablet*, 12 Oct. 1935, News and Notes.
14. *Tablet*, 14 Dec. 1935, News and Notes and 21 Dec. 1935, News and Notes.
15. *Sunday Times*, 30 June 1935, 'Italy and Abyssinia' by Scrutator; 14 July 1935, 'Abyssinia – and Europe' by Scrutator; 28 July 1935, 'Italy and Abyssinia' by Scrutator.
16. *Sunday Times*, 1 Sept. 1935, '4 September' by Scrutator and 6 Oct. 1935, 'The Condemned War' by Scrutator.
17. *Sunday Times*, 8 Dec. 1935, 'The Appeal for Peace', by Scrutator.
18. *Sunday Times*, 24 Nov. 1935, 1st l.a., 'Britain and Sanctions'.
19. *Sunday Times*, 15 Dec. 1935, 'Abyssinian Peace Plan' by Scrutator.
20. *Sunday Times*, 22 Dec. 1935, 'Public Opinion Wins' by Scrutator.
21. *New English Weekly*, 10 Oct. 1935, Notes of the Week and 'Whither is Europe Drifting?' by C.H. Norman.
22. *New English Weekly*, 24 Oct. 1935, Notes of the Week.
23. *Truth*, 28 Aug. 1935, 1st l.a., 'The Problem of Sanctions' (unsigned).
24. *Truth*, 16 Oct. 1935, 1st l.a., 'Can Sanctions Succeed?' by Plain Dealer; 27 Nov. 1935, Entre Nous, 'Oil'; 4 Dec. 1935, 1st l.a., 'The Mad Dog of Europe' by Plain Dealer.
25. *Truth*, 6 Jan. 1936, Entre Nous.
26. *New Statesman*, 10 Aug. 1935, 1st l.a., 'The League or the Duce?'; 24 Aug. 1935, 1st l.a., 'League, Duce and Empire' and 17 Aug. 1935, Comments.
27. Kingsley Martin Papers, Dalton to Martin, 24 Sept. 1935.
28. *New Statesman*, 7 Sept. 1935, 1st l.a., 'For League or Empire?'; 21 Sept. 1935, 1st l.a.,

'Socialists and Sanctions'; 28 Sept. 1935, 1st l.a., 'Do Sanctions Mean War?'.
29. *New Statesman*, 5 Oct. 1935, Comments and 1st l.a., 'The Crusade for Civilisation'.
30. Kingsley Martin Papers, Martin to K. Zilliacus (undated).
31. *New Statesman*, 26 Oct. 1935, 1st l.a., 'Cold Heads and Cold Feet'.
32. For example, *New Statesman*, 23 Nov. 1935, 1st l.a., 'The Day of Ignominy' and 30 Nov. 1935, 1st l.a., 'Mr Baldwin's Foreign Policy'.
33. *Time & Tide*, 28 Sept 1935, 1st l.a., 'Italy and the World'; 5 Oct. 1935, 1st l.a., 'The League and Sanctions'; 12 Oct. 1935, Review of the Week; 23 Nov. 1935, Review of the Week.
34. Norman Angell Papers, Angell to Behrens, 5 June 1935.
35. Sir J. Evelyn Wrench Papers, ad.ms.59579, BM, 'Diary of Balkan Visit', 15 Sept. 1935.
36. Sir J. Evelyn Wrench Papers, ad.ms., 59544, B.M., Rothermere to Wrench, 23 Jan. 1936.
37. Sir Angus Watson, *On Building a Christian State*, p. 11.
38. *Spectator*, 11 Oct. 1935, 1st l.a., 'The Danger of Weak Sanctions'; 25 Oct. 1935, 1st l.a., 'A Critical Ten Days'.
39. *International Affairs*, Jan.–Feb. 1936, p. 53 (vol. XV, No. 1).
40. *The Economist*, 29 Feb. 1936, 1st l.a., 'Europe at War'; 24 Aug. 1935, 1st l.a., 'Italy Says "No"'.
41. *The Economist*, 12 Oct. 1935, 1st l.a., 'Over the Rubicon'.
42. *The Economist*, 19 Oct. 1935, 1st l.a., 'The League in Action'; 26 Oct. 1935, 1st l.a., 'The League Stays Its Hand'; 23 Nov. 1935, 1st l.a., 'Mr Baldwin's Victory'.
43. *The Economist*, 14 Dec. 1935, 1st l.a., 'The Paris Blunder'.
44. *The Economist*, 21 Dec. 1935, 1st l.a., 'The Triumph of Public Opinion'.
45. *Saturday Review*, 23 March 1935, Notes of the Week.
46. *The Economist*, 29 Feb. 1936, Notes of the Week.
47. *Time & Tide*, 29 Feb. 1936, Review of the Week.
48. *Spectator*, 28 Feb. 1936, News of the Week; *New Statesman*, 15 Feb. 1936, Comments and 8 Feb. 1936, 1st l.a., 'The Shift of the Balance'.
49. *Tablet*, 25 Jan. 1936, News and Notes.
50. *Observer*, 9 Feb. 1936, 1st l.a., 'Europe and Security'.
51. *Observer*, 1 March 1936, The World: Week by Week, 'The Rhineland'.
52. *Truth*, 5 Feb. 1936, 1st l.a., 'Three Years of Nazism' by Plain Dealer and 26 Feb. 1936, Entre Nous.
53. *Sunday Times*, 9 Feb. 1936, 1st l.a., 'The Search for Security' and 23 Feb. 1936, 'Defects of the League' by Scrutator.
54. Nicolson, *Diaries, 1930–1939*, pp. 248–9 and 254.
55. Baldwin Papers, 171 p. 262, Rhondda to Baldwin, 30 June 1936.
56. *Time & Tide*, 14 March 1936, Review of the Week.
57. *Time & Tide*, 21 March 1936, 1st l.a., 'Will They Fight?' and 28 March 1936, 1st l.a., 'Cobwebs and Steel'.
58. *Time & Tide*, 4 April 1936, 1st l.a., 'The Watch on Westminster'.
59. *Spectator*, 13 March 1936, Notes of the Week and 1st l.a., 'The German Challenge'.
60. *Spectator*, 20 March 1936, 1st l.a., 'Does Germany Mean Peace?' and A Spectator's Notebook by Janus.
61. *New Statesman*, 14 March 1936, Comments and 1st l.a., 'Is There a Way to Peace?'.
62. *New Statesman*, 21 March 1936, 1st l.a., 'British Policy and Public Opinion'.
63. Jones, *Diary*, pp. 179–82 (entry for 8 March 1936).
64. Jones, *Diary*, p. 181 and Gilbert and Gott, *The Appeasers*, p. 88.
65. *International Affairs*, Special Supplement, April 1936, p. 18 (record of Chatham House meetings on 18 March and 2 April 1936).
66. Hutton, *Is It Peace?*, p. 149.
67. *The Economist*, 14 March 1936, 1st l.a., 'Peace on the Razor's Edge' and Notes of the Week.
68. *The Economist*, 21 March 1936, 1st l.a., 'Germany at the Council Table'.
69. Layton, 'Whither Europe?' in *Challenge to Democracy*, pp. 7–23.
70. *The Economist*, 11 April 1936, 2nd l.a., 'Poisoner or Policeman?'

71. *The Economist*, 25 April 1936, 2nd l.a., 'The Parting of the Ways'.
72. *British Weekly*, 12 March 1936, Notes of the Week: 'The New Crisis' and 19 March 1936, Notes of the Week: 'A Neutral Zone'.
73. *New English Weekly*, 12 March 1936, Review of the Week.
74. *New English Weekly*, 26 March 1936, 'The Franco-Soviet Pact' by A.S. Elwell-Sutton.
75. *Truth*, 11 March 1936, 1st l.a., 'Wacht am Rhein' by Plain Dealer.
76. Ibid.
77. *Truth*, 18 March 1936, 1st l.a., 'Hitler's Dilemma and Ours' by Plain Dealer, and 25 March 1936, 1st l.a., 'Thoughts on the White Paper' by Plain Dealer.
78. *Tablet*, 14 March 1936, 2nd l.a., 'A Breach of Promise' and 28 March 1936, News and Notes.
79. *Tablet*, 4 April 1936, 'The Re-making of Europe' by C. Dawson.
80. *Sunday Times*, 8 March 1936, 1st l.a., 'Treaties Torn Up' and 'For National Safety' by Scrutator.
81. *Sunday Times*, 15 March 1936, 'The Crisis and Its Cause' by Scrutator; 22 March 1936, 'Is Herr Hitler a Realist?' by Scrutator; 29 March 1936, 'Britain and European Peace' by Scrutator.
82. *Sunday Times*, 29 March 1936, 1st l.a., 'Hitler's Choice'.
83. *Observer*, 8 March 1936, 1st l.a., 'Herr Hitler's Double Stroke'; 15 March 1936, 'Settle or Fight?' by J.L. Garvin; 22 March 1936, 'Not Now – But . . .' by J.L. Garvin.
84. Watkins, *Britain Divided*, p. vii.
85. Woodruff letter to author, 12 May 1977.
86. Woodruff letter to author, 12 May 1977 and interview with Woodruff 26 March 1977.
87. Woodruff letter to author, 12 May 1977.
88. *Tablet*, 8 Aug. 1936, The World: Week by Week – 'Revolution and the Fleet' and 25 July 1936, The World: Week by Week – 'Civil War in Spain'.
89. *Tablet*, 1 Aug. 1936, The World: Week by Week – 'The Spanish Tragedy'.
90. *Tablet*, 15 Aug. 1936, The World: Week by Week – 'Surreptitious Support'.
91. *Tablet*, 5 Sept. 1936, The World: Week by Week – 'The Charge of French Intervention' and 10 Oct. 1936, The World: Week by Week – 'Non-Intervention'.
92. *Tablet*, 13 Feb. 1937, The World: Week by Week – 'The First Intervention'.
93. *Tablet*, 10 Oct. 1936, The World: Week by Week – 'Non-Intervention' and 5 Sept. 1936, The World: Week by Week – 'All I Mind About is Gibraltar'.
94. *Observer*, 20 Sept. 1936, The World: Week by Week – 'Heroes of the Alcazar' and 'The Two Forces'; and 4 Oct. 1936, The World: Week by Week – 'Burgos and Madrid'.
95. *Observer*, 10 Jan. 1937, 'A 3,000-Mile Tour of Spain' by Nigel Tangye.
96. *Observer*, 27 June 1937, leader page article, 'The Spanish Situation' by Arthur Bryant.
97. *Observer*, 11 Oct. 1936, The World: Week by Week – 'Russian Intervention' and 'Portugal and Neutrality', and 'Moscow Dooms Neutrality' by the Diplomatic Correspondent (George Glasgow); 3 Jan. 1937, 'The Spanish Peril' by J.L. Garvin.
98. *Observer*, 20 Dec. 1936, The World: Week by Week – 'International War in Spain'.
99. *Observer*, 5 Sept. 1937, leader page article, 'Lying and Counter-Lying' by Arthur Bryant and 19 Sept. 1937, The World: Week by Week – 'An Old Adam'.
100. *Saturday Review*, 1 Aug. 1936, Through the Looking Glass.
101. *Saturday Review*, 13 March 1937, 1st l.a., 'Spanish Stalemate'.
102. *Saturday Review*, 26 April 1937, 2nd l.a., 'Franco's Armada' and 6 Nov. 1937, 1st l.a., 'Mr Eden's Speech'.
103. *Truth*, 29 July 1936, 1st l.a., 'Hopeless Spain' by Plain Dealer and 12 Aug. 1936, 1st l.a., 'Ruffians Versus Ruffians' by Plain Dealer.
104. *Truth*, 12 Aug. 1936, 1st l.a., 'Ruffians Versus Ruffians' by Plain Dealer.
105. *Truth*, 9 Dec. 1936, 1st l.a., 'Britain and the Spanish War' by Plain Dealer.
106. *Truth*, 30 Dec. 1936, 1st l.a., 'Facing the Future' (unsigned).
107. *Truth*, 24 Feb. 1937, Entre Nous.
108. *Truth*, 21 April 1937, 1st l.a., 'Labour's Castle in Spain'.
109. *Truth*, 2 June 1937, Entre Nous.

110. *Sunday Times*, 2 Aug. 1936, 'The Spanish Civil War' by Scrutator.
111. *Sunday Times*, 4 Oct. 1936, 'The Spanish Tragedy' by Scrutator.
112. For example, *Sunday Times*, 11 Oct. 1936, 1st l.a., 'Keep Clear!'.
113. *Sunday Times*, 10 Jan. 1937, 'Right Way with Spain' by Scrutator.
114. *Sunday Times*, 25 Oct. 1936, 1st l.a., 'The Powers & Spain'.
115. *Sunday Times*, 2 Aug. 1936, 'The Spanish Civil War' by Scrutator and 2 May 1937, 'Neutrality & Peace' by Scrutator.
116. *Sunday Times*, 2 May 1937, 'Neutrality & Peace' by Scrutator.
117. *Spectator*, 7 Aug. 1936, 2nd l.a., 'Europe and Spain'.
118. Ibid.
119. *Spectator*, 16 Oct. 1936, Notes of the Week.
120. *Spectator*, 23 Oct. 1936, 1st l.a., 'Brussels and Moscow'.
121. *Spectator*, 11 Dec. 1936, 2nd l.a., 'An International War' and 19 Feb. 1937, Notes of the Week.
122. *Spectator*, 30 April 1937, Notes of the Week; 7 May 1937, Notes of the Week; 21 May 1937, Notes of the Week. (The absence of a leader on Guernica was also characteristic.)
123. *Spectator*, 4 June 1937, 1st l.a., 'After Almeria'.
124. *Spectator*, 25 June 1937, 1st l.a., 'Germany's Aims'.
125. Layton, 'Whither Europe?' in *Challenge to Democracy*, p.18.
126. Hutton, *Is It Peace?*, pp.185–99.
127. *The Economist*, 8 Aug. 1936, 1st l.a., 'The Spanish Cauldron'.
128. *The Economist*, 15 Aug. 1936, 1st l.a., 'The Spanish Tragedy'.
129. *The Economist*, 22 Aug. 1936, 1st l.a., 'Spain and Britain'.
130. *The Economist*, 10 Oct. 1936, Notes of the Week.
131. *The Economist*, 5 Dec. 1936, 3rd l.a., 'The Fascist Offensive'.
132. *The Economist*, 3 July 1937, 1st l.a., 'Europe's Poker Game'.
133. Ibid.
134. *The Economist*, 11 Sept. 1937, 2nd l.a., 'Britain and the Powers'.
135. *The Economist*, 19 March 1938, 1st l.a., 'The Shadow of the Sword'.
136. *Time & Tide*, 1 Aug. 1936, Review of the Week.
137. *Time & Tide*, 8 Aug. 1936, 1st l.a., 'Find the Culprit'.
138. *Time & Tide*, 28 Nov. 1936, 1st l.a. 'Spain and the Powers'.
139. *Time & Tide*, 5 Dec. 1936, Review of the Week.
140. *Time & Tide*, 5 Dec. 1936, 1st l.a., 'Forced by Its Own Supporters . . .'.
141. *Time & Tide*, 1 May 1937, Review of the Week, and 12 June 1937, Review of the Week.
142. *Time & Tide*, 10 July 1937, 1st l.a., 'Spain and the Powers'.
143. *Time & Tide*, 19 March 1938, 2nd l.a., 'Spain Next?'.
144. Kingsley Martin, *Editor*, pp.224, 225.
145. Passfield Papers, Beatrice Webb Diaries, entry for 14 Sept. 1936.
146. *New Statesman*, 1 Aug. 1936, 1st l.a., 'Trenches across Europe'.
147. *New Statesman*, 8 Aug. 1936, 1st l.a., 'Non-Intervention' and 22 Aug. 1936, 1st l.a., 'One-Sided Neutrality'.
148. *New Statesman*, 24 Oct. 1936, 1st l.a., 'The Drift in Europe'.
149. *New Statesman*, 2 Jan. 1937, 1st l.a., 'Hunger Breeds War'.
150. *New Statesman*, 8 May 1937, 1st l.a., 'Guernica and Ourselves'.
151. *New Statesman*, 5 June 1937, 1st l.a., (unsigned), 'The *Deutschland*'.
152. *New Statesman*, 26 June 1937, Comments.
153. Kingsley Martin Papers, J.M. Keynes to Kingsley Martin, 1 July 1937.
154. *New Statesman*, 3 July 1937, 1st l.a., 'The Last Chance in Spain'.
155. *New Statesman*, 10 July 1937, 'British Foreign Policy' by J.M. Keynes and 1st l.a., 'The Policy of Delay' by Kingsley Martin.
156. Kingsley Martin Papers, J.M. Keynes to Kingsley Martin, 9 August 1937.
157. *New Statesman*, 9 April 1938, 1st l.a., 'The Folly of Britain'.
158. Kingsley Martin Papers, A. Werth to Kingsley Martin, 2 Sept. 1938.

CHAPTER VI: 1938 – THE *ANSCHLUSS* AND THE CZECH CRISIS

1. *Observer*, 17 May 1931, 'Peace and "Drifting Backwards"' by J.L. Garvin.
2. *Observer*, 14 July 1935, 'Power and Peace' by J.L. Garvin.
3. *Tablet*, 5 Jan. 1935, 2nd l.a., 'The Independence of Austria'.
4. *Tablet*, 2 May 1936, The World: Week by Week – 'The Coup Feared in Austria'.
5. *Sunday Times*, 29 July 1934, 'Murder Most Foul' by Scrutator and 1st l.a., 'An Affair For Austrians'; 9 Feb. 1936, 1st l.a., 'The Search for Security'.
6. *Truth*, 21 June 1933, 1st l.a., 'The Fruits of Hitlerism' by Plain Dealer.
7. *Time & Tide*, 4 Aug. 1934, 1st l.a., 'A New Watch on the Rhine'; *New Statesman*, 4 Aug. 1934, 1st l.a., 'The Austrian Problem'; *The Economist*, 4 Aug. 1934, 3rd l.a., 'Gangster Politics in Europe'; *Spectator*, 3 Aug. 1934, 1st l.a., 'Hindenburg and Dollfuss' and 2nd l.a., 'Germany's Foreknowledge'.
8. *New Statesman*, 2 May 1936, 1st l.a., 'The End of Collective Security'; *Time & Tide*, 24 July 1937, Review of the Week – 'Germans, Austrians and Czechs'.
9. *Observer*, 22 Nov. 1936, '*Not* as in 1914' by J.L. Garvin and 23 May 1937, 'Empire and Europe' by J.L. Garvin.
10. *Tablet*, 27 Nov. 1937, The World: Week by Week – 'The Two Paths'.
11. *Saturday Review*, 27 Nov. 1937, 3rd l.a., 'The Problem of Germany'.
12. *Truth*, 22 Jan. 1936, 1st l.a., 'A Continent in Confusion'.
13. *Observer*, 13 March 1938, 'The Austrian Drama' by J.L. Garvin.
14. *Observer*, 20 March 1938, 'No War and Why' by J.L. Garvin.
15. *Observer*, 29 May 1938, 'The Czech Peril' by J.L. Garvin.
16. *Tablet*, 19 March 1938, The World: Week by Week – 'The Incorporation of Austria'.
17. *Tablet*, 19 March 1938, The World: Week by Week – 'The Unchanging Feature of German Policy'.
18. *Sunday Times*, 13 March 1938, 'A Black Day for Europe' by Scrutator.
19. *Sunday Times*, 20 March 1938, 'Grave Issues of Peace or War' by Scrutator.
20. *Sunday Times*, 13 March 1938, 1st l.a., 'Law of the Jungle'.
21. *Sunday Times*, 13 March 1938, 2nd l.a., 'Air Urgencies'.
22. *Saturday Review*, 19 March 1938, 1st l.a., 'Austria *Fuit*' and 26 March 1938, 1st l.a., 'British Foreign Policy'.
23. *Truth*, 16 March 1938, Entre Nous – 'Troublous Times'.
24. *Truth*, 16 March 1938, 1st l.a., 'Hitler's *Coup*'.
25. *Spectator*, 18 March 1938, 1st l.a, 'After Austria'; *The Economist*, 19 March 1938, 1st l.a., 'The Shadow of the Sword'; *New Statesman*, 19 March 1938, 1st l.a., 'The Inescapable Facts' by Kingsley Martin and 'Where to Say "Halt"' (unsigned); *Time & Tide*, 19 March 1938, 1st l.a., 'The Austrian Tragedy'; *Tribune*, 18 March 1938, 'Zero Hour Now! Save Peace and Sack Chamberlain' (unsigned).
26. *Truth*, 30 May 1934, Entre Nous – 'A Great Democrat'.
27. *Observer*, 6 March 1932, 'Dr Masaryk' by the Diplomatic Correspondent (i.e., George Glasgow).
28. *Sunday Times*, 4 April 1937, 'Germans and Czechs' by Alan H. Brodrick.
29. *Time & Tide*, 31 July 1937, 1st l.a., 'The Central European Crisis'.
30. *Economist*, 27 Feb. 1937, News of the Week – 'Reconciliation in Czechoslovakia'.
31. Hutton, *Danubian Destiny*, p.29.
32. *New Statesman*, 11 July 1936, 1st l.a., 'The End of Collective Security'.
33. *Time & Tide*, 26 June 1937, Review of the Week – 'Czechoslovakia – What Policy?'.
34. *Spectator*, 29 Oct. 1937, 1st l.a., 'Czechoslovakia and Berlin'.
35. *Observer*, 22 Nov. 1936, 'Not As In 1914' by J.L. Garvin.
36. *Observer*, 23 May 1937, 'Empire and Europe' by J.L. Garvin and 12 Dec. 1937, 'Fear and Folly' by J.L. Garvin.

37. *Truth*, 17 Feb. 1937, Entre Nous – 'The Empire of Mittel-Europa'.
38. *Truth*, 22 Jan. 1936, 1st l.a., 'A Continent in Confusion' by Plain Dealer.
39. Kingsley Martin, *Editor*, pp.264, 265–6.
40. Dalton Papers, diary entry for 8 April 1938.
41. *New Statesman*, 19 March 1938, 'Where to Say "Halt"' (unsigned).
42. *New Statesman*, 26 March 1938, 'A Positive Peace Programme' by J.M. Keynes.
43. *New Statesman*, 26 March 1938, 'On Not Fighting Fascism' by C.E.M. Joad.
44. Dalton Papers, diary entry for 8 April 1938.
45. *New Statesman*, 27 Aug. 1938, 'Comments'.
46. *New Statesman*, 17 Sept. 1938, 'London Diary' and 3 Sept. 1938, 1st l.a., 'Blind Man's Bluff'.
47. Rolph, *Kingsley*, p.246.
48. Kingsley Martin Papers, Alexander Werth to Kingsley Martin, 2 Sept. 1938.
49. Kingsley Martin Papers, Kingsley Martin to G.E.R. Gedye, 1 Sept. 1938.
50. Kingsley Martin Papers, J.M. Keynes to Kingsley Martin, 26 Aug. 1938.
51. Kingsley Martin Papers, J.M. Keynes to Kingsley Martin, 11 Sept. 1938.
52. Rolph, *Kingsley*, p.232.
53. Kingsley Martin Papers, Kingsley Martin to J.M. Keynes, 13 Sept. 1938.
54. *New Statesman*, 17 Sept. 1938, 2nd l.a., 'A.R.P.' by Kingsley Martin.
55. Kingsley Martin Papers, Kingsley Martin to J.M. Keynes, 19 Sept. 1938.
56. *New Statesman*, 17 Sept. 1938, 1st l.a., 'Flight Into the Unknown'.
57. *New Statesman*, 24 Sept. 1938, 'Comments' and 1st l.a., 'The Surrender to Hitler'.
58. *New Statesman*, 8 Oct. 1938, 1st l.a., 'The New Europe'.
59. *New Statesman*, 15 Oct. 1938, 1st l.a., 'Stock-Taking'.
60. Rolph, *Kingsley*, p.246.
61. Dalton Papers, Journal, pp.12–17, entry for 19 Oct. 1938.
62. From discussion following A.J. Toynbee, 'After Munich: The World Outlook', *International Affairs*, Jan.–Feb. 1939, p.94.
63. Wilson Harris, *Life So Far*, pp.251–2.
64. *Spectator*, 1 April 1938, 1st l.a., 'Europe After Chamberlain'.
65. *Spectator*, 2 Sept. 1938, 1st l.a., 'The Fate of Europe'.
66. *Spectator*, 16 Sept. 1938, 1st l.a., 'Germany's Next Move'.
67. *Spectator*, 16 Sept. 1938, 2nd l.a., 'Air Raid Protection'.
68. *Spectator*, 23 Sept. 1938, 'Dismemberment or Destruction?'.
69. *Spectator*, 23 Sept. 1938, 1st l.a., 'What Hitler's Victory Means'.
70. *Spectator*, 23 Sept. 1938, 1st l.a., 'A Respite – And After'.
71. *Spectator*, 7 Oct. 1938, 1st l.a., 'The Price of Peace'.
72. Wilson Harris, *Life So Far*, p.252.
73. *Spectator*, 7 Oct. 1938, 2nd l.a., 'Defence To-day'.
74. *Spectator*, 14 Oct. 1938, 1st l.a., 'Facing the Facts'.
75. *The Economist*, 12 March 1938, 4th l.a., 'The Bastion of Europe'.
76. *The Economist*, 28 May 1938, 2nd l.a., 'A Crisis Averted'.
77. *The Economist*, 19 March 1938, 1st l.a., 'The Shadow of the Sword'.
78. *The Economist*, 10 Sept. 1938, 1st l.a., 'Mediation Means What?'.
79. *The Economist*, 17 Sept. 1938, 1st l.a., 'Hope From Despair'.
80. *The Economist*, 24 Sept. 1938, 1st l.a., 'Vain Sacrifice'.
81. *The Economist*, 1 Oct. 1938, 1st l.a., 'Eleventh-Hour Reprieve'.
82. *The Economist*, 15 Oct. 1938, 1st l.a., 'Counting the Cost'.
83. *The Economist*, 8 Oct. 1938, 1st l.a., 'The Price of Peace'.
84. *Time & Tide*, 2 April 1938, Review of the Week.
85. *Time & Tide*, 28 May 1938, 1st l.a., 'War Was Near'.
86. *Time & Tide*, 30 July 1938, 1st l.a., 'Official Optimism – A Dangerous Drug'.
87. *Time & Tide*, 3 Sept. 1938, 1st l.a., 'Great Britain's Role'.
88. *Time & Tide*, 17 Sept. 1938, Review of the Week – 'The Crisis'.
89. *Time & Tide*, 24 Sept. 1938, 2nd l.a., 'The Crisis and the Public'.
90. *Time & Tide*, 24 Sept. 1938, Review of the Week – 'The Anglo-French Discussions'.

91. *Time & Tide*, 24 Sept. 1938, 1st l.a., 'Civilisation is Warned'.
92. *Time & Tide*, 1 Oct. 1938, Review of the Week – 'The Issues at Stake'.
93. Viscountess Rhondda, 'Introduction' to *Time & Tide Anthology*, p. 14.
94. *Time & Tide*, 8 Oct. 1938, 1st l.a., 'If We are to Survive' and 15 Oct. 1938, 1st l.a., 'The New Europe – German Edition'.
95. *Tribune*, 29 July 1938, 'Where Peace Hangs by a Thread' by a Special Correspondent.
96. *Tribune*, 2 Sept. 1938, 1st l.a., 'Hitler Germany Means War'.
97. *Tribune*, 30 Sept. 1938, 'Britain's Freedom Is Now At Stake'.
98. Hadley, *Munich: Before and After*.
99. Ibid, p. 9.
100. Ibid, pp. 9, 62–8.
101. *Sunday Times*, 15 May 1938, 1st l.a., 'The Henlein Visit'.
102. *Sunday Times*, 29 May 1938, leader page article, 'Czechoslovakia and Europe' by P. Etienne Flandin.
103. *Sunday Times*, 12 June 1938, 'The Czechs and the Germans' by Virginia Cowles.
104. *Sunday Times*, 31 July 1938, 'Lord Runciman's Task' by Scrutator.
105. *Sunday Times*, 11 Sept. 1938, 'Hitler's Choice To-morrow' by Scrutator.
106. *Sunday Times*, 11 Sept. 1938, 1st l.a., 'Crisis Still Continues'.
107. *Sunday Times*, 18 Sept. 1938, 'The Premier's Valiant Mission' by Scrutator.
108. *Sunday Times*, 25 Sept. 1938, 1st l.a., 'The War Peril' and 'Still Hope For Peace' by Scrutator.
109. *Sunday Times*, 2 Oct. 1938, 'The Morrow of Peace'.
110. *Sunday Times*, 2 Oct. 1938, 'The Peace – and After' by Scrutator.
111. *Sunday Times*, 2 Oct. 1938, 1st l.a., 'The Morrow of Peace' and 9 Oct. 1938, 1st l.a., 'The Defences of Britain'.
112. *Sunday Times*, 2 Oct. 1938, 'The Peace – and After', by Scrutator.
113. Astor Papers, Draft of an article entitled either 'Back to First Principles' or 'League or No League' by J.L. Garvin.
114. *Observer*, 29 May 1938, 'The Czech Peril' by J.L. Garvin.
115. *Observer*, 10 July 1938, 'Steady – and Strong' by J.L. Garvin.
116. *Observer*, 28 Aug. 1938, 'The Way' by J.L. Garvin.
117. Astor Papers, J.L. Garvin to Viscount Waldorf Astor, 30 Aug. 1938.
118. Astor Papers, Waldorf Astor to J.L. Garvin, 1–2 Sept. 1938.
119. Astor Papers, J.L. Garvin to Waldorf Astor, 6 Sept. 1938.
120. *Observer*, 11 Sept. 1938, 'Face to Face', by J.L. Garvin.
121. Astor Papers, J.L. Garvin to Waldorf Astor, 6 Sept. 1938.
122. Ibid.
123. *Observer*, 18 Sept. 1938, 'A World At Stake' by J.L. Garvin.
124. Astor Papers, J.L. Garvin to Waldorf Astor, 21 Sept. 1938.
125. *Observer*, 2 Oct. 1938, 'What It Means' by J.L. Garvin.
126. *Observer*, 9 Oct. 1938, 'Make Sure' by J.L. Garvin.
127. *Observer*, 2 Oct. 1938, 1st l.a., 'London in the Crisis'.
128. Astor Papers, J.L. Garvin to Waldorf Astor, 3 Nov. 1938.
129. *Tablet*, 28 May 1938, The World: Week by Week – 'The Need for Revision'.
130. Interview with D. Woodruff, 26 March 1977.
131. *Tablet*, 24 Sept. 1938, The World: Week by Week – 'The Radical Solution'.
132. *Tablet*, 24 Sept. 1938, 1st l.a., 'Mr Chamberlain's Great Effort'.
133. *Tablet*, 1 Oct. 1938, The World: Week by Week – 'The Hesitations of the Smaller Powers'.
134. *Tablet*, 8 Oct. 1938, 1st l.a., 'After Munich'.
135. *Tablet*, 8 Oct. 1938, The World: Week by Week.
136. *Truth*, 4 May 1938, Entre Nous and 18 May 1938, Entre Nous.
137. *Truth*, 18 May 1938, Entre Nous.
138. *Truth*, 31 Aug. 1938, 1st l.a., 'Europe on Edge'.
139. *Truth*, 7 Sept. 1938, 1st l.a., 'Still on Tenterhooks'.
140. *Truth*, 14 Sept. 1938, Entre Nous.

141. *Truth*, 21 Sept. 1938, 1st l.a., 'Chamberlain and Hitler'.
142. *Truth*, 21 Sept. 1938, Entre Nous –'Czechoslovakia'.
143. *Truth*, 28 Sept. 1938, Entre Nous –'German Confidence'.
144. *Truth*, 5 Oct. 1938, 1st l.a., 'What Munich Means' and 2nd l.a., 'Runciman on Czechoslovakia'.
145. *Truth*, 5 Oct. 1938, 'Air Bases of the Powers' by Nigel Tangye.
146. *Truth*, 19 Oct. 1938, 1st l.a., 'The Way to Peace'.
147. Taylor, *Origins*, p. 235.
148. Hadley, *Munich*, p. 93.
149. Hadley, *Munich*, p. 87.

CHAPTER VII: 1939

1. *Spectator*, 18 Nov. 1938, 1st l.a., 'The New Barbarism'.
2. For example, see the *Observer*, 13 Nov. 1938, The World: Week by Week – 'Savage Work in Germany'.
3. *New Statesman*, 18 March 1939, Comments – 'The Spirit of Munich'.
4. *New Statesman*, 25 March 1939, 1st l.a., 'After Appeasement'.
5. *New Statesman*, 1 April 1939, 1st l.a., 'Poles Apart'.
6. *New Statesman*, 8 April 1939, Comments – 'Britain and Germany' and 1st l.a., 'The New Policy'.
7. *New Statesman*, 20 May 1939, Comments – 'War or Peace Aims?'; 3 June 1939, 1st l.a., 'What the Alliance Would Mean' and 19 Aug. 1939, 1st l.a., 'August 1938 – August 1939'.
8. *Tribune*, 31 March 1939, 1st l.a., 'Peace Is Yours – If You'll Take It' by H.J. Hartshorn, and 6 April 1939, 'The Polish Guarantee' by Konni Zilliacus.
9. *Time & Tide*, 18 March 1939, Review of the Week – *'Mein Kampf* Marches On'.
10. *Time & Tide*, 1 April 1939, Review of the Week – 'Wanted – A New Premier' and 25 March 1939, 1st l.a., 'Divided We Fall'.
11. *Time & Tide*, 1 April 1939, Review of the Week – 'Wanted – A New Premier'.
12. *Time & Tide*, 8 April 1939, Review of the Week – 'A United Country'.
13. *Time & Tide*, 29 April 1939, Review of the Week – 'Semi-Appeasement'.
14. Ibid.
15. *The Economist*, 18 March 1939, 1st l.a., 'The Agony of the Czechs'.
16. *The Economist*, 18 March 1939, Topics of the Week – 'Britain and Russia'.
17. *The Economist*, 25 March 1939, 1st l.a., 'England Awake'.
18. *The Economist*, 25 March 1939, 2nd l.a., 'Business Not As Usual'.
19. *The Economist*, 25 March 1939, 1st l.a., 'England Awake'.
20. *The Economist*, 8 April 1939, 1st l.a., 'Britain Girds Her Loins' and 8 July 1939, 2nd l.a., 'England and Eastern Europe'.
21. *The Economist*, 5 Aug. 1939, 1st l.a., 'The Parliamentary Watchdog'.
22. *The Economist*, 26 Aug. 1939, 1st l.a., 'Double Cross Roads'.
23. *Spectator*, 27 Jan. 1939, 1st l.a., 'The Shadow of Crisis'.
24. *Spectator*, 17 March 1939, 1st l.a., 'The Rape and After'.
25. Wrench, *I Loved Germany*, pp. 17, 269.
26. *Spectator*, 24 March 1939, 1st l.a., 'Britain's Rejoinder'.
27. *Spectator*, 7 April 1939, 1st l.a., 'The Next Step'.
28. *Spectator*, 14 July 1939, 'A Spectator's Notebook' by Janus, and 18 August 1939, 1st l.a., 'The War of Nerves'.
29. Wrench, *I Loved Germany*, pp. 173, 268.
30. *Observer*, 8 Jan. 1939, 'From Munich to Rome' by J.L. Garvin.
31. *Observer*, 19 March 1939, 'The Truth' by J.L. Garvin.
32. Astor Papers, J.L. Garvin to Waldorf Astor, 16 March 1939.
33. *Observer*, 19 March 1939, 1st l.a., 'The Cabinet and the Crisis'.
34. Astor Papers, J.L. Garvin to Waldorf Astor, 20 March 1939.
35. *Observer*, 9 April 1939, 'Grave Hours' by J.L. Garvin.

36. Astor Papers, J.L. Garvin to Waldorf Astor, 19 June 1939.
37. *Observer*, 4 June 1939, 'Russia's Choice' by J.L. Garvin.
38. *Observer*, 11 June 1939, 'New Peace Moves' by J.L. Garvin.
39. Astor Papers, J.L. Garvin to Waldorf Astor, 29 June 1939.
40. *Observer*, 2 July 1939, 'What Danzig Means' by J.L. Garvin.
41. *Observer*, 9 July 1939, 'Premier and Cabinet' by J.L. Garvin.
42. *Observer*, 27 Aug. 1939, 'Climax' by J.L. Garvin.
43. *Sunday Times*, 1 Jan. 1939, 'Looking Back – and Forward' by Scrutator.
44. *Sunday Times*, 19 March 1939, 1st l.a., 'Parting of the Ways in Foreign Policy' and 'Hitler's Word' by Scrutator.
45. *Sunday Times*, 26 March 1939, leader page article, 'The Government's Foreign Policy' by Lord Kemsley.
46. *Sunday Times*, 26 March 1939, 'What Next?' by Scrutator.
47. *Sunday Times*, 2 April 1939, 1st l.a., 'Why We Gave Our Assurance to Poland'.
48. *Sunday Times*, 2 April 1939, 'The Pledge to Poland' by Scrutator.
49. *Sunday Times*, 2 July 1939, 'Danzig & Tientsin' by Scrutator.
50. Gilbert, *Churchill*, Vol. V, p. 1094.
51. *Sunday Times*, 3 Sept. 1939, 1st l.a., 'Hitler's Challenge and Britain's Response'.
52. *Tablet*, 25 March 1939, The World: Week by Week – 'The Art of Threatening Europe'.
53. *Tablet*, 25 March 1939, 1st l.a., 'The British Initiative'.
54. *Tablet*, 22 April 1939, 1st l.a., 'The Enemies of Peace'.
55. *Truth*, 17 Feb. 1939, Entre Nous – 'Economic Appeasement'.
56. *Truth*, 17 March 1939, Entre Nous – 'Mailed Fist in Czechoslovakia' and 'Our Plain Duty'.
57. *Truth*, 24 March 1939, 1st l.a., 'Up Against It'.
58. *Truth*, 7 April 1939, 1st l.a., 'Britain's Wider Frontiers'.
59. *Truth*, 5 May 1939, Entre Nous – 'Problem of Danzig'.
60. *Truth*, 14 April 1939, 1st l.a., 'Britain and the Balkans'.
61. *Truth*, 7 July 1939, Entre Nous – 'Churchill and the Government'.
62. *Truth*, 7 July 1939, 1st l.a., 'The Tenth Hour'.
63. For example, in 1944 W.W. Hadley (despite his own views as expressed in the *Sunday Times*) recalled that 'The British guarantee of Poland was accepted by a united Parliament and endorsed by all sections of the public. It was the measure of the nation's resolve to resist further German aggression.' (Hadley, *Munich*)

CHAPTER VIII: CONCLUSION

1. Middlemas, *Diplomacy*, passim.
2. Gannon, *British Press*, p. 7 and Hadley, *Munich*, p. 93.
3. Gannon, *British Press*, pp. 30–1.
4. For Voigt's obsession with Mediterranean security, see Gannon, *British Press*, p. 85.
5. Astor Papers, J.L. Garvin to Waldorf Astor, 31 Aug. 1933.
6. Astor Papers, J.L. Garvin to Waldorf Astor, 28 April 1934.
7. *Observer*, 20 April 1933, 1st l.a., 'Germany and Britain'. See also *Observer*, 7 May 1933, 'Whither Germany?' by J.L. Garvin.
8. *New Statesman*, 6 May 1933, 2nd l.a., '"Adolf Hitler Will Give You . . .?"'.
9. *New Statesman*, 15 July 1933, 1st l.a., 'The Meaning of Fascism'.
10. *New Statesman*, 30 Sept. 1933, 1st l.a., 'The League and Germany'.
11. *New Statesman*, 3 Feb. 1934, 1st l.a., 'Is It Peace?'
12. *Truth*, 10 May 1933, 1st l.a., 'Hitler Comes To Stay' by Plain Dealer.
13. *Sunday Times*, 14 May 1933, 'New Challenge to Europe' by Scrutator.
14. *Time & Tide*, 21 Oct. 1933, 1st l.a., 'Stand By The Treaties!'.
15. Taylor, *Origins*, p. 235.
16. Colvin, *Chamberlain*, p. 64.
17. Howard, *Continental Commitment*, pp. 120–1.

BIBLIOGRAPHY

MANUSCRIPT SOURCES

Private Papers

Norman Angell Papers
Lord (Waldorf) Astor Papers
Baldwin Papers
Hugh Dalton Papers
B.H. Liddell Hart Papers
H. Kingsley Martin Papers
Passfield Papers
Templewood Papers
J. Evelyn Wrench Papers

Interviews and Unpublished Letters

Interviews with:
Roland Bird
Lord Brooke of Cumnor
Graham Hutton
Douglas Jay
Goronwy Rees
George Strauss
Douglas Woodruff

Letters from:
Graham Hutton
Douglas Jay
Ursula Slaghek (née Garvin)
Donald Tyerman
Douglas Woodruff

PRINTED SOURCES

Weeklies and Sunday Newspapers

The British Weekly
The Economist
The Listener
The Nation
The New English Weekly
The New Statesman (from 1931 the *New Statesman and Nation*, from 1934 incorporating the *Week-End Review* as well)
The Saturday Review
The Spectator

The Tablet
Time & Tide
Tribune
Truth
The Week-End Review
The Observer
The Sunday Times

Reports and Documents

Political and Economic Planning Report on the British Press, London, 1938
Royal Commission On The Press Report, 1947–1949, HMSO, 1949
Woodward, E.L. and Butler, Rohan, ed., *Documents On British Foreign Policy 1919–1939*, Third Series, HMSO, 1949 etc.

PRINTED SECONDARY WORKS

Books

Allen, Warner, *Lucy Houston, D.B.E.*, London, 1947
Arendt, Hannah, *The Origins of Totalitarianism*, New York (Meridian Books ed.), 1962
Attenborough, John, *A Living Memory: Hodder and Stoughton Publishers 1868–1975*, London, 1975
Bartlett, Vernon, *Nazi Germany Explained*, London, 1933
—— *If I Were A Dictator*, London, 1935
—— *I Know What I Liked*, London, 1974
Bracher, Karl D., *The German Dictatorship*, London (Penguin ed.), 1970
Brooks, Collin, *Can Chamberlain Save Britain?*, London, 1938
Bullock, A., *Hitler, A Study in Tyranny*, London (Penguin ed.), 1963
Camrose, Viscount, *British Newspapers And Their Controllers*, London, 1947
Caute, David, *The Fellow Travellers*, London, 1973
Cockburn, Claud, *In Time of Trouble*, London, 1956
—— *Crossing The Line*, London, 1958
Collier, Basil, *The Defence of the United Kingdom*, HMSO, 1957
Colvin, Ian, *Vansittart in Office*, London, 1965
—— *The Chamberlain Cabinet*, London, 1971
Cowling, Maurice, *The Impact of Hitler*, Cambridge, 1975
The Economist, 1843–1943, Oxford, 1943
Feiling, Keith, *The Life of Neville Chamberlain*, London, 1946
Gannon, Franklin R., *The British Press and Germany 1936–1939*, Oxford, 1971

Garvin, Katharine, *J.L. Garvin*, London, 1952
Gehl, Jürgen, *Austria, Germany and the Anschluss, 1931–1938*, Oxford, 1963
Gibbs, N.H., *Grand Strategy*, Vol.I, London (HMSO), 1976
Gilbert, Martin and Gott, Richard, *The Appeasers*, London, 2nd ed., 1967
—— *The Roots of Appeasement*, London, 1966
Granzow, Brigitte, *A Mirror of Nazism*, London, 1964
Graves, Robert and Hodge, Alan, *The Long Week-End*, London (Penguin ed.), 1971
Hadley, W.W., *Munich: Before and After*, London, 1944
Halifax, Earl of, *Fulness of Days*, London, 1957
Harris, H. Wilson, *Life So Far*, London, 1954
—— *Ninety-Nine Gower Street*, London, 1943
—— *The Peace in the Making*, London, 1919
Henderson, Nevile, *Failure of a Mission*, London, 1940
Hitler, Adolf, *Mein Kampf*, London, 1972
Howard, Michael, *The Continental Commitment*, London (Pelican ed.), 1974
Hudson, Derek, *Writing Between the Lines*, London, 1965
Hutton, Graham, *Is It Peace?*, London, 1936
—— *Danubian Destiny*, London, 1939
Hyams, Edward, *The New Statesman*, London, 1963
Jones, Thomas, *A Diary With Letters 1931–50*, Oxford, 1954
Layton, Walter, *Allied War Aims*, London, 1939
Liddell Hart, B.H., *The Memoirs of Captain Liddell Hart*, Vol. I, London, 1965
Mairet, Philip, *A.E. Orage*, London, 1936
Marquand, David, *Ramsay MacDonald*, London, 1977
Martin, Kingsley, *Editor*, London, 1968
—— *Fascism, Democracy and the Press*, London, 1938
Middlemas, Keith and Barnes, John, *Baldwin*, London, 1969
Middlemas, Keith, *Diplomacy of Illusion*, London, 1972
Mowat, Charles L., *Britain Between the Wars, 1918–1940*, London (University Paperback ed.), 1972
Mowrer, Edgar A., *Germany Puts the Clock Back*, London, 1934
Muggeridge, Malcolm, *The Thirties*, London, 1940
Nicolson, Harold, *Diaries and Letters, 1930–1939*, ed. Nigel Nicolson, London, 1966
Northedge, F.S., *The Troubled Giant*, London, 1966
Orwell, George, *An Age Like This* (The Collected Essays, Journalism and Letters, Vol. I), London (Penguin ed.), 1970

Price, G. Ward, *Years of Reckoning*, London, 1939
Rees, Goronwy, *A Bundle of Sensations*, London, 1960
—— *A Chapter of Accidents*, London, 1972
Robertson, E.M., ed., *The Origins of the Second World War*, London, 1973
Rolph, C.H., *Kingsley*, London, 1973
Rowse, A.L., *All Souls and Appeasement*, London, 1961
Schoenbaum, David, *Hitler's Social Revolution*, London, 1967
Sharf, Andrew, *The British Press and the Jews Under Nazi Rule*, Oxford and London, 1964
Shirer, William, *Berlin Diary*, London, 1941
Slessor, John, *The Central Blue*, London, 1956
Speer, Albert, *Inside the Third Reich*, London, 1975
Spender, Stephen, *World Within World*, London, 1951
Stansky, Peter, and Abrahams, William, *Journey to the Frontier*, London, 1966
Steed, Henry Wickham, *The Press*, London, 1938
Symons, Julian, *The Thirties*, London, 1960
Taylor, A.J.P., *The Origins of the Second World War*, London, 1961
—— *English History, 1914–1945*, London (Pelican ed.), 1970
Templewood, Viscount, *Nine Troubled Years*, London, 1954
Thomas, Hugh, *The Spanish Civil War*, London (Pelican ed.), 1968
Thomas, William Beach, *The Story of the Spectator*, London, 1928
Vallance, A., and Postgate, Raymond, *Those Foreigners*, London, 1937
Vansittart, Robert, *The Mist Procession*, London, 1958
Voigt, F.A., *Unto Caesar*, London, 1938
Watkins, K.W., *Britain Divided*, London, 1963
Watson, J. Angus, *My Life*, London, 1933
—— *On Building a Christian State*, London, 1935
Watt, D.C., *Personalities and Policies*, London, 1965
Webster, C., and Frankland, N., *The Strategic Air Offensive Against Germany, 1939–1945*, Vol. I, HMSO, 1961
Wheeler-Bennett, J.W., *Munich*, London, 1963
Wiskemann, Elizabeth, *The Europe I Saw*, London, 1968
Wood, Neal, *Communism and British Intellectuals*, London, 1959
Wrench, J.E., *I Loved Germany*, London, 1940
—— *Geoffrey Dawson and Our Times*, London, 1955
—— *F. Yates-Brown*, London, 1948
Young, Kenneth, ed., *The Diaries of Sir Robert Bruce Lockhart*, Vol. I, London, 1973

206

Articles

Barry, Gerald, 'The Mirage of Isolation', *Challenge to Death*, London, 1934

Layton, Walter, 'Whither Europe?', *Challenge to Democracy*, London, 1936, 7–23

Toynbee, A.J., 'Peaceful Change or War? – The Next Stage In The International Crisis', *International Affairs*, Jan.–Feb. 1936

—— 'Germany and the Rhineland', *International Affairs*, Special Supplement, April 1936

—— 'The Issues in British Foreign Policy', *International Affairs*, May–June 1936

INDEX

Somme, Battle of the, 4
South Africa, 19
Soviet Union (Russia), 9, 10, 14, 28, 30, 33, 39, 45, 47, 57, 69, 72, 75, 76, 78, 80, 97, 100, 103, 105, 109, 138, 140, 157–8, 160, 163, 177, 178
intervention in Spain, 108–10, 113, 120
Spanish Civil War (1936–39), 2, 26, 37, 39, 46, 49, 57, 58, 59, 61, 62, 63, 64, 87, 88, 106–20, 168, 175, 178
Spectator, 5, 7, 11–16, 17, 19, 52–3, 55, 57, 59, 60, 62, 63, 65, 69, 72, 74, 75, 79, 81, 82, 83, 85, 86, 89, 93, 95, 97, 100, 112–14, 122, 125, 127, 129, 135–7, 150, 153, 159, 168, 176, 178, 179, 181, 183
Stalin, Josef, 154
Stalinism, 28
Steed, Wickham, 9, 35, 36, 38
Stoddart, Jane T., 40
Strachey, John, 27
Strauss, George, 46
Streicher, Julius, 10
Stresa Conference ('Stresa Front') (April 1935), 68, 78, 79, 80, 81, 86, 88
Sudetenland (Sudeten problem), 2, 25, 26, 30, 119, 120, 121, 126–52, 168
Suez Canal, mooted closure of (1935–36), 93, 94, 95, 181
Sunday Times, 5, 34–7, 39, 43, 50, 51, 54, 56, 58, 61, 62, 71, 73, 76–7, 80, 81, 84, 85, 88, 89, 91, 92, 98, 99, 104–5, 107, 111–12, 122, 123, 124–5, 126, 128, 142–4, 151, 161–2, 164, 165, 168, 174–5, 177, 179, 181, 183

Tablet, 2, 37–9, 44, 55, 88, 90, 97, 103–4, 107, 109, 111, 121–2, 123, 124, 128, 147–8, 150, 163, 165, 166, 168, 178, 181, 183
Tangye, Nigel, 55, 59, 108, 149
Taylor, A.J.P., 175–6
Third International, 92, 107
Thomas, Ivor, 134
Time & Tide, 5, 7, 11, 21–4, 53, 57, 61, 65, 70, 72, 75, 80, 81, 82, 83, 85, 86, 89, 94, 97, 99, 100, 116–17, 122, 125, 127, 138–40, 141, 151, 156–7, 160, 167, 168, 172, 175, 178, 179, 181, 183
Times, The, 139, 143, 148
Toynbee, Arnold, 17, 18, 20, 63, 95, 185 n.41 and 44
Tribune, 9, 46–7, 60, 65, 112, 120, 122, 125, 126, 127, 129, 140–1, 156, 159, 165, 166, 176, 177, 178, 183
Truth, 2, 5, 29–31, 50, 65, 71, 73, 77, 78, 80,

81, 82, 83, 85, 86, 89, 92, 93, 98, 103, 105, 107, 109–11, 122, 123, 125, 126, 128, 148–9, 151, 163–5, 166, 174–5, 177, 183
Truth Publishing Company, 29
Tyerman, Donald, 17

Vallance, Aylmer, 28, 133
Versailles, Treaty of (1919), 4, 8, 9, 10, 15, 20, 21, 22, 25, 27, 28, 30, 31, 36, 38, 40, 44, 45, 46, 53, 67, 68, 73, 74, 75, 77, 83, 84, 96, 97, 99, 100, 101, 102, 104, 105, 121, 150, 153, 155, 169, 175–6, 178
revisionism, 13–14, 20, 21, 22, 24, 26, 27, 29–30, 31–3, 36, 38–9, 40, 41, 42, 46, 68, 69, 73, 79, 80, 85, 98, 121, 132, 134, 142, 150, 153, 154, 158, 160, 162, 173–4
Voigt, F.A., 21, 42, 171

Wadsworth, P.B., 34
Ward Price, G., 67
Wareing, E.B., 35
Watkins, K.W., 106
Watson, Sir J. Angus, 11–14, 95, 188 n.5
Weald, Geoffrey, 50
What would be the Character of a New War, 50
Webb, Beatrice, 24, 25, 117
Wedgwood, Veronica, 21
Week-End Review, 4, 7, 8, 24, 42–3, 52, 183
Wells, W.J., 60
Werth, Alexander, 29, 43, 119–20, 132
West, Rebecca, 21
'Western Air Pact', 67, 69, 70, 71, 76, 84, 85
Wilkinson, Ellen, 46
Wilson, Sir Arnold, 15, 41, 42, 159
Wilson, Woodrow, 13
Wiskemann, Elizabeth, 25, 27, 29
Women's Social and Political Union, 21
Woodruff, Douglas, 2, 24, 31, 38–9, 104, 107–8, 122, 123, 124, 147–8, 163, 165, 168, 188 n.6
Woolf, Leonard, 134
Woolf, Virginia, 66
World War I (Great War), 3, 4, 9, 12–14, 17–18, 22, 23, 24, 28, 31, 33, 40, 44, 48, 49, 68, 112, 144, 170, 172, 177, 179, 180, 181
World War II, 17, 21, 23, 117
Wrench, Sir J. Evelyn, 7, 11–15, 41, 42, 49, 95, 100, 112, 159, 180
I Loved Germany (1940), 14

Zilliacus, Konni, 28

For Product Safety Concerns and Information please contact our EU
representative GPSR@taylorandfrancis.com
Taylor & Francis Verlag GmbH, Kaufingerstraße 24, 80331 München, Germany

www.ingramcontent.com/pod-product-compliance
Lightning Source LLC
Chambersburg PA
CBHW050706280326
41926CB00088B/2819